Mike,
Thanks for taking
the time to meet w.
me at the Stoneleigh
again thanks for a
Wonderful chat

A MOST IMPROBABLE

Millionaire

LAYNIE D. WEAVER

Published in the United States by BookBaby

7905 N. Crescent Boulevard

Pennsauken, New Jersey 08110

www.bookbaby.com

This book is a work of nonfiction.

Book design by BookBaby

Cover concept by C. Courtney Weaver

Cover photography © 2019 by Marcus Casian of Casian Photography

ISBN: 978-1-09837-890-5

eISBN: 978-1-09837-891-2

First Paperback Edition 2021

To my family:

Chip, Sharon, Courtney, Kaycee, McKenna, and Connor

In memory of:

Del Matthews

and Bruce O'Neil

CONTENTS

Introduction   1

The Immortal   3

Chapter 1: The Son   7

Chapter 2: The Student   14

Chapter 3: The Serviceman   20

Chapter 4: The Editor   22

Chapter 5: The Hawaii Bellhop   29

Chapter 6: The California Bellhop   40

Chapter 7: The Salesman   44

Chapter 8: The Runner-Up   48

Chapter 9: The Partner   53

Chapter 10: The Manager   59

Chapter 11: The Dog Lover   62

Chapter 12: The Tour Guide   65

Chapter 13: The Proprietor   70

Chapter 14: The Weatherman   74

Chapter 15: The Snowmobiler   80

Chapter 16: The Speaker   87

Chapter 17: The Boss   91

Chapter 18: The Competitor   97

Chapter 19: The Customer   102

Chapter 20: The Outsider   111

Chapter 21: The Statistician   114

Chapter 22: The Entertainer   120

Chapter 23: The Entrepreneur   124

Chapter 24: The Rancher   128

Chapter 25: The Patient   133

Chapter 26: The Restaurateur   139

Chapter 27: The Friend   143

Chapter 28: The Guest   150

Chapter 29: The Eyewitness   154

Chapter 30: The Catch   161

Chapter 31: The Family Man   166

Chapter 32: The Collector   173

Chapter 33: The Curator   181

Chapter 34: The Oregon Developer   187

Chapter 35: The Visionary   190

Chapter 36: The Employer   193

Chapter 37: The Carnie   197

Chapter 38: The Baller   203

Chapter 39: The Fundraiser   209

Chapter 40: The Gentleman   214

Chapter 41: The Host   219

Chapter 42: The Traveler   224

Chapter 43: The Mogul   235

Chapter 44: The Lucky   243

Chapter 45: The Mentor   249

Chapter 46: The Giver   258

Chapter 47: The Silent Partner   267

Chapter 48: The Prey   271

Chapter 49: The Problem Solver   276

Chapter 50: The Challenged   280

Chapter 51: The Underdog   283

Chapter 52: The Adaptable   287

Chapter 53: The Free Spirit   289

Chapter 54: The Human   295

Chapter 55: The Simple Man   298

Chapter 56: The Homeless   305

Chapter 57: The Crime Fighter   309

Chapter 58: The Disappointed   315

Chapter 59: The Optimist   319

Chapter 60: The Contented   324

Chapter 61: The Rich   327

Afterword   331

Acknowledgements   332

Bibliography   336

Photo Credits   353

About the Author   356

INTRODUCTION

Within ten minutes of talking to Jim Schmit, you'll learn that he has a Teacup Yorkie named Gidget, he drives a rare Doval Shadow, he rides a road bike for exercise, he lost his $50 million real estate empire following the 2009 economic recession, and he might be the most authentically happy person you may ever meet.

At one time, he traveled by private jet socializing with international celebrities while wearing tailor-made suits and shiny gold jewelry. Now, Jim makes business calls from a public picnic table by the San Clemente pier and chats with strangers walking by while wearing a tattered, spandex cycling outfit. He may also be found based in his motor coach in central Oregon or near Lake Tahoe wearing walking shorts and a Hawaiian shirt. With him always are a yellow pad, pen, mobile phone, and Gidget.

"I'm the happiest guy I know, and I can't rub two nickels together," Jim says, amused with himself. And he sincerely means it.

One may interpret Jim's amusement with his ragtag situation as a revelation. He openly admits that he's happier now living a simpler life, free from managing dozens of businesses, maintaining seven homes, and controlling countless collections. It is also quite possible that Jim is amused with his current state of affairs because of the projects he has underway that may leave him even wealthier than before.

The truth is, no matter what he does or doesn't have, where he is or isn't, or who has or hasn't been good to him, Jim Schmit has a gift. He sees the positive in life and lives each day indisputably content. The life of Jim Schmit is a lesson in happiness and this book is his case study.

THE IMMORTAL

"I want to live forever!" Jim says. "I've had the most unbelievable life and I don't want it to end. I plan to be frozen."

The year 2040 is the estimated date for the first revival of a human from cryopreservation, or the freezing of a human to preserve for future recovery. If Jim is still alive in 2040, he will be 99 years old. If not, he hopes to be a human popsicle, awaiting his turn to be thawed. He believes science and technology will provide answers to not only revive people from their frozen state but make them functional far into the future.

"They already freeze and thaw embryos. I'm just a giant embryo. I have no doubt science can advance to revive people," Jim laughs.

Jim plans to join the likes of Dr. James Bedford, said to be the first frozen in 1967, and baseball legend Ted Williams, purportedly one of the most famous frozen. Through Alcor, one of the largest cryopreservation companies in existence, individuals have the choice to cryopreserve their brain or their whole body. An individual attains a membership, ranging from $80,000 to $200,000, depending on the requested service, by verifying proof of funding is available upon their death. In addition, all living Alcor members, estimated at over 1,000 individuals, pay annual dues to support ongoing research and advancement of the science behind cryogenics.

One thing is for certain: to gamble on cryopreservation, these individuals not only have hope in the future of science and technology, but they also have hope in humankind. They also have plenty of money—something

Jim is lacking at the moment, although that is of little concern to him as he anticipates he'll have plenty of money soon.

When asked how he would feel if he woke up decades from now and knew nobody on Earth, Jim shrugs and says, "I will meet new people." He then ponders the scenario that he'll wake up and some of the younger women he dated will finally be his age. He smiles and adds, "Wouldn't that be interesting!"

For a man who proclaims he has never had a bad day in his life, he does have a single regret to address and one final hope. The hope will be revisited, but the regret is that he failed to keep a journal of his unbelievable adventures. Jim is on the path to remedying this regret by chronicling his stories in this book, which may double as a condensed diary of his past life and serve to jog his memory when he wakes from his long, cold, immortal nap.

In the event cryopreservation falters and Jim's revival is unattainable, his sunny outlook on life will be frozen in the words on these pages. His entertaining stories and positive perspective may inspire those of us in need of being more appreciative of every day, moment, and breath. Given enough people read his story, the guidance within may encourage a kinder, more loving world community now and in the future when the unfrozen may walk alongside us.

PART I – RAGS

Learn to let go. That is the key to happiness. – Buddha

Chapter 1:

THE SON

The two Christmas trees Christmas

James Robert Schmit began his storied life in the small port town of Escanaba on Michigan's Upper Peninsula. Well before Jim arrived in the early 19th century, pioneers began filtering through the area and created a small trade center on the west bank of the Little Bay Noc. By 1830, settlers began erecting picturesque churches to compensate for the raucous saloons. The town was formally organized during the early Civil War years; it arose and still relies on shipping commerce. Escanaba was, as many American cities were, centered first on accessibility to water and resources and then on the ever-evolving transportation systems that linked the country more closely together over the decades.

The American Dream originally involved the privilege of religious freedom and the opportunity to fulfill one's basic needs. Over time, the symbiotic relationship of a shelter to keep one safe from the elements and a job to keep one sheltered grew into the monstrous business of real estate, and with it an ever-expanding style of homes and architecture.

The modest log cabin may be the most iconic of American structures, memorializing days of survival and self-reliance, hope, and progress. Originally made from the land by pioneer hands and popularized during westward expansion, log cabins were intended to serve as temporary shelters until more permanent edifices could be afforded and built. However, thousands of log cabins are still built each year—a nod to Manifest Destiny.

In 1941, an ordinary log cabin sheltered Evelyn and William John Schmit Jr. and their two sons through Escanaba's bone-chilling winters and mild summers. Although basic, it was equipped with some modern conveniences like the luxury of running water.

That summer, the Schmits welcomed their third son, James Robert, into the world. The young couple, with their growing family of boisterous boys, was still working towards establishing themselves somewhere between their daily grind and their American Dream.

The extended Schmit family had also carved out a comfortable living in Escanaba. Many of the Schmits were living an upper-class life; one Schmit ran tugboats on the Great Lakes, another was in finance, and Jim's grandfather became the President of Escanaba First National Bank.

Only a few months after Jim's birth, America entered World War II. While many Americans fought overseas, the Schmit family was fighting a battle at home. Evelyn became sick with cancer not long after Jim was born, and after several years of fighting to regain her health, she required in-hospital care.

The hospital did its best to remain void of germs, so as young children the brothers were restricted from visiting their mother. As a result, the impressionable boys were relegated to limited and distant conversations with her that provided little comfort. Jim's sole recollection of his mother is seeing her peek out a second-floor hospital window to talk with him and his brothers.

The boys would wait outside in the cold for a glimpse of their mother at the window, and as a substitute for hugs and kisses, "she would toss Hershey bars from the window. They would hit the ground and break up into perfect bite-sized pieces. That is all I remember of my biological mother," Jim recollects.

Evelyn passed on October 28, 1945, at the young age of 31. "She didn't have a chance to be a mother to us," explains Jack Schmit, the middle son and three years Jim's senior. To this day, a Hershey chocolate bar reminds Jim of the love of a mother he never truly knew.

Other Escanaba memories are limited for Jim, except for two distinct recollections. One day the kid next door, Butchie, was pulling a new red wagon around. That shiny wagon captured Jim's five-year-old eyes, and it was all he could think about.

"I wanted that red wagon and so I took it. I hid it under our porch. I knew it was wrong, but I wanted it. I'll never forget that," Jim recalls.

One of Jim's older brothers caught him red-wagon-handed and advised he tell their dad. The wagon was soon returned to Butchie, and Jim was humbled by an early life lesson: Do not lie, cheat, or steal. As a consequence, Santa did not visit Jim that year.

Jim spent a different, happier Christmas at his grandfather's house, which was decorated with two magnificent Christmas trees that stood from floor to ceiling. This lavish holiday display overwhelmed and delighted him as he marveled at the tall trees.

"I couldn't believe that one house could have two Christmas trees," Jim says.

The pageantry of these trees represented wealth and success to Jim, and the image remained etched in his mind, so much so that he would come to consider them symbolic of his future. Jim's appreciation of the shinier side of life and the glamour of nice things had just begun. What's more, he had learned early that he had to earn his goods—not take them.

Around the time of the two-Christmas-trees Christmas, and not long after his mother passed, Jim's father remarried. The new blended family included the three brothers, a new step-sister, and many future half-sisters. Together, they ventured out to settle on the West Coast.

Jim doesn't recall much about why they moved or the actual move itself, but the trip involved a car full of kids, a new mother, and a two-wheeled trailer full of their possessions. Jim's brother Jack remembers the trip as the time "I put my mark on Jim," referring to the moment when he knocked Jim in the forehead with some snow skis, leaving him with a small scar.

After a short period of highway nomadism, the Schmits settled in Puyallup, Washington, about eight miles east of Tacoma along the Puyallup River. The Puyallup tribe, which means *the generous people*, was the original inhabitants in the fertile Puyallup Valley.

Around 1862, after bringing his family west from Ohio via the Oregon Trail, American pioneer Ezra Meeker discovered the Puyallup valley was ideal for growing hops to brew beer. He was influential in developing the town of Puyallup, formally incorporated in 1890, and about 60 years later welcomed the Schmits. On a clear day, Mount Rainier serves as a scenic backdrop to the town best known for growing daffodils and hosting the Washington State Fair.

The Schmit family lived a simple life and faced the typical daily challenges to make ends meet. John was a stern father and an intelligent, hardworking man. He initially found work on a mink farm and soon acquired a farm of his own. His regular paycheck, however, came from Kaiser Aluminum in Tacoma, and he left much of the farm work to his growing sons.

Kaiser Aluminum was established by one of America's foremost industrialists in the mid-twentieth century. Henry J. Kaiser was known as a key Western entrepreneur, driven by determination, innovation, pragmatism, and grit. He excelled in myriad industries from building Liberty ships for America's military to building dams on the Western frontier, elevating tourism in Hawaii, and organizing the Kaiser Permanente Medical Group. He was considered a miracle man by some because of his extraordinary ability to conquer the impossible as he skillfully navigated markets, politics, labor issues, and the media with no more than an eighth-grade education.

In its first year of business, Kaiser Aluminum made more than $5 million in 1946, about $66 million in 2021 dollars. Jim's father was one of many workers contributing to the success of the Kaiser Aluminum business less than a decade later. By the mid-1960s, company profits neared $59 million, or over $480 million in 2021 dollars, to become Kaiser's most prosperous long-term enterprise.

While their dad was working, Jim's stepmother kept the house and took care of her growing brood of daughters, and the three Schmit sons ran the family farm and took care of themselves. Although he was still a boy, Jim was growing up fast and was expected to contribute on the farm like his older brothers. He was a lean kid used to working from dawn until dark. His curious eyes were set close together, and he had brown hair that glinted yellow and red in the sun.

Jim says, "I worked at least eight hours a day, in addition to school."

Apart from school and church, his time was spent taking care of the animals; cleaning, caring, feeding, then repeat. There was no time for kids' play, not even with his brothers. Sports were indisputably out of the question. In pay for their hard work, the brothers earned a roof over their heads and dinner, albeit not the most delicious meals.

The family dynamics were uniquely segregated. The sisters were kept away from the brothers, to the point that they ate at separate dinner times and dawdled in different rooms during the short time they were all under the same roof awake. The boys labored to keep up the farm or were out trying to make a little money at neighboring farms and businesses to buy themselves shirts, pants, shoes, and socks along with any items they desired. They were left to fend for themselves and often had to rummage for their own breakfasts and lunches. Jim recalls rooting through discarded food put out behind the grocery store. Big bags of old bread could be scavenged, and mold easily picked out of the best pieces to make an edible lunch for school.

He remembers, "I would sit alone at lunch. I didn't want anyone seeing my sad sandwich. The other kids all had nice bread with peanut butter and jelly and all I had was moldy bread."

Jim also remembers eating rotten eggs for some meals that his stepmother prepared. The few meals he did eat at the family table required every bite consumed before leaving. For the most part, this was never an issue for the hardworking boys, but on occasion it would prove a challenge to clean his plate when the meal featured tomatoes and peas, Jim's least favorite foods.

"My pants had these big cuffs at the bottom, so I would hide tomatoes or peas in the cuffs of my pants and after dinner I'd walk to the door trying not to drop any of it. Then I'd empty my cuffs in the yard. I never got caught," Jim smiles.

Occasionally, Jim would receive food from Ms. Hazel Hanson, who ran the nearby chicken hatchery where Jim worked regularly.

"Ms. Hazel was a blonde-haired older lady. She would drive by in her yellow 1953 two-door Chevy Continental with a white hard top and twin exhaust pipes. She would toss out a paper sack in the ditch for me full of good food."

In the brown paper sack would be much welcomed fresh bread smeared with thick jelly and delicious peanut butter and a candy bar.

Jim eventually found a way to have a jelly sandwich like the other kids. He learned to be resourceful and began making his own jam from a berry bush he passed on the way to school and spread it on the best pieces of discarded grocery store bread. Jim admits that once he could bring more socially acceptable lunches, "I would show off my jelly sandwich while I ate so the other kids could see." It was one of his first successful forays into problem-solving.

Jim simply wanted to be a normal kid, but even with his normal lunches he remained shy. He mostly kept to himself and to his ensemble of closest friends: the pigs, sheep, ducks, geese, rabbits, and minks on the farm.

Chapter 2:

THE STUDENT

Senior year at Puyallup High School

Other than a gift of $5 at Christmas, money was provided about as often as hugs in the Schmit family, which was never. For extra money, Jim worked at neighboring farms cleaning chicken coops and shearing sheep. He typically saved and spent this hard-earned money on necessities like clothes. On rare occasions, he would buy his favorite candy bar—a Big Hunk. In one instance, Jim decided to save his money to make his first business investment.

Nobody knew better than Jim that farm work was never done and physically demanding. Jim began to think about how he could make his chores easier and faster, so he could make more money.

He remembers, "I saw these electric sheep shearers in the Sears Roebuck Catalogue and I thought about how fast I could shear sheep with those electric shearers. I saved my money for a while, because they were expensive, and bought some."

Once the electric shearers were purchased, Jim practiced and became a talented shearer. He started marketing his services to other neighboring farmers and found consistent work shearing sheep.

"I could remove a fleece in one piece without buttonholes," he says, referring to nicks to the sheep's skin. "The hardest part of the job was catching the sheep."

Having spent so much time in the company of farm animals, the barns and fields provided a comfort to Jim that his house never did. Taking care of his sheep proved gratifying and purposeful for Jim and, in one case, a source of newsworthy pride: "I made the front page of the *Tacoma Tribune* when my ewe, Grandma, had triplets."

Jim attributes his tireless work ethic to these early days working on farms. "Hard work is all I knew for the first years of my life. It also taught me common sense. It's surprising how far common sense can take a person," he says.

In the early 1950s, news arrived in Puyallup that Jim's grandfather, William John Schmit, back in Escanaba, was ill. Jim wanted to see his grandfather and ask him a very important question in person, and so he started saving his sheep shearing money for a trip to Michigan. Jim saved and saved and saved enough to buy a train ticket, two new loaves of bread, a jar of peanut butter, and a jar of jelly. At the age of 12, Jim started his 2,000-mile trip alone to visit his grandfather with just $3 in his pocket (about $30 in 2021).

The journey began in Tacoma, Washington, and by North Dakota, Jim says, "I ran out of one ingredient. I needed more food because we weren't even halfway to Escanaba."

In talking with the train conductor, Jim learned that the train would stop briefly in Minot, North Dakota. He would have a total of 15 minutes to make it to the grocery store a few blocks from the train station and back to the train for the rest of the journey. As the train rolled to a stop, Jim hopped down and took off running. He followed the train conductor's directions and found the store, but his lungs had nearly frozen.

Unaccustomed to the frigid temperatures of North Dakota, and in his haste, Jim had forgotten to wear his jacket. That level of cold was nothing he had ever felt. He purchased his food and then had no choice but to run back to the depot in the icy air, and he barely made it.

Once on board he remembers being in severe pain from the cold on his skin and in his lungs as if being frozen alive. Looking back, Jim thinks of that icy North Dakota sprint and says quite matter-of-fact, "I almost died."

Jim made it to his grandfather's home in Escanaba with very little food left. It was there that he asked his grandfather his burning question.

"How do you have two Christmas trees when most people have only one? How do you make money?" Jim asked. Jim's grandfather presented him with some simple, straightforward advice: Invest in real estate at a young age.

After a few days, some good meals, and those golden words, Jim returned west—ending his only vacation away from the farm during his formative years. He was back to work and back to school. Grandfather Schmit would live quite a bit longer, passing at the age of 74 in April 1963. Jim never had a chance to see him again.

While Jim began honing his business skills on the farm, he also began testing his negotiating skills around town. About a mile away from his house in the middle of the woods lived an old, reclusive doctor and his young, mentally disabled daughter. Jim remembers the doctor driving his 1928 Hupmobile around town with his daughter in the back. The man kept very much to himself and took care of his daughter; however, his asocial behavior attracted the jeers and teasing of local bullies.

In response, the recluse would yell and threaten the tormenting kids with a shotgun in hand whenever they ventured too close to his property. Jim always liked that old car and would occasionally ask the doctor about it. He never joined in on the name calling like some of the other boys.

"Jim was a dealmaker from early on, and one of his first deals was purchasing that old Hupmobile off of that doctor," says Jim's brother, Jack.

Jim credits his first car purchase to simply being nice to the old guy while others were mean. That, and paying attention. When Jim saw the doctor driving around in a new vehicle, he realized he could make the fellow a deal for the old one. He wanted the vehicle and the man wanted to sell it. Jim was beginning to recognize that being observant, polite, inquisitive, and proactive could result in a win-win situation.

"I don't remember how much it was, probably between $25 and $35, or between $230 and $320 in 2021 dollars. I didn't have much money so it couldn't have been very expensive." Jim says.

In school, Jim maintained average grades, never having the luxury of being able to study. His homework was farm work. The only extracurricular activity he was allowed to participate in was the Future Farmers of America.

Puyallup High School had an active Future Farmers of America program with competitions scheduled at the Washington State Fair right on their home turf in town. One year, Jim qualified for the tractor and trailer driving competition. "You picked out your own tractor and they would attach a manure spreader. I had to drive through a course, weave around stakes, and back up. I was really good at it." Jim laughs, "I was the Washington State FFA Manure Spreader Backer Upper Champion, or something like that."

In a short time, Jim acquired his second vehicle at a cost of about $50. He rescued a 1935 International Pickup sitting useless in some bushes, and it became his shop project. After relocating it to the high school, Jim rebuilt the motor and painted the body red with a paintbrush. He was determined to get it running for transportation purposes as well as for a passing grade in shop class.

With his shop grade on the line and his teacher watching, Jim turned the ignition over, expecting the truck to start as it had the day before. It clicked but did not start. Confused, he started poking around the engine and discovered a problem with the spark plugs. Once back in place, the engine fired up and the truck was mobile.

Jim says, "I think some of my classmates messed with the spark plugs to tease me. I drove that pickup, but the paint job was so bad I would park it far away in the parking lot at school so it would look like a nice red pickup."

Outside of school and the farm, Jim spent a good deal of his time in church with his family. His pious upbringing was full of Catholic traditions and customs, although much of this puzzled him as a boy. The concept of everyone being a sinner did not make sense to him. He had learned from taking Butchie's red wagon to not lie, cheat, or steal. Nevertheless, he was required to go to confession before communion, though he felt he had nothing to confess. So, he came up with a routine statement for each confession.

"Bless me Father for this is my sin," Jim would say.

"Yes, son. What have you done?" came the reply.

"I have had immoral thoughts towards a woman. ..." he would continue on.

Jim would repeat that for every confession, as it was the closest thing to truth as he could devise. On occasion, Jim admits, it may have been a true confession.

On religion, Jim explains, "The thing that makes sense to me is the Ten Commandments. I really believe in those Ten Commandments. But I would not say I am religious, really. I'm not Christian. Well, I guess I'm kind of Christian, just in case. It's all kind of confusing to me."

Despite his detachment to the rituals of religion, Jim subconsciously upholds the seven heavenly virtues like a saint. The question is, why? And the answer starts with his struggle through childhood.

As Jim reminisces about his less-than-ideal upbringing, he simply states, "I wasn't a happy kid. I had a lousy childhood. I took that and turned it completely around. I believe my unhappy childhood made me appreciate the rest of my life."

When it comes to his childhood past, or any past, Jim doesn't dwell much on what has happened. He doesn't overanalyze the impact it may have had on his life decisions. He doesn't blame anyone for where he is now and does not play a victim to his past. He believes that is all a waste of time and energy.

"You can't change anything in the past." Jim says.

Jim accepts the past is the past and lives in the present, always looking forward.

One spring day in Puyallup, Jim received his high school diploma with his school mates under the motto, "We're the class that's first in line— nineteen hundred and fifty nine!" His diploma was his ticket to a new life.

Chapter 3:

THE SERVICEMAN

"My life didn't start until boot camp. The military was like a vacation," Jim says.

The Coast Guard's boot camp ironically introduced Jim to free time and free will. He entered boot camp right out of high school to discover he was no longer a slave to the family farm; he was a serviceman in the military. The military offered time off, comfortable living quarters, free clothes, and three square meals a day. For Jim, boot camp was easy living.

In signing up for Coast Guard service, Jim felt he was fulfilling his American civic duty. While he was in high school, The Reserve Forces Act of 1955 had been established and signed by President Dwight D. Eisenhower to ensure the United States had enough ready reservists available for national emergencies and defense. Only a decade removed from World War II and on the heels of the Korean War, battle-ready young men were a high priority for the nation. To keep the military prepared to mobilize in the event of a national emergency, young men were enlisted to complete six months of mandatory military training and serve as reservists for a period of eight years.

Or as Jim says, "I went to the Coast Guard to do my six-by-eight."

Jim started his six-by-eight in Alameda, California, with Delta-28 on what was then known as Government Island. While the other guys were doubled over in exhaustion, the physical demands of boot camp were comparable to working long hours on the farm for Jim. When the others were out on liberty skipping their study time, for the first time in his life Jim had a chance to actually study. He stayed focused on the duty at hand, which helped him succeed beyond his own expectations.

"I broke some Delta-28 physical and scholastic records during boot camp. It wasn't that hard, either," he says.

For part of his service, Jim spent time on the United States Coast Guard Cutter *Dexter*, a Casco-class ship designed with a shallow draft to operate in and out of small harbors and atolls. The *Dexter* was originally commissioned in 1941 to the Navy then transferred to the Coast Guard five years later. She would serve many roles and after a stint on the East Coast and a period of decommission, she found a new home and duty in Alameda, California, as a United States West Coast training vessel starting in 1958.

For the most part, serving his six months in the Coast Guard was not extremely memorable, but for one particular instance. Jim surmises, "I can remember this like yesterday. We went out to do a rescue during a storm. It was so stormy that just about every person on the boat was seasick. I got lucky and didn't get sick, but the waves were thrashing the boat and we were getting tossed. It was exciting to me, but then again, I wasn't sick. I'll never forget the Captain came over a loudspeaker and said he was also sick and that he had never been sick before. He told all of us to hang on, we'll get through it. When the Captain gets seasick, it must be a pretty serious storm."

Jim's military service passed in a blink, and he continued to complete his reserve duty over the next eight years. Reserve duty consisted of between two and four weeks of service each summer plus regular meetings every month.

Most of all, Jim learned during and after the Coast Guard that his life was just beginning. His daily schedule was no longer dictated by farm work or military schedules. His meals no longer had to be rotten eggs, moldy bread, gooey tomatoes, and nasty green peas. Jim had the freedom to make his own decisions, good or bad. His next decision was college.

Chapter 4:

THE EDITOR

The 1950s closed with Alaska and Hawaii becoming the 49th and 50th states respectively, and NASA (the National Aeronautics Space Agency) introducing the first American astronauts. As Americans jitterbugged into the 1960s, the nation was in the midst of a presidential election. Jim found himself intrigued with Senator John Kennedy from Massachusetts and distinctly remembers thinking how interesting it would be to meet this man.

Jim did not have much time to follow politics as he was working two jobs to put himself through Olympic College in Bremerton, Washington. Between the ice cream shop, the car wash, and school, he tried out for the basketball team.

"I was never able to do sports in high school. The only team I was part of was the Future Farmers' of America debate team. But I liked sports and I was really quick. I thought I would give basketball a try," Jim remembers.

Jim was the first to arrive and the last to leave every Olympic College basketball tryout practice, and he worked hard. Although his skills didn't measure up, nor his 5'8" frame, he landed the last spot on the squad. The coach had chosen him over several other more talented players based on his positive attitude and work ethic. The coach knew the more skilled players could learn a lot from Jim's fortitude.

"I wasn't a good player. I was more like the inspiration for the team," Jim says.

Jim enjoyed the sport. He liked the pace of the game and the team camaraderie. He was always dedicated to his basketball practices and games but didn't see much court time. "We were ahead by 50 points or something like that in one game, and they put me in for a few minutes. It was the only time I played. I knew I would never be a professional basketball player, but maybe I could own a team." Jim was on the basketball team for only one season; jobs and school monopolized his time.

When it came to academics, Jim had a little catching up to do because he'd never had time to study in high school. While he aced the scholastics in boot camp, his college placement test scores were low in some subjects. He found himself in a remedial English class and although a bit disappointed, he embraced the class.

When the English professor assigned homework to write an article as if each student were the Editor of the college newspaper, Jim took it seriously. The professor had announced that the best article would be published in the college newspaper the *Ranger Roundup*.

Jim was exploring various topics for his assignment when his coworkers at the ice cream shop looped him in on their standard scheme of taking $10 from the register drawer each shift.

"I was brought up that you don't lie, cheat, or steal. I didn't agree with the other workers. They were stealing. I don't steal," Jim remembers. "Well, except one other time, kinda."

Jim continued his shift, leaving all the shop money in the register drawer where it belonged. The owners of the shop took notice that more money was consistently made during Jim's shifts and after observing this ongoing trend, they offered him a manager position. His trustworthy and reliable character eventually led to the offer of a partnership in the ice cream shop. He declined and kept working as a manager because he wanted to stay focused on college.

Meanwhile, with his ice cream and car wash employment savings, he made his very first home investment in 1960 by purchasing a 24-foot trailer. He and his two roommates lived in the Bremerton RV park, which was owned by the Belmont family, who happened to have a lovely daughter named Sharon. Enamored by Sharon, Jim began to court his first girlfriend with the little free time he had. He wanted to be a good man for her. In addition to the stunt his co-workers were playing, Jim started to observe those lacking a moral compass.

As a result of this awareness, Jim began witnessing and was disturbed by what seemed like a common college practice—most of his fellow students were cheaters. This observation became the topics of his English assignment. He decided to interview his fellow students on why and how they cheated and their opinions on cheating itself.

Jim learned that they had answers on their pencils, in their friends' collars, and in other clever hiding places. He gathered his research, carefully crafted his article, and submitted his assignment. After reading Jim's article, entitled *Students Voice Opinions on Cheating*, the professor commended his talent for reporting and selected his work to be published in the *Ranger Roundup* newspaper. The article resulted in a path Jim had not foreseen.

Jim reflects, "Thanks to bonehead English, I became the Editor of the *Ranger* newspaper and was given a chance to do some neat things I never otherwise would have done. Good things can always come from bad things. You just have to be willing to see it."

As the Editor, he earned a small scholarship, allowing him to quit his car wash job. Unexpectedly, this position presented the opportunity to attend a college editors' conference in San Diego, California, in the spring of 1961. It also required he stay attentive to current events and national politics, which he found surprisingly interesting.

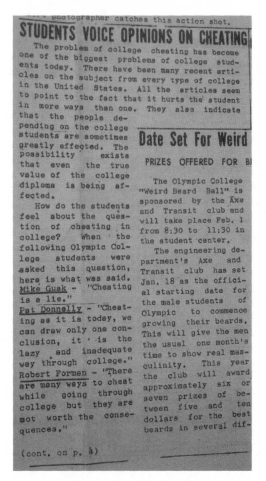

... photographer catches this action shot.

STUDENTS VOICE OPINIONS ON CHEATING

The problem of college cheating has become one of the biggest problems of college students today. There have been many recent articles on the subject from every type of college in the United States. All the articles seem to point to the fact that it hurts the student in more ways than one. They also indicate that the people depending on the college students are sometimes greatly effected. The possibility exists that even the true value of the college diploma is being affected.

How do the students feel about the question of cheating in college? When the following Olympic College students were asked this question, here is what was said. Mike Guak - "Cheating is a lie." Pet Donnelly - "Cheating as it is today, we can draw only one conclusion, it is the lazy and inadequate way through college." Robert Forman - "There are many ways to cheat while going through college but they are not worth the consequences."

(cont. on p. 4)

Date Set For Weird

PRIZES OFFERED FOR B

The Olympic College "Weird Beard Ball" is sponsored by the Axe and Transit club and will take place Feb. 1 from 8:30 to 11:30 in the student center.

The engineering department's Axe and Transit club has set Jan. 18 as the official starting date for the male students of Olympic to commence growing their beards. This will give the men the usual one month's time to show real masculinity. This year the club will award approximately six or seven prizes of between five and ten dollars for the best beards in several dif-

Ranger Roundup article

At the conference in Southern California, Jim felt like a little pipsqueak from Olympic College. However, he found the courage to raise his hand and offer up an idea during one of the sessions focused on empowering youth in reporting. He said to the crowd, "I think students should be able to attend major press conferences like other media outlets."

The response to his idea was positive, so positive in fact, the group decided to act. The crowd of students voted to pick a representative from a big college to attend a presidential press conference. Jim hadn't met the chosen representative before, but he seemed nice.

Jim says, "Since it was my idea, they gave me the task of writing the letter to the Press Secretary for the President of the United States of America. I wrote and sent the letter asking if this other guy could attend a presidential press conference."

To Jim's surprise, he received a response. The recently elected, President John F. Kennedy, felt this was a good idea, with one exception: he requested Mr. Jim Schmit attend because he had authored the letter. Jim was formally invited by the President of the United States to attend a speech at the University of Washington's Hek Edmonds Pavilion in Seattle in November of 1961.

That year, the Cold War had heated up. The Bay of Pigs invasion failed in April, East Germany built a wall to divide East and West Berlin in August, and at about the same time the Soviet Union reportedly began nuclear testing. On November 16, 1961, President John F. Kennedy arrived at Boeing Airport in Seattle to deliver a major foreign policy speech at the University of Washington.

Jim bought a striped suit jacket, pants, and shoes at the local Salvation Army. In the pre-dawn hours, Jim dressed and started his Fiat 600, which was an accomplishment itself, to catch the ferry to Seattle to meet President Kennedy. Jim reminisces, "I had my press pass and was ready to go. The ferry left at 6:00 am and the conference was in the early afternoon. I wanted to be on time, which means I was going to be really early. It was still dark while I was waiting for the ferry and I was first in line with my Fiat. I drove onto the ferry and the workers told me to turn off my engine. But I couldn't, because the car would only start on a hill. I told the guys that I couldn't turn the car off because I was going to see the President of the United States—and if I turned the car off, it wouldn't start again. They told me they would push me off the ferry. So, I turned off the engine for the ferry ride. When they pushed me off the ferry, I got the engine running and I was on my way to see the President."

Jim made it to the Hek Edmundson Pavilion, sure to park on a hill, and wove through the crowds to find his place with the press. When the time had come, he found himself only a dozen feet away from President Kennedy while he made his speech.

The President's speech honored higher education and addressed current affairs. Having opened during the first year of the American Civil War, the University of Washington's 100th anniversary offered the perfect platform for emphasizing education. It also allowed the Kennedy administration to connect with America's youth and address the current state of world affairs. An excerpt from the speech reflects the complicated political climate the United States was navigating in 1961:

> This nation made a basic commitment to the maintenance of education, for the very reasons which Thomas Jefferson gave, that if this nation were to remain free it could not remain ignorant. The basis of self-government and freedom requires the development of character and self-restraint and perseverance and the long view. And these are qualities which require many years of training and education. ... [O]ur people realize that this country has needed in the past, and needs today as never before, educated men and women who are committed to the cause of freedom. So for what this university has done in the past, and what its graduates can do now and in the future, I salute you. ...

> In 1961 the world relations of this country have become tangled and complex. One of our former allies has become our adversary—and he has his own adversaries who are not our allies. Heroes are removed from their tombs—history rewritten—the names of cities changed overnight.

> We increase our arms at a heavy cost, primarily to make certain that we will not have to use them. We must face up to the chance of war, if we are to maintain the peace. We must work

with certain countries lacking in freedom in order to strengthen the cause of freedom.

Not only was Jim present for the speech, but President Kennedy also selected him to ask a question. "I'm there at the press conference, and the Kennedy administration was very focused on the youth vote, so I was a big deal. President Kennedy chose me to ask a question when I raised my hand, but I can't remember what I asked him. I just remember the moment."

Not long after he attended the press conference and briefly spoke to President Kennedy, Jim recognized something important. "I realized I had planted the seed about meeting the President and it came true. Then I started to plant all sorts of seeds," Jim says with a smile.

Chapter 5:

THE HAWAII BELLHOP

Jim was barely making ends meet, but he managed to hold down his job, attend school, fulfill his editor duties, buy a '54 Pontiac with white seats, and purchase an engagement ring for his lovely girlfriend Sharon. He doesn't recall anything special about the proposal other than cost of the ring. "I bought the ring in Tacoma. It was $50 total, I paid something like $4 a month."

Life was on track, until "one day I was working in the ice cream shop and saw Sharon ride by in a '57 Chevy with a sailor. I'll never forget that. She dumped me for a '57 Chevy. And that was it," says Jim.

Soon thereafter, he got the ring back and left Bremerton for Seattle in devastation. His plan was to finish college at the University of Washington, but things don't always go as planned. "I moved into an apartment in Seattle with two other friends but couldn't afford my one-third of the rent. Earl and Nina Johnston managed the apartment and I ended up negotiating a deal to work off my rent. I would take out the trash, clean, and repair things. It worked out pretty well," Jim explains.

Earl Johnston was a tall, impressive man, with a domineering voice. He proved to be a great influence on Jim's life and a good friend over the years. Jim observed that Earl seemed to always know the right things to say. Everyone liked Earl.

Through college, Jim had remained shy. In reality, for much of his life his closest friends had been farm animals, affording little in refining the art of conversation. Relating to people took additional study and adjustment for Jim. Yet, he observed in Earl something he found curious, "Earl could talk to anyone. He told me to start talking to people; that I would learn a lot. So I did, and he was right. He taught me to open up."

Jim never quite made it back to college. Instead, he bought a '55 Red T-Bird to get himself back and forth to his job as an expediter at Boeing. Jim ordered the office supplies for the company, which was founded in 1916 as a military and commercial aircraft manufacturer in the Puget Sound.

"It was an impressive amount of supplies. Boeing had offices all over Seattle, and we would buy a half truckload of pencils or two trucks of paper," Jim says.

Jim wasn't the only Schmit to work at Boeing. His brother Jack Schmit started out sweeping floors and ended his career decades later as a Boeing vice president.

Between Boeing and his odd jobs around the apartment building, Jim stayed busy as Seattle readied to host the 1962 World's Fair. With a population of approximately 550,000 residents, Seattle was expecting to accommodate possibly 10 million visitors over a six-month period and carry on the tradition of hosting this momentous event on the world stage.

The World's Fair has a colorful history, numbering over 100 fairs in more than 20 countries. The 1851 Great Exhibition, showcasing the famous Crystal Palace in London's Hyde Park, is considered the inaugural World's Fair. The event actually originated from a combination of popular industrial trade shows, national fairs, art competitions, technological exhibits, and carnival-like attractions. These events ignited the world's taste for cultural pageantry, family entertainment, technological demonstrations, and possibly most of all, worldwide marketing for the host city and nation.

The golden age of World's Fairs, between 1880 and World War I, is responsible for the original Ferris wheel (Chicago 1883) and the Eiffel Tower (Paris 1889). The spectacle, glamour, and popularity of future World's Fairs never quite reached the popularity of its golden age again, as organizers had less to offer attendees due to radio programming, improved transportation, and the introduction of movies. Still, noteworthy and inspirational World's Fairs did take place after the golden age, including the 1939 New York World's Fair, which not only introduced new art deco designs and broadcast television, but also provided hope for the survivors of the Great Depression. By the time it was Seattle's opportunity to host, the World's Fair was being planned amongst Cold War tension.

Seattle's 1962 Century 21 Exposition opened on April 21. The Space Needle and Monorail still stand today as Seattle's most recognizable landmarks. President Kennedy christened the event from afar, welcoming guests to enjoy Seattle's achievement.

Jim summed up his World's Fair experience bluntly: "I rode the Monorail. I did all the stuff."

More memorable to him was an attraction separate and apart from the World's Fair—the Jones' Fantastic Museum. The museum was located right near one of the Fair's gates and it stayed in Seattle for about 20 more years. The slogan for the Jones' Fantastic Museum purported it to be full of "Things weird and strange from all over the world. Amazing. Amazing. Amazing. Wild, weird, wonderful. Weirdatorium."

The recorded voice enticing customers to enter and look around was backed by shrill laughs and a funeral trumpet played by creator Doc Jones, *Collector of the Weird*. The museum hosted innumerable quirky collections and items such as side show attractions, automatons, unusual inventions, human oddities, funhouse mirrors, Captain Hook's hook, a bicycle air conditioner, a petrified space man, the popular laughing lady known as Laffing Sal, and the nine-foot tall mummified Viking Olaf the Giant, among countless other items.

Jim says, "I remember the penny arcade stuff was cool. There was a full-sized, real-looking mechanized elephant. And I remember seeing Olaf." This odd museum made more of an impression on Jim than the extravagant World's Fair next door, with one exception.

In the shadows of the Space Needle, amongst the plethora of tents and exhibits of far-off places and people, 21-year-old Jim found himself standing by a pink-and-white striped Jeep marketing the islands of Hawaii. The infant 50th State was showcasing its paradise destination and *Aloha* way of life. It didn't take much convincing before Jim and his two friends to decide they were all moving to Hawaii.

Jim's rationale for moving across the ocean was, "It was exciting! We were going to pick pineapples." He also admitted that adding distance between himself and his first heartache might help, too. "I couldn't get over Sharon."

A guy managing the Hawaii booth negotiated a trade with Jim: he proposed swapping the pink-and-white striped Jeep for Jim's '55 red T-bird. Jim thought this was a perfect idea, after all they would really stand out in a pink-and-white striped Jeep in Hawaii. The exchange made the move even more motivating. Not much later, Jim and his two buddies found themselves in economy-class accommodations on the *President Wilson* cruising their way to Hawaii with the Jeep stashed somewhere in the cargo hold.

Accompanying Jim was Fred Swanson, a shy, handsome guy and the son of a Seattle car dealer. Along with one other fellow, the three friends began their journey to Hawaii and discussed their future. Jim explains, "I was a good climber. I figured I could make money picking pineapples out of the trees. That was my plan."

The *President Wilson* was a part of the American President Lines fleet converted from ocean liners to war vessels during World War II and then back to ocean liners. In 1963, the *President Wilson* was operating on the Sunshine Route, a 39- to 42-day cruise from "California to the Orient." The voyage from San Francisco to Honolulu took five days. First-class passengers enjoyed a pool and lounge on the promenade deck with the economy accommodations located on the lower decks—meager in comparison.

The three perused the economy class decks, mingling with passengers and enjoying the fresh ocean air. Entertainment on the boat ranged from movies to dances, to deck sports and parties. One night there was a talent contest held amongst the economy class passengers. Jim and his buddies entered the contest and planned out an improvised skit.

"I have always been athletic like a gymnast and could make myself stiff as a board," Jim explains.

His buddies wrapped Jim up in toilet paper to look like a mummy. His friends carried him out on stage by the shoulders and feet, set his heels down, and tipped him up straight as if he were a flagpole, never a bend or break in his joints. There he stood, petrified in front of the crowd. The music started and he began singing *The Mummy Song*:

> You ought to see what they did to my mummy
> Pulled his organs out of his tummy
> Put 'em in spice, whacked 'em in a jar
> Painted him up with sticky tar
> Wrapped him in linen from his head to his toes
> Pulled his brains out of his nose
> That's not all the embalmers did
> They buried my mummy in a pyramid

Other acts preceded and followed, but at the end of the night Jim won the contest and with it a bump up to First Class. "It was great! I had a room all to myself with a real bed with nice sheets. I went to dinner with tablecloths and china and talked to interesting, first-class people. They would ask about me and I would explain how I won a first-class cabin. They thought that was great and I became a minor celebrity on the boat," Jim laughs. "But I made sure to take care of my friends and get them some good food. I didn't forget about them."

The crew of friends arrived jobless in Honolulu on the island of Oahu. While waiting for the pink-and-white striped Jeep to be offloaded, they looked around and noticed there were pink-and-white striped Jeeps everywhere.

"I thought we were going to be so different with our Jeep, but it ends up everyone drove them in Hawaii back then. I would have been better off keeping the red T-bird. That guy swindled me," Jim admits.

Once loaded into their ordinary pink-and-white striped Jeep, their job searches began.

"When I got to Hawaii, I learned that my pineapple picking job wasn't going to work because pineapples don't grow on trees. And the only jobs available were in hotels," Jim says.

The Hawaii islands were experiencing a boom in tourism in the 1960s credited to the growth of air travel and an intense marketing campaign to promote the destination to middle-income American households. Hawaii also became and remains a popular vacation destination for Japanese travelers.

Jim applied at a hotel as a bellhop and was rejected. Then another, and another, and another. He discovered he wasn't a competitive candidate because he didn't have any hotel experience and could not speak Japanese. He got a book on how to speak Japanese, so he could fake-speak Japanese during job applications. After some practice, he learned a few basic Japanese phrases and figured he sounded pretty good.

Jim's next employment attempt was at The Waikikian Hotel. Built in 1956, the hotel was designed in *tiki-style* architecture known for its casual appeal and tropical gardens. It was the antithesis of colossal resorts and high-rise complexes soon to take over the Honolulu landscape. At the same time The Waikikian Hotel was opening, Henry Kaiser, founder of Kaiser Aluminum, was working on a mega-complex next door.

When Kaiser retired to Hawaii in the early 1950s, Kaiser Motors purchased Willys-Overland Motor Company. In 1959, Willys-Overland Motor Company began producing the Jeep Surrey Gala—the pink-and-white striped Jeeps. These Jeeps were made from old postal truck surplus parts and cleverly repurposed for use as delivery trucks and transportation rentals for resort patrons, including guests staying at Henry Kaiser's Hawaiian

Village Hotel resort. Jim was driving around in a Kaiser creation while he was attempting to get a job next door to Kaiser's resort.

Jim submitted his application for a bellhop position at The Waikikian Hotel and was invited to the office of Hotel Manager Jim Nafler. Mr. Nafler dressed daily in a Hawaiian shirt and white slacks and looked like he should have been famous. He kept a tidy office and intimidated Jim somewhat with his good posture and confidence. During the interview, Nafler asked Jim several questions. He seemed pleased when he asked Jim if he spoke Japanese, and Jim rattled off his string of phrases.

"It ended up Jim Nafler was fluent in Japanese. I was caught, but I needed a job and told him I would work free for two weeks to at least get some experience. Then they could decide if they wanted to keep me," Jim remembers.

Nafler agreed to those terms and in four days' time, Jim had learned every detail of his duties and then some. He was a good worker and a smart kid, and Nafler couldn't deny it. Soon after hiring Jim, Nafler was so impressed with him, he arranged for Jim to take on a manager position at the hotel across the street instead of bell-hopping at The Waikikian. Nafler believed he was giving Jim a chance at a better job. Jim followed Nafler's advice and applied for and got the Assistant Manager position at the Driftwood Hotel. Jim mastered his Assistant Manager duties, proving he was a quick learner and capable employee. Jim also made sure to take care of his buddies; he helped one get a job as a pool boy and the other get a job in charge of hotel linens.

However, Jim kept hearing the bellhops talk about their tips, and in doing the math, Jim was certain he could hustle and make more money as a bellhop than an Assistant Manager. When Jim heard that one of the bellhops at The Waikikian was about to quit, he crossed the street to ask Nafler if he could take that position. Nafler pointed out that moving from a manager to a bellhop was a step backwards, but Jim had made up his mind. He wanted to be a bellhop because he could make more money than as a manager, thanks to tips. Nafler fulfilled his request and Jim quickly became the top bellhop at The Waikikian Hotel.

A few memorable individuals were among Jim's customers. The movie *In Harm's Way*, released in 1965, was filmed at Pearl Harbor. Jim and another bellhop, James, may have played a bigger role in that movie than anyone realizes.

Jim remembers, "John Wayne and Kirk Douglas stayed at The Waikikian while they were filming. John Wayne would get so drunk at the hotel bar that his nose would turn purple. James and I would take him to his room every night because he couldn't walk. Then he would be bright-eyed and bushy-tailed at 7 o'clock the next morning and go to work."

Jim recalls another person without a famous name or famous face. This hotel guest was an American who conducted a lot of business in Japan. He stayed at The Waikikian as his layover when traveling back and forth.

"This guy was a class act. He would show up about once a month and I would check him in and he would always tip me $5. He was sharp and wore a nice gold nugget watch. I think he recognized that I was too smart to be a bellhop, so he gave me some advice. He told me to go back to the mainland and make more money." Jim kept the advice in mind.

Guests came and went at The Waikikian and Jim fell into a natural routine of taking care of everyone. One early morning around 8:00 a.m., Jim was strolling along a cement walkway by the beach on the way to work and he passed an outdoor restaurant. Even today he can visualize the moment when a restaurant worker, who had been setting the tables, shared troubling news as he passed by.

It was November 22, 1963, and for Jim, "It was a life-changing moment. I was shocked. There was something about this event that really affected me, more than anything else up to that moment of my life. I'll never forget that moment when I heard that President Kennedy had been assassinated."

The assassination of President Kennedy left a cloud of gloom and despair over the United States for months. Americans were battling with disbelief, grief, anger, and fear, tangled with the uncertainties of the ongoing Cold War. Coping with this tragic event proved difficult for many. America needed a distraction from itself and unbeknownst to the melancholy nation, a distraction was on the way.

The British invasion of American pop culture officially began when the Beatles made their famous debut on the Ed Sullivan Show in New York on February 9, 1964. While the band had become somewhat accustomed to its hysterical fan base mobbing them around England and parts of Europe, they had doubts about how they would be received in America. Consequently, they were pleasantly surprised to find the same pandemonium upon their reception in the United States.

On the 50th anniversary of the Beatles' first visit to America, *The Beatles Bible* website quotes Paul McCartney saying, "There were millions of kids at the airport, which nobody had expected. We heard about it in mid-air. There were journalists on the plane, and the pilot had rung ahead and said, 'Tell the boys there's a big crowd waiting for them.' We thought, 'Wow! God, we have really made it.'"

Upon disembarking from the plane, the Beatles were greeted by 5,000 frantic fans—mostly girls, squealing and waving signs from the upper deck of the newly renamed John F. Kennedy Airport in New York. Nearly 200 reporters were on hand to capture the event. The Beatles would end up meeting similar chaos from their adoring fans everywhere they went in the United States. America's Beatlemania had officially begun.

According to Jim, one day he was called into Jim Nafler's office and informed that the Beatles were stopping, unannounced, in Hawaii and staying at The Waikikian. Nafler stressed that it was important to keep this a secret and that Jim would be their personal assistant. After their debut in the continental United States, the four Beatles and their manager arrived in Hawaii. They retreated to The Waikikian's penthouse rooms A, B, and C for a few days and did not come out. Jim delivered cigarettes, food, and any necessities or luxuries they desired. He also picked up after them a little and kept them comfortable.

"I couldn't help but tell my roommates that I was taking care of the Beatles. I planned to take their cigarette butts and matchbooks and other things and sell them for extra cash. And the sheets…the plan was to cut up the sheets and sell the pieces when they left," Jim says.

Eventually, the Beatles decided to venture out of the hotel and go to the beach. Jim set out grass mats and umbrellas and escorted the Beatles down to a lovely patch of sand. Jim noticed as they waded into the ocean, "They were lily white—white as ghosts. And they had this shaggy hair. They were out swimming when a lady arrived and put her mat nearby. She made a comment on how she didn't want these *drowned rats* next to her. I said, 'No ma'am, these are the Beatles.' And she said, 'I don't care if they are the bug worms.' I moved their mats away from her a little. She had no idea who the Beatles were," Jim says.

After a few days tucked away in The Waikikian, it seemed the Beatles were missing the limelight of fame. Jim says, "They asked where the girls were and moved to another hotel to get the attention they were seeking."

Jim explains how he snagged the sheets off their beds and sold them to his roommate for a flat price. Jim's roommate cut the king-sized sheets into one-inch squares and put an advertisement in the *Honolulu Star Bulletin* and made good money from that enterprise.

It was a profitable plan that worked out seamlessly until Jim was fired for stealing the sheets. He did pay for the sheets later on out of his paycheck. However, like Butchie's red wagon, this incident reminded Jim to never lie, cheat, or steal, and this time the lesson stuck for good.

Jim's encounter with the Beatles was eye-opening. Their level of fame was entertaining, but not desirable, he felt. Jim did not necessarily want to aim for that kind of life, although he thought it might be fun to dabble in it on occasion. While the Beatles made an impression, it was the guest with the gold nugget watch that would have the greatest influence on him.

"One day the gold nugget watch businessman stopped in for an overnight stay. He looked at me and said, 'I don't want to see you here when I stop in next time.' He was serious. But it helped me make a big decision," Jim says.

Chapter 6:

THE CALIFORNIA BELLHOP

At last, Jim heeded the gold nugget watch owner's counsel and headed back to the mainland on the first plane ride of his life to start making money after a year in Hawaii. He got an apartment in Redwood City, California, on Redwood Avenue and was now working at The Cabana Hotel.

The Cabana Hotel in Palo Alto, California, was originally financed by actress Doris Day. It was ornately decorated with Greek goddess statues, elaborate fountains, and bellmen in togas. Jay Sarno designed and built the hotel, a precursor to his famous Caesar's Palace in Las Vegas. The Cabana Hotel opened in 1962, and three short years later on August 31, 1965 Jim was again working as a bellhop and his hotel was preparing to host several famous guests.

"I heard the Beatles were coming to The Cabana, so I went and talked to the manager because I had helped them before. It was a big deal," Jim says.

The Beatles were staying in Palo Alto following two shows at the Cow Palace in San Francisco. It would be their final stop on their second American tour. As the Beatles' popularity grew, their privacy diminished and chaos reigned before, during, and after their appearances. The Cabana Hotel did everything it could to prepare for the anticipated mayhem. The special security detail for the Beatles' approximately 25-hour stay in Palo Alto cost over $125,000 in current dollars, or $15,000 at the time. The hotel itself hired almost 200 security guards, including some of the football players from the University of Santa Clara.

Jim recalls, prior to the Beatles arrive to the hotel, "There were kids everywhere and the hotel was mobbed. The fans had put soap in the fountains and there were soap suds all over the place."

When the Beatles finally arrived, frantic fans climbed on top of the limousine, denting the roof. To Jim's surprise, when he saw the band, "They recognized me from Hawaii. They only stayed one night. I helped them out. It was a little like déjà vu."

Given the fan fiasco displayed upon the Beatles' arrival, a special plan was devised for their departure. "The original plan was to bring the limo in behind a wedge of police cars. The Beatles would get in and drive out. I suggested putting them in the linen truck. The linen truck could drive up through the kids to the back of the hotel and The Beatles could use the truck to escape the hotel."

The hotel decided to go with the linen truck plan. Once the Beatles were loaded in the truck and safely off the property, the hotel announced to the fans that the group had already left. The disappointed fans eventually trickled away. According to the *Palo Alto History* website:

> The Beatles made a slick getaway. Plans were announced that the Beatles were to be whisked out of their suite in room 810, down the northside elevator, past the Cabana kitchen, and out through the service entrance. Sure enough, two decoy limos and a truck were stationed out front, prompting many fans to wave goodbye to vehicles that they mistakenly thought John, Paul, George, and Ringo were inside. Instead, the boys were sent by police out the southside entrance. 'Where's the car?' asked Paul, upon arriving, only to be directed into a white and blue 1.5-ton delivery truck ... A photograph of two of Palo Alto female fans, 14-year-old Rocky Keith and 13-year-old Sue Moore, was

printed in the *Palo Alto Times* the next day, [they were] sobbing with joy because they happened to see the Beatles exit. But most of the girls on the other side of the hotel were not so lucky—and were forced to console themselves by later purchasing pieces of Beatle bedsheets sold in the Cabana parking lot.

Jim was not part of the bedsheets scheme this time around. He had learned his lesson before. He elaborates a bit more on the getaway. "My friend Earl Johnston happened to work as a car salesman for the Bob Sikes Dodge Dealership then and we arranged that to be the transfer point. The linen truck took the band there and transferred them to their waiting limo."

Palo Alto Times headlines following the Beatles departure

Most of Jim's time working at The Cabana Hotel was less exciting, but he had started dating a girl he really liked. He also continued his good Catholic duties by attending church and confession regularly. He had never spent the night with her, but found himself repeating the same confession he did as a boy:

"Bless me Father for this is my sin."

"Yes, son. What have you done?"

"I've had immoral thoughts towards a woman...." And so on.

However, instead of the confession merely ending with forgiveness or with the assignment of prayers to repent, this priest would inquire more about his lady. Jim would provide details of his pretty girlfriend, thinking it strange but sharing with the priest in the sacred tradition of Catholic confession. It wasn't long after that that Jim found the priest in bed with his girlfriend. "I never went to confession again. I lost faith in the morality of Catholicism, church, and especially confession," Jim says.

Instead of dwelling on the breakup, Jim was ready to move forward and create opportunities for himself. Remembering what his grandfather had told him about investing in real estate at a young age, Jim began working towards that goal. First, he wanted to educate himself, so he could make a wise investment.

Jim saved his money and started taking real estate classes at Anthony Schools. He had just turned 25 years old—old enough to be serious about his occupation and young enough to still follow his grandfather's advice. Jim's hotel and bellhop days were over.

Chapter 7:

THE SALESMAN

In the early 1960s, Jim recalls, "I used the money I had earned from the hotel to go to the Anthony Schools and learn about real estate, but not with the idea of being a real estate salesman. I was going to be a finance guy." While Jim was attending classes in the San Francisco Bay Area, he saw a flyer with information that captured his attention: *Tahoe Paradise. Lots $100 down and $39 a month.* "I found out where Lake Tahoe was, and I borrowed a car from Earl and drove up to check out Tahoe Paradise," Jim says.

Jim arrived to a place that Mark Twain described approximately 100 years before as "the fairest picture the whole world affords." He immediately fell in love with Lake Tahoe. "I had $500 in a savings account and I spent a lump of it on 339 Apalachee Drive and another lot as investments. It had a lake view and was across from the airport. I eventually built a chalet on it."

Lake Tahoe is a deep glacial lake straddling the California and Nevada state borders. Geologic shifting of the Earth's crust about two to three million years ago sculpted the basin in which Lake Tahoe tranquilly rests today at the north end of the Sierra Mountain range. The snowy mountain peaks mirrored in a sapphire blue lake make a breathtaking sight. With a maximum depth of 1,645 feet at an elevation of 6,225 feet, Lake Tahoe is the second deepest lake in the United States and the highest lake of such size.

The clarity of Lake Tahoe typically reaches an incredible 70-foot depth today, although this measure is a drastic reduction from the 100-foot clarity first measured in the late 1960s. The inevitable land use modifications that come with population growth have consequently stressed the Lake Tahoe Basin ecosystem and left impacts in the water and the land—an unfortunate side effect of being a highly desirable place to live. Lake Tahoe, however, not only attracts those seeking nature's majestic wonders and pine-scented air but also attracts those flocking to the glitzy, commercialized casinos lined up along the Nevada border.

The 1954 federal ban on slot machines nationwide, except in Nevada, shut down casinos in San Francisco and Los Angeles and turned Lake Tahoe into a popular destination for gamblers. Since then, Lake Tahoe has increasingly become more of a tourist destination, necessitating more locals to settle in and provide services for the tourists. With incredible foresight, a dapper California businessman named Jim Wilson set the groundwork for developing a large swath of land south of Lake Tahoe.

As a young man, Wilson had successfully established Wilson Builders to profit from the demand for subdivision development around the Sacramento and Redding, California, areas. No stranger to Lake Tahoe, thanks to childhood excursions in his father's Model-A Ford over the unpaved Highway 50, it occurred to Wilson that the small community of Meyers was a location ripe for development. In 1953, just a year before Lake Tahoe became a gambler's paradise, he and a group of other businessmen created the Tahoe Paradise Corporation with long-range development plans.

The 20-year plan outlined a strategy for turning 1,600 acres of virgin land near the base of Echo Mountain into a vibrant and attractive community with residential, commercial, and recreational land uses. By 1960, the construction was well underway and would transform the southern Lake Tahoe region. With Wilson's vision, the value of those 1,600 acres of land in Meyers escalated from its original assessment of $300,000 in 1953 to $12 million by 1962 or approximately $2.9 million to $103 million in 2021 dollars.

In the two following decades, land development continued to flourish around Lake Tahoe. The full-time population was approximately 10,000 residents in 1960 and increased fivefold over the next 20 years. The population boost was also due in part to the popularization of winter sports—the 1960 Winter Olympics were held at the nearby Squaw Valley resort, nestled in the peaks west of Lake Tahoe.

Tahoe Paradise salesman Jim McGraw, who worked for Wilson, couldn't help but notice Jim's obvious excitement about purchasing 339 Apalachee Drive. McGraw suggested Jim Schmit try selling lots since he was so enthusiastic about buying some. Jim deflected explaining his plan was to go into finance. Nevertheless, McGraw casually handed him a stack of sales brochures, unknowingly activating Jim's new career path. Those brochures set in motion a series of events that in short turn would make Jim Schmit the boss of Jim McGraw.

Jim was still quite shy at the time he was recruited to sale property, so instead of making a verbal sales pitch to people while handing them a brochure, he devised a different plan. He wrote his contact information on each brochure and slid one under every apartment door in his building in Redwood City, California. He also posted one on the building's bulletin board. By the time he got back to his own apartment, after delivering the flyers in his first endeavor in real estate marketing, the phone was ringing—he had his first customer.

Lou Gracie, a bartender at Mel's Bowl in Redwood City, was interested in buying a lot. Jim acted fast and went down to talk to Lou immediately. "I called McGraw at Tahoe Paradise that day and told him I had a buyer. The next day Lou Gracie went to Tahoe with me. I borrowed a car from Earl again—he loaned me an old Cadillac."

Lou and Jim drove up to Tahoe and Lou committed to buying the lot. It was Jim's first sale, and soon to be his first partnership. Jim says, "I asked Lou if he would help me sell. The Tahoe Paradise deal for the buyer was $100 down and $39 each month. The salesman kept $45 out of the initial $100 down and nearly half of the monthly $39 payment, or $17.50. I proposed that Lou keep the flat $45 commission and I would keep the monthly commission for each lot sold. The lots cost around $5,000 each so the note on each lot was approximately 10 years. I was making $210 on each lot I sold for 10 years."

Lou agreed and used his bartending network to sell beverages as well as land to many of his regular customers. It worked! In a blink, Jim was gainfully employed as a property salesman out of the Tahoe Paradise San Francisco office at 117 Montgomery Street. The San Francisco branch was key to generating sales because it was believed that city people were the ones that had the money to afford mountain homes.

The sales model he had with Lou worked so well that Jim recruited others. "I had people bird-dogging for me. Mostly bartenders. It was the same agreement I had with Lou; they would keep the $45 flat sales payment, and I would keep the contingent commission. I would get paid monthly commissions and pretty soon I had sold nearly three hundred lots. It added up fast; I was making good money."

Making $210 a year on a single lot was not extravagant. But making around $60,000 a year from 300 sales a year in the early 1960s was something. Constant sales kept Jim traveling back and forth between San Francisco and Lake Tahoe. With his strategy in play, Jim became the top salesman for Tahoe Paradise in his first year on the job, earning around half a million dollars in 2021 money. His various partners made plenty of cash, too. At 25 years old, Jim had followed his grandfather's advice and invested in real estate young. The experience also served as Jim's introduction to the value of partnerships and his awakening to the earning potential found in selling real estate.

Chapter 8:

THE RUNNER-UP

As a result of his hard-earned success, Jim was chosen as the top real estate salesmen to attend the Sales Master Awards in San Francisco around late 1966, an honor in itself. He was accompanied by other top salesmen from various disciplines, one of whom would be named the year's Sales Master and receive the exceptionally generous prize of $25,000, a new car, and a trip around the world. Of course, everyone wanted that prize, including Jim.

It came time to announce the winner, and the runner-up was…Jim Schmit. He was incredibly flattered, but also slightly disappointed that he didn't win that incredible top prize. However, the runner-up was provided the opportunity to take a trip to Hawaii and have lunch with Henry J. Kaiser. It certainly did not compare to a trip around the world, but it was a good consolation prize.

Jim found himself on a plane back to Hawaii to collect his second-place prize. Despite his success, he was recently troubled about some of his latest failed ideas. In a short time around Lake Tahoe, Jim had earned a *golden boy* reputation, or someone for whom *everything he touched turned to gold.* That was only because he was embarrassed about his failed ideas and kept the duds to himself. In reality everything he touched was not turning to gold. These secret failures and the embarrassment he felt were on his mind as the plane touched down in Hawaii, only a few years after he had been a bellhop at The Waikikian waiting on men with gold nugget watches and cutting up the Beatles' bed sheets for a few bucks. The Waikikian was located next to Kaiser's own hotel in Honolulu. On this trip to Hawaii, Jim would be one of Henry Kaiser's guests, not a bellhop.

Born in 1882, Kaiser had over 80 years of life experience and knowledge that he was willing to share with young Jim Schmit and the other dozen entrepreneurs lucky enough to receive an invitation to the luncheon. Kaiser hosted the lunch at his Oahu home and Jim recollects that on the drive there they passed "all this pink construction equipment near his house. It was a shocker." It had puzzled Jim to see such bright pink machines, the same pink as the striped Jeep he owned when he lived in Hawaii. Unbeknownst to Jim, he had been driving around in a Kaiser Jeep just a few years before.

The attendees enjoyed their lunch and chatted easily with each other. Then Kaiser rose and took the podium. Kaiser introduced himself and covered the typical formalities of the event, then brought up his topic explaining how he wanted to talk to all of them about how everything he touched turned to gold. This rang loud and clear with Jim as he was struggling to maintain his *golden boy* reputation.

Jim recalls that Kaiser followed that statement saying, "That is the biggest bunch of bull crap I have ever heard in my life. Everybody knows of Kaiser Aluminum, Kaiser Gypsum, Kaiser Steel, Kaiser this and Kaiser that. But what about the Kaiser car, the Kaiser boat, the Kaiser such and such?" Kaiser continued listing a number of Kaiser enterprises unfamiliar to the crowd. The mogul continued, "Fifty percent of everything I have ever tried has failed. If you haven't failed, you haven't done anything."

Jim can still picture it. "When Henry J. Kaiser said that, he pointed right at me. It was exactly what I needed to hear."

This single sentiment, spoken by one of America's master entrepreneurs, changed Jim's whole life. Jim's perspective on failure transformed entirely with Kaiser's words. He went from being scared of failure to anticipating, expecting, and almost appreciating failure. In a sense, failure validated that he was trying. Jim ultimately realized that true failure wasn't trying something new and having it not work out; true failure was not trying at all. What many people consider failure, Jim merely considers lessons. From then on, Jim explains, "I became honest about my failure. It didn't bother me. I knew I was trying, and I wasn't afraid to try new things. Of course, I wouldn't try to fail, but I wouldn't mind if it happened. And I wouldn't mind telling people about it."

Kaiser also mentioned a daily routine that had kept him productive throughout his life, saying, "Have a business plan every day. I go into each day knowing what I'm going to do. I do the simple things first to set the momentum of productivity. Then move on to the harder things."

Jim immediately started to plan his days, which gave him focus and the structure necessary to achieve big goals. In fact, Jim's daily plans, as they were when he started this practice decades ago, are still carefully listed on his ever-present yellow legal pads. His life revolves around a yellow pad filled with contact information of friends and associates, meeting times and dates, travel plans, to-do lists, brainstormed ideas, and countless other details that keep him moving forward and excited to wake up each day. Despite the ubiquitous technologies of present-day smartphones, touch pads, and laptop computers, which he has as well, Jim feels nothing quite compares to his yellow pad—nor ever will.

That single lunch provided Jim the priceless privilege of hearing Henry J. Kaiser pass along tips and advice on how he became one of America's most successful businessmen. After only a few short hours, Jim was inspired to open himself up to all opportunities and be ready for them with a plan each day. Jim concludes, "I was the real winner as the runner-up."

PART II – RICHES

No one has ever become poor by giving. —Anne Frank

Chapter 9:

THE PARTNER

After some thought, Jim decided he loved Lake Tahoe so much that he wanted to live at 339 Appalachee Drive permanently and he moved up to the mountains as winter was looming. Jim says, "The other realtors told me I would starve because it's impossible to sell land in Tahoe during the winter—they thought I was crazy. But I moved anyway." Jim also recalls watching a *60 Minutes* episode reporting that undeveloped land opportunities were a bad investment. The conditions and timing were not in his favor, but he had a plan.

While Jim didn't know it at the time, a man by the name of Tom Fields would play a key role in his future. "I think I met Tom at a sales meeting at 117 Montgomery Street in San Francisco," Jim reminisces. "That office was right across the street from the Playboy Bunny Club where the girls wore the bunny costumes with the tails. I'd go with the guys after work every once in a while."

Tom obtained his real estate license while teaching physical education and mathematics in the Bay Area town of Pleasanton, California. He worked for Tahoe Paradise selling mountain property on the weekends and during the summer to make a few extra dollars on top of his teacher's salary. It did not take long for Tom to realize that between school and weekend sales trips, the dual work schedule was quite demanding.

Tom says, "Our properties were advertised in the San Francisco Metro area, and a lot of our potential buyers worked on the weekends. As a teacher, I could not take weekdays off to show the properties in Lake Tahoe. Instead, I referred clients to Jim since he was living up there, and we'd split the commission. I could still teach and sell property."

Over time, it became apparent that Tom and Jim worked well together; they balanced each other. Tom had an eye for details and Jim was a big-picture visionary. Tom was good about managing the money and Jim was great about finding investment opportunities. Tom was focused on the present and Jim was always looking ahead. Tom's half-Portuguese roots left him short-tempered and ready for action, while Jim remained mild-mannered through all the ups and downs.

Tom admits, "I was sort of infamous in our partnership for writing letters and berating people. It never bothered Jim. He let me write my letters and it all turned out okay."

"He never sat still," Jim says. "There's thinkers and doers, and Tom was and always has been a doer. I like that about him. I liked his work ethic. He's also smart and athletic and a great golfer."

As different as they were, they had several things in common: Jim and Tom were both just starting out, willing to take calculated risks, and had the energy, drive, and naivety of youth on their side. In addition, and maybe most important, they earned each other's trust and respect because they had the same values and did not underestimate honest, hard work.

Tom remembers the challenges of real estate at the time. "There was a lawsuit in the 1960s triggered because properties were being sold as investments. Jim decided that it would make more sense to sell property not as an investment, but to actually be used by the owner. We would be selling to people who wanted to have and use a mountain cabin."

This shift in strategy meant Jim and Tom were selling to a different clientele. They had more prospective buyers and no longer had to focus on the city-based, upper echelon clients. As a result, Tom's remote real estate arrangement did not last long. In a fitting move, he relocated up to Lake Tahoe to take the Dean of Students job at the new Tahoe Paradise College, a school pioneered by Jim Wilson. Mr. Wilson, who also owned Tahoe Paradise Real Estate, had opened the college independently, adding another attractive element to the growing Meyers community. Released to a number of papers, the Associated Press announced: "The four-year, coeducational college will be housed in the Tahoe Paradise Motel, near the base of Echo Summit about four miles south of Lake Tahoe. Students will live in some motel rooms, with the larger rooms used for classes."

Tom was ready to greet the young students in the fall of 1967 when the college opened its doors. However, he had a unique challenge ahead of him in dealing with young college students. The mid- to late-'60s were a trying time for America, which resonated loudly with college-aged kids. In 1964, America was on the eve of inviting itself to save South Vietnam from communism. Meanwhile, Ken Kesey's Merry Pranksters were scooting around in their psychedelic painted bus, handing out LSD and inspiring the rise of tie-dyed hippies. In June, Congress passed the Civil Rights Act of 1964, and in December, Martin Luther King, Jr. received the Nobel Peace Prize for his peaceful leadership role in fighting for African-American rights and equality. America was the embodiment of incongruity and strife. This era fashioned a generation of peace-loving beatniks intent on freeing their minds and bodies through music, sex, hallucinogens, and anti-establishment groups.

While mountain living buffered out some of the political and racial tension faced in cities across the United States, the instability was prevalent no matter where one lived. The nation was in the middle of a Civil Rights Movement predicated on racial equality, and the shift was gaining momentum through both non-violent protests and civil unrest.

Tom recollects upon starting his position as the Dean of Students at Tahoe Paradise College in 1967, "At that time, college campuses were struggling with turmoil—war, riots, and drugs." Tom soon realized that the majority of his time was spent counseling students as the Dean. He recognized the importance of that role. However, he missed being in the classroom.

Tahoe Paradise College also employed Jim Schmit as the gymnastics coach and a teacher for business classes such as salesmanship and marketing. Jim remembers, "I hadn't been trained, but I taught myself gymnastics and so I was good at teaching the students. I could do an iron cross on the rings. I could stand on a block, then jump straight up, do a back flip, and land right back on that block."

Despite Jim's small frame, he was a powerhouse of athleticism. To a certain degree, Jim was genetically fortunate, but he also was proactive in trying to live healthily. Jim never strayed into the excessive drinking or drug use that was so rampant in the 1960s and '70s.

"I was such a square; I still am. I once had too much wine and had my one and only hangover the next day. I felt like I had wasted a day of my life. I never wanted to do that again." Still, Jim admits that he certainly likes wine and enjoys a glass or two on occasion.

In addition to coaching and sales, Jim was evolving into a clever marketing strategist—far removed from the shy guy that slid flyers under doors at his apartment building just a few years prior. He had become known for employing unusual ways to attract clients and would master one of the great and seemingly impossible challenges of mountain real estate—winter sales.

Jim encouraged Tom to consider doing more in real estate. "I would make $40 a day teaching at the college while Jim would make $400 the same day in commissions," Tom says. The earning potential had a lot to do with Tom's decision to move back into real estate part-time. Jim spearheaded real estate sales with Tom's assistance between teaching and counseling students.

Years before Jim and Tom were on the scene, Jim Wilson bought a large block of land south of Lake Tahoe at a good price and divided it into 5,500 lots. The lots were about a quarter of an acre and started out at $5,000 (or just over $40,000 in 2021), the same as when Jim first got into real estate. Tahoe Paradise plotted, sold, and developed the land in sections starting with roads and infrastructure. Once one section was largely sold, they would start plotting and developing the next section of housing.

To fuel winter sales, Jim decided to introduce some seasonal charm to the cold, snow-covered lots. He talked to a local contractor about the cost of building a cozy wooden cabin, 24 feet x 36 feet, or a total of 864 square feet. Don Jack, the contractor, quoted him $3,800 for the structure, and Jim had one built as a showpiece for potential buyers. It would give clients something tangible and appealing to see, feel, touch, and picture themselves enjoying.

Tom recalls their strategy, "We put together a shell of a cabin that people could finish as a do-it-yourself project. We were selling to folks with average incomes. When we gave them four walls, they could see themselves finishing it. It was like a jumpstart." Jim and Tom also lined up electrical, plumbing, and other professional contractors in case the customers were not do-it-yourself inclined. The new cabin owners had an instant list of local resources to call upon and help fulfill the vision for their little cabin, whether they chose to leave it basic or add every modern convenience available. The cabins could be customized to meet whatever was in the eye of the beholder. All Jim and Tom now had to do was find the beholders.

Jim put up a sign along the snowy Highway 50 advertising cabins for $3,997. He would light up a campfire by the sign, have hot dogs on hand, and provide free snow mobile rides for anyone that stopped. "I had the first snowmobile in Tahoe. It was fun to take people out in the snow and show them around."

Jim breaks it down, "The cabin cost the buyer $3,997. I only made about $200 on the cabin. Of course, then they'd ask, what about the property? It was kind of like selling a Polaroid camera—you make the money off the film. I gave the cabin away, and then we'd make money on the property."

"It was the same deal as before, $100 down and $39 a month. But for people that wanted a cabin, we added $50 to the monthly payment. In the end, they paid $100 down and $89 a month. Now, not only had the buyer made an investment, but they had a mountain cabin retreat." Jim explains.

Winter sales increased dramatically, and the Tahoe Paradise sales team was now quite busy year round. Jim had a sales team working overtime and was splitting commissions with his colleagues. He also found himself actively recruiting salesmen and women. "We would sell 30 or 40 lots in a single weekend," Jim remembers. The money started to pour in.

The ingenious concept transformed property sales. Until then, winter sales in Tahoe had seemed impossible, so these cabins came to be known as the Impossible Cabins. Tom explains, "Jim never looked at the money. It was the art of the deal that was fun for him. Jim liked putting people in properties when they thought they couldn't afford it. He could make it happen; he would take the impossible and turn it around."

Tom reflects, "You know, I got one of my schoolteacher friends to buy an Impossible Cabin, and he spent about $20,000 on the land and cabin after all the original costs and additional upgrades and conveniences. He sold it a few years back for $250,000 on top of over 40 years of rental income. We were so fortunate to be in real estate at that time."

Chapter 10:

THE MANAGER

The Impossible Cabins became enormously successful and Jim was offered a sales manager position at Tahoe Paradise. Jim recalls of his boss and owner of Tahoe Paradise, "Jim Wilson was a really big-time guy, real admired, real dynamic…and very wealthy. He always dressed like a million bucks and anyone that saw him knew he was an important guy. He had a big home on the lake and an elegant wife. She was a kind and gentle person."

Wilson had a business partner, Bob Watson, who Jim also looked up to. Like Wilson, Watson was a sharp dresser, always in a suit and tie, according to Jim. He was also "a real family man. I wasn't brought up in a happy family. Bob was always talking about his family and it was clear how important that was to him. While he was a successful man, it was clear that family was always more important to him than money. I still remember that."

Mr. Wilson offered Jim one of two payment options for the sales manager position: either a monthly salary of $2,500 plus 2 percent of sales and reimbursement on travel, or commission at 8 percent of sales and nothing else. Jim immediately picked the second option. Mr. Wilson reminded him that they had only logged $1 million in sales the year prior and advised that even though Jim was accountable for about half of those sales and did very well, he should consider the math and the stability a salary offered. He also informed Jim that every other sales manager had opted for the salary in the past. Although Jim had his answer, Mr. Wilson suggested he sleep on it.

"People warned me that I wouldn't last six months as the sales manager. Maybe they were a little jealous because I was younger than the rest of them, I don't know," Jim says. What people were saying did not matter to Jim. He was confident he could handle the position and increase sales.

After sleeping on it, Jim stuck with the 8 percent commission. He was confident his work ethic, creativity, and willingness to learn would deliver. Jim knew, without a doubt, that Tahoe Paradise could sell a lot more property than they had the year before. He felt he was just getting started.

In his first year as the sales manager, Jim continued the momentum he had created with Impossible Cabins. He inspired new marketing ideas and the company tried various methods to get people to stop in—from pony rides to free helicopter tours. Jim led the charge and the sales team was right in line with him. "All my salespeople were extremely motivated. We were all making money. I remembered McDonalds kept track of how many burgers it sold. I copied McDonalds and started keeping track of how many lots we sold. It made the staff excited."

At the end of the first year, Jim and his sales team brought in $8 million in property sales (approximately $66 million in 2021 dollars), equating to roughly $640,000 (approximately $5 million in 2021 dollars) in earnings for Jim due to his 8 percent sales commission. This was more than three times the $190,000 he would have earned with the salary plus 2 percent sales commission option. They were far more successful than any of them would ever have imaged—except maybe for Jim Schmit. "The company owed me so much money I didn't get it all at once. I would get huge checks every month, and even then they couldn't afford me. Eventually, I don't remember exactly how it worked out, but I took over Tahoe Paradise Real Estate."

The once shy farm boy had easily and quickly mastered property sales, and truly found his place in the world. Jim succeeded in real estate because he believed wholeheartedly in what he was selling. He made sure he created an opportunity for both parties: the client got an excellent deal on a property and the seller was compensated fairly. It was the classic win-win philosophy. Plus, Jim simply liked entertaining people. He enjoyed the work.

"I realized how much fun it was to talk to people after I came out of my shell. It's fun to hear their stories," Jim raises his eyebrows, "and you just never really know who you may meet."

Chapter 11:

THE DOG LOVER

Tippy, Jim's constant companion

"I've had people say they want to be reincarnated as one of my dogs," Jim laughs.

Jim is extraordinarily kind and loving to everyone, but especially to his pets. He seemed to understand the health benefits of dog ownership long before studies explained how dogs make life better. According to the *Research on Health and Happiness of Dog Owners*, dogs "make you smile more. They force you to move. They encourage you to be more mindful and present. They make you feel loved…science has shown that dogs improve your physical, mental, and emotional health."

There was one partner in Jim's life no other person could match, his trusted confidant Tippy. This lucky dog was afforded the good life. Tippy was the first of many, but possibly the most special of all of Jim's four-legged companions. "I don't even know how I got her. I probably got her as a puppy in Lake Tahoe. I was really, really attached to her."

Tippy was a mutt. She looked like a mix of German Shepherd, Samoyed, and Labrador. Jim called her his Shamoloyed. Tippy was Jim's partner in crime on many adventures.

One particular memory starts with a dawn hike up through Desolation Valley to fish in Heather Lake. Jim and Tippy hiked up the rugged terrain to the quiet lake nestled between craggy peaks and a few green pines at 9,280 feet. Jim hauled up a rubber raft and pole for fishing. Once at their destination, he took to floating and fishing and Tippy stayed on the shore to sniff around and dip in and out of the water. Unknowingly, they were both in store for an unusual yet brief downpour.

Jim says envisioning the memory, "I heard this engine, but there were no motorized vehicles allowed up there. I looked around—then I looked up, and there was a plane flying over real low. Pretty soon it was raining fingerling trout—they were planting the lake. These little fish landed in my boat and were flopping around. Those guys dumped them right on top of me."

Although not his initial fishing plan, Jim may have had his best fishing day ever catching around 50 fish in mere seconds without bait. He placed those flopping baby trout in the lake to grow up and be ready for his next trip to Heather Lake.

When Tippy and Jim had had enough fishing and sunning, they started the hike back down. Mid-way through the hike, Jim noticed Tippy was limping.

"Her paws were soft from swimming and were being torn up by the granite rocks. She was too big to carry so I took my socks off and made pads for her feet." They both made it safely down from the lake, with Tippy wearing socks. It took a couple of days for her to recover.

For work, Jim would drive a van and Tippy had her spot in the back where she would lay down near the door. It bothered Jim that she did not have a view. He decided to have a window put in by the door so Tippy would have a view from her favorite spot. He had customized the vehicle for his dog.

Tom Fields mentions, "Jim always has a dog. At one point he had his dog in his will."

Other friends describe Jim as someone who "anthropomorphizes his dogs" and "is a great dog trainer."

Jim had a secret admirer in the little girl that lived next door, Laura Larson. She remembers Tippy well. "Tippy used to run after Jim's car when he was driving away. I remember he was tired of it and once, as he was driving away, he opened the car door and hit the brakes, and Tippy ran into the door. She never did that again."

Laura also remembers, "We had a sliding glass door at our house and Tippy would come over and beg for food at that door. We liked her, so we would give her food. But one night, she came over with a note on her collar that said, 'Please don't feed me because I'm already too fat.'" She adds, "Tippy also wore a very nice turquoise and silver collar. Someone stole that collar. But Jim got her another one."

Since he brought Tippy home, Jim has kept a furry companion by his side. The loss of these friends is heartbreaking for Jim, but his happiness in caring for his pups outshines the loss of each one.

Jim explains, "There's all sorts of studies out there that prove having a dog makes you happier. I totally agree with that. I truly enjoy taking care of a dog. I'm never alone and they are good company. I even feel guilty leaving my dog alone for too long."

Jim smiles considering one other memory of Tippy, "Sometimes I would take her on the snowmobile. She had her own goggles."

Chapter 12:

THE TOUR GUIDE

Harrah's
LAKE TAHOE

Jim, a friend, Pam, and Rick Barry in 1970
at Harrah's Hotel and Casino

Snowmobiles came about in the early twentieth century for the utilitarian function of getting people and things around on snow-covered land. These early versions were automobile adaptations, with tracks instead of wheels, and typically an enclosed cabin to keep the drivers and passengers protected from the elements.

The personal, open-cockpit, two-seater snowmobile became available in the 1950s, but these models were heavy and slow. Technological advancements through the 1960s introduced lighter and faster variations, attracting a different clientele—those less interested in functionality and more interested in fun. The new recreational sport of snowmobiling had been born.

Jim discovered snowmobiling soon after he moved to Lake Tahoe. "I had the first ones in Tahoe—they were like a tractor, really old-fashioned."

In 1966, snowmobiling was still novel and snowmobiling tour companies did not exist unless you knew Jim Schmit. It wasn't long before Harrah's Resort and Casino teamed up with Jim to coordinate snowmobile tours for special guests.

Harrah's is credited for turning what was once a seasonal gambling destination into a year-round attraction by making a deal with a bus line out of Sacramento in the 1950s to shuttle folks to Lake Tahoe. Like many other hotels, clubs, and casinos, Harrah's brought in mega-stars to entertain guests and draw in more clientele. Frank Sinatra and the Rat Pack, the Supremes, Wayne Newton, the Righteous Brothers, Elvis Presley, Bill Cosby, and more were invited to perform. They were paid and treated well.

"Bill Harrah was the importer for Ferrari and Rolls Royce for Reno, Nevada—he owned Modern Classic Motors. I bought several cars from there: including one of Bill's personal Ferraris. That's actually where I met Bill. He arranged for me to go to a show at the Casino, and we became friends," Jim says.

As their friendship evolved and Bill learned of Jim's snowmobiling pastime, Bill would have his hotel staff call Jim to take special guests on tours. Jim liked doing it because he got to meet interesting people and it was fun.

In 1966, two years after making his first appearance on *The Tonight Show,* Bill Cosby was headlining at Harrah's in Lake Tahoe. As noted in Mark Whitaker's 2014 biography *Cosby: His Life and Times,* "He was paid $20,000 a week. Driving up to the casino, he saw the name 'Bill Cosby' at the top of the marquee for the first time.... The casino owner greeted him as a prince, putting him up in one of the ritziest suites at the resort. Feeling flush for the first time in his life, Cosby splurged by buying one of Harrah's private fleet of Rolls Royces for $35,000."

To add to the princely treatment, Harrah's arranged a special outing for Cosby. Jim remembers, "Harrah's called me and asked me if I would take Bill Cosby snowmobiling. I thought, this will be neat. He seems like a fun guy."

Jim loaded up his snowmobiles and found himself out in the spring snow talking through basic snowmobile operations with Bill Cosby. He had selected a good place to ride with good trails. Jim told Cosby it was important he stay behind him so he wouldn't get stuck in the deep snow.

Jim and Cosby started their tour buzzing around trees and enjoying the fresh mountain air. After some time, Cosby pulled away from Jim and headed on his own path. Sure enough, Cosby found himself stuck in the snow, immobile, and helpless. Jim turned back and helped dig out the snowmobile and reminded Cosby to stay behind him to avoid another mishap. But like before, Cosby veered off track and was soon wedged into another hole. Jim doubled back and helped him dig out…again. Jim repeated his instructions, believing Cosby knew better by then. They continued on their tour churning up the spring snow and when they were headed toward their destination, Cosby split off again and got stuck a third time.

"I knew he was stuck, but I pretended I didn't notice and kept going to the end of the trail. I left him there. He had to walk back, alone," Jim says with a soft giggle. "He just wouldn't follow along like I asked. The walk couldn't have been more than a mile or so. He was very upset."

That next day Harrah's called Jim again. They asked if Jim would provide another snowmobile tour. Despite his frustrating experience with Bill Cosby, Jim was cooperative. He decided to go to the same place and provided the same directions—explaining that the rider was to follow along behind him.

Pam and Rick were a young couple and somewhat new to the Lake Tahoe experience. Rick recalls, "I remember I was invited to go to Harrah's at the end of the season in 1966. I was asked if I wanted to go snowmobiling—I love speed and power; it sounded fun."

"I met Rick Barry right there by the Tippy's Tavern sign." Jim clearly pictures that day.

Pam also remembers first meeting Jim. "The hotel gave us Jim's name for snowmobiling, so we met up with him. He was so small compared to Rick," Pam smiles at the memory.

At 6'7" Rick towered almost a foot over Jim. Rick was taller than just about everyone, but his basketball teammates on the San Francisco Warriors—renamed the Golden State Warriors in 1971. As Rick was wrapping up his first professional basketball season in early 1966 at 21 years old, he was named the National Basketball Association's Rookie of the Year. He had emerged as a clear competitor with a bright professional basketball career ahead.

Out in the snow, after Jim walked them through operational instructions, they fired up the snowmobiles and started along the trails. Jim vividly remembers, "Here I had this professional athlete on a snowmobile, and I figured he would be worse than Cosby. But every time I looked back he was right behind me just as I had asked. It surprised me a little."

Jim could tell Rick genuinely liked snowmobiling and decided to show him a few different maneuvers, including a small jump, to demonstrate the machines' capabilities.

"When I took people on tours," Jim says, "I always drove my racing snowmobile, which was a very powerful machine and gave them my older, slower models. I remember I had a race that next weekend and the prize money was really good. I was pretty sure I would win. I had the best machine around."

Rick had other ideas. "I talked Jim into letting me try out his race snowmobile. It was fast and powerful—I wanted to ride it. Jim knew I was a professional athlete and that I could physically manage the snowmobile."

Rick was convincing enough for Jim to acquiesce and let him try out his racer. But after speeding around and getting a feel for the more powerful machine, Rick continued pushing his limits.

"There was this little jump. I did it a few times fine, and then...I hit it off to the side where there was no trail—there was a tree," Rick remembers.

Fortunately, Rick was not hurt, but the damage to the snowmobile made it impracticable to race.

Rick says, "I felt horrible about it. I told him I would pay for it. I did not know I had wrecked the snowmobile he was going to race that weekend."

While Jim was a bit bummed about the circumstances of that day, he doesn't regret any of it. "I met two of my best friends because of that snowmobile crash. Something good always comes out of something bad. You just have to be willing to see it."

Pam recalls, "Jim was very kind and invited us back again. He was always a very generous host to us. He knew Lake Tahoe, so he was really good about showing us around." Their friendships continued to develop as Pam and Rick regularly returned to Lake Tahoe.

Chapter 13:

THE PROPRIETOR

The Market Campus Shopping Center

Given his financial bonanza in real estate, Jim acquired a large piece of undeveloped land at the junction of U.S. 50 and CA 89. He explains, "I was a young pup, and I wanted that lot because I knew this little town could use some more stores and services."

Still a few years shy of the age of 30, Jim bought and developed the Market Place Shopping Center to serve a variety of needs for the community. In addition to a basic convenience store, over time the Market Campus Shopping Center would grow to include a laundromat, grocery store, Tippy's Tavern, Schmit's Sports Sales, a barber and beauty shop, Tahoe Paradise Real

Estate offices, a hotel, and a post office. A sample Impossible Cabin shell was also put up on-site for people to see, plus the Rough and Ready Room—a restaurant grill where people cooked their own steaks.

"The restaurant grill was different. I came up with this idea that you give the customers a piece of raw steak and they would cook it themselves on the open grills. And we had a salad bar too. It became pretty popular."

Jim had also received intel that the men's U.S. track and field Olympic qualifiers were coming to stay in Meyers so they could train at the top of nearby Echo Mountain for the 1968 Olympics to be held in Mexico City. At an altitude of 7,377 feet, the summit of Echo Mountain was 28 feet higher than Mexico City, and the United States Olympic Committee saw a great benefit to having Olympians train at a proper altitude. When the U.S. Forestry Department, owner of the land, signed off on the plan to build a track on Echo Summit, they requested the land be left as natural as possible. The track oval was six lanes with trees towering in the center field.

With this insight, Tom recalls, "Jim called up the Olympic Committee to ask them how he could help. They said they needed shuttles to get the athletes, coaches, and spectators back and forth from Meyers up to the track on the mountain." Of course, Jim said he had a great place for the shuttles to pick up and drop off passengers coming and going to the high-altitude training facility on Echo Summit.

By the late summer of 1968, Olympic qualifier athletes had arrived with hardy appetites and money to spend. With the shuttles staging at the Market Campus Shopping Center, Jim was ready for these guests.

Tom says, "We had a line around the shopping center for people waiting to get on the shuttle bus, and we had salesmen handing out mountain real estate brochures. Some of those people actually came back and bought property."

The Olympic qualifiers also brought with them an intense media in light of recent events. Only months earlier, on April 4, 1968, Martin Luther King, Jr. was assassinated. The Nobel Peace Prize winner had brought a sense of calm and pride to the Civil Rights Movement, and his death ignited a feeling of despair for many African-Americans that, in some cities, manifested in destructive riots. Two short months later, on June 6, another civil rights figure, Robert F. Kennedy, was targeted and killed during the 1968 presidential campaign season.

Racial tensions were high, and many of America's elite track and field athletes competing for a position on the U.S. Olympic team were Black and conflicted about representing the United States. To give the athletes space to focus, restrictions were established for press and media interactions with the athletes. An August 16, 1968, article from *The Spokesman Review* entitled 'Olympic Camp's Press Ban Unpopular' explains, "Here the athlete is first and only. In an age of promotion, where individual athletes are vigorously exploited for the purpose of sponsors, this indeed is a Tahoe Paradise. The beauty and inspiration of the site aside, it is the community interest and cooperation and the direction of the Olympic Committee program by Bill Bowerman, that makes the Echo Summit camp a success."

Although much was going on elsewhere in the United State, the remote training location and serene surroundings left special and positive memories for many of the athletes. As stated in Bob Burns' book, *A Track in the Forest: The Creation of a Legendary 1968 Olympic Team,* "It was a troubling and confusing time in 1968. For a few brief weeks a California mountaintop provided a remarkable group of individuals shelter from the storm."

Ultimately, there were those whose dreams were dashed on Echo Summit and those who would go to Mexico City and make history. The Men's Olympic Track and Field Team would go on to break six world records and collect 12 Olympic gold medals in Mexico that October.

There every day to play a small role in making the experience a success were shuttles waiting in the Market Campus Shopping Center to haul the Olympic crowds up and down the winding mountain road. Without fail, the athletes and staff had snacks and drinks and real estate pitches to keep them entertained.

After the Olympians left, Jim needed some new ideas to get people to stop in. He decided to make the Market Place Shopping Center memorable by turning the huge pine tree on the property into the World's Biggest Christmas Tree.

Jim smiles, "That's what I called it, anyway. It was huge! I hired these guys to come out with a crane and put lights up all the way to the top. And when you came over the mountains, driving east into Tahoe, you could see it. It looked great!"

The Market Campus Shopping Center and its World's Biggest Christmas Tree would serve as the center of Jim's universe into the 1970s. Ideas, products, and people would arrive; some would stay and some would go, yet the shopping center remains to this day. It still serves the purpose that Jim envisioned decades ago, standing as a gateway for visitors coming to enjoy South Lake Tahoe.

Chapter 14:

THE WEATHERMAN

OCT 1968

Enjoying the snow

In addition to managing his Market Campus Shopping Center businesses, Jim was coaching and teaching at Tahoe Paradise College and receiving an education of his own. He had developed an interest in weather forecasting upon moving to the mountains, and Professor John James, the college's weather expert, mentored Jim in refining his weathercasting skills.

"I became his protégé. On top of teaching, John was responsible for reporting the weather to a dozen or so radio stations and news channels daily," Jim remembers.

After a short apprenticeship, Professor James found Jim competent enough to serve as his weatherman substitute when he was out of town. Jim would faithfully wake up extra early and drive out and record all the climate measurements from the various weather stations the professor had set up in the area and then share the reports with the partner radio stations and news channels.

The diverse topography of eastern California is known for extremes of hot and cold and dry and wet, given its valleys and mountains. The Northern and Southern Coastal Mountain ranges and the Sierra Nevada mountain range, with their nooks and crannies, create numerous sub climates throughout the state and into neighboring regions.

The Sierra Nevada Mountains, Spanish for snow-covered mountains, cradle Lake Tahoe in a northern basin. These mountains host some of the nation's highest peaks, including the tallest mountain in the contiguous United States, Mt. Whitney, at 14,505 feet. The Sierras are also home to the resplendent Yosemite National Park full of majestic views carved by ancient glaciers. In general, the Sierra Nevada Mountains have a gentle sloping western side green with flora and a steeper, arid eastern face as a result of a rain shadow effect.

Lake Tahoe is known for perfect summers with mild temperatures washed in mountain sunshine and the lake warm enough to plop in and enjoy. The winter weather, however, can be harsh. The region consistently collects plenty of snow, with an average of 400 inches over the season to feed a number of winter ski resorts stamped into north facing slopes around the Lake. Winter weather systems originate off the California coast, where the Pacific Ocean can churn up storms like a factory. These cloudy masses march up and over the Sierra Nevada Mountains, and when the warm, moist air of the Pacific meets the dry cold air of the mountains, the storm releases snowy precipitation leaving powdery peaks in its wake. These systems can come and go in dramatic or passive fashion. Despite the technological advances in storm tracking and measurements, the weather can still be unpredictable in the Sierras.

The Sierra Nevada Mountains are, after all, the setting of an infamous story memorialized in the name Donner Pass situated northwest of Lake Tahoe along current day Interstate 80. The Donner party of 81 pioneers set out from Springfield, Illinois, in the late spring of 1846 for the promised land of California. They decided to take the Hastings Cut-off route, a supposedly new, quicker route through the mountains. A late start, a few delays, and an early blizzard left the Donner party snowbound on Halloween just east of the pass with only one hundred miles to go to reach their destination.

Snow had already piled several feet deep, yet a number of successive storms passed through in November burying them further. By mid-December, a team of 15 individuals set out to seek help between the lull in the storms. Equipped with homemade snowshoes and a weeks' worth of food, the rescue team dwindled to seven, with the survivors reaching a ranch on the western side of the mountains 33 days later. Meanwhile, their family and friends remained wedged in by snow walls near Donner Lake living in makeshift structures and awaiting the winter to break so they could continue west. The weather did not cooperate for the stranded party, and Patrick Breen stated in his diary from that time, "No living thing without wings can get about."

Diminishing food supplies required alternative options for survival. While some resorted to eating boiled animal hides and gnawing on leftover bones, others turned to cannibalism and began eating the frozen corpses of the deceased. The first of four rescue parties would arrive in February, and the last survivor would be found in April. In the end, only half of the Donner Party would survive that tragic winter.

Unlike the mountain summits, such as Donner Pass, the Lake Tahoe basin receives respite from many of the snowstorms due in part to its location further east of the peaks. Additionally, the moderating effect of Lake Tahoe, which never freezes over, keeps the air temperature milder around its shore.

Jim still enjoys the cycle of weather, predicting and anticipating the forecast, tracking incoming storms, the uncertainty of what will really show up, and then the surprise in seeing what does. Under Professor James' guidance, he was learning the science behind Lake Tahoe's weather patterns and becoming a keen observer of Mother Nature.

In 1968, the ski season was off to a slow start and ski resorts near Tahoe had opened up late. However, by mid-December, there was an estimated three feet of snow, enough to play in and crank up the ski lifts, with more collecting as Christmas approached. Then a few weeks later, temperatures plummeted, winds blew, and snow fell.

And fell.

And fell.

And fell.

The Lake Tahoe area was blasted by the cold breath of winter and walloped with snow for a 48-hour period starting January 23, 1969. Nevertheless, Jim had weather duties to fulfill since the Professor who was out of town. Jim recalls the storm as if it were yesterday, "It snowed over six feet. I'm sure of it. I called it a *no-walker*. But that morning it took me hours to get out of my house. I had to use a dry cleaning bag to get out of the house."

He explains that after finally digging out the doorway, he would dig to a point to make sure that the snow wouldn't collapse, then throw the dry cleaning bag on that portion of snow, shimmy on top of the somewhat stable surface, and repeat; all the way to his mountain jeep, which he had to dig out as well.

"I finally escaped my house and made it up to my first weather station around noon. By that time, the sun had been on the snow a few hours and it had melted and settled. I recorded 5'11" of fresh snowfall. I know it was over 6 feet earlier that morning. It would have broken records." However, Jim abided by the weatherman's code and reported exactly what he measured.

It was indeed only the start of the snow. The article 'Hoping for another Winter of '69' published in the *Sierra Sun* records, "Snowfall totals soared to nearly 300 percent of normal as a powerful jet stream drove storm after storm into the mountains.... The big storms of 1968–69 set plenty of weather records in Nevada and dumped 601 inches of snow at the Central Sierra Snow Lab near Donner Pass."

Donner Pass got eleven straight days of snow. It snowed so much the houses were completely buried. People were trapped in their homes. Or, for those returning home after the storm, some people had to find their houses by poking long sticks in the snow to tap the roofs. After digging themselves out of their wooden igloos, the winter turned into a fruitful spring with raging rivers and brimming lakes. Residents welcomed the sun and warmer weather.

During the milder months of 1969, as Tom was finishing up his second year as Dean of Tahoe Paradise College, Jim told him to hop in the car; he wanted to show him something. Jim drove them out to a beautiful lakefront property with a quaint wooden cabin and an undeveloped lot next door. Jim proposed to Tom that they buy the property together. Tom was hesitant.

"I thought, yeah right. I don't have the money to do this!" Tom remembers. "On top of not making much money at the college, I was very frugal. But Jim showed me I could do both, invest and still be frugal. Especially if I had a good partner."

At the time, Jim was cash poor himself, but it was such a nice property he wanted to figure out a way to purchase it. The property was owned by a widow named Erma Mace, whose recently deceased husband had been a land developer in Sacramento. She was asking $39,500 cash, or approximately $280,000 in 2021 dollars.

Though Tom and Jim did not have enough cash immediately available to meet the seller's demands, Jim's win-win strategic mind began to compute their options. Jim figured they could each pay $5,000 up front for 25 percent down and then ask to finance the balance. To appease Mrs. Mace, who really wanted all cash, they would offer her $40,000 for the property, or

$500 more than she had asked. Jim proposed the idea to Tom, who agreed, and then to Mrs. Mace.

Sold!

"Mrs. Mace thought we were so nice because we were offering more. She agreed to the arrangement," says Jim.

Their generosity made her more willing to commit to them as buyers and, therefore, more willing to negotiate a payment plan. She got more money and sold the property, and Jim and Tom secured the property in a way that was financially affordable for them. It was another win-win and the two friends were now partners in a new, lakefront investment.

Ultimately, Jim moved into the lakefront property holding the old Tahoe cabin with knotty pine walls and agreed to pay $22,000 of the $40,000. Tom agreed to his share at $18,000 and took the empty lot. Tom recollects: "Jim sold that house a few years later or traded it. I kept my lot and eventually paid it off. In 1973, I got a permit to build a small five-bedroom house, which I still own, use, and enjoy today with my family. It's a simple house. That property is now worth $1.5 million. And to think I was stressed about $18,000 when Jim envisioned it all. I would have never done that if it wasn't for Jim. I wouldn't have seen the finish. He has a way of making things happen. He can see opportunity and make deals."

Chapter 15:

THE SNOWMOBILER

Winter fun

As the memorable year of 1969 concluded with snowfall records out west, the Woodstock Music Festival in the east, the Beatles finishing up what would be their final album across the pond, and the first human footprints made on the moon, Jim had grown accustomed to making tracks of his own.

Between win-win deals, buying and developing property, and teaching at the college, Jim would spend a lot of his free time snowmobiling.

Within a handful of years after moving to Lake Tahoe and discovering snowmobiling, Jim's new winter pastime had developed into a local competitive sport. The United States Snowmobile Association was founded in Wisconsin in 1965 to support snowmobile safety and competitions by establishing uniform race rules. It was the early adopters, like Jim, that helped bring the hobby to different snowy locations and push the young sport into popularity.

The program for the 1971 $10,000 Castrol Cup Snowmobile Race sums up a little of Lake Tahoe's competitive snowmobiling history:

> From a small group of dedicated members in 1966 enthused about a new sport that was just beginning to capture the imagination of Americans across the country, the South Lake Tahoe Snowmobile Association has grown into the largest group in the 13 states of the Western Division of the United States Snowmobile Association. The Association started with five charter families: including Jim Schmit, Schmit's Sport Sales; Bill Ramsey, C&R Automotive; Mildred Buel; William V.D. Johnson, El Dorado County Supervisor; and Vic Colvin, who has since moved from Lake Tahoe. Today, the Snowmobile Association has more than 100 families.

> This year's $10,000 Castrol Cup Race is the most ambitious project the Association has undertaken. It is a long way from their first race in 1967 when only 35 entries were registered and about 300 spectators watched.

> By 1970, their club race had grown to 110 entries that attracted more than 3,000 spectators.

Jim recalls the very first event in 1967, "We set up a racing course on the golf course near the grocery store. There weren't many racers, but it was fun. We set up a hill climb, and my ski friends helped set up the skijoring with a ramp. Then we started riding our snowmobiles off the ramp."

Skijoring is when a skier is pulled by a horse and rider, or in some cases a dog or dogs, through an obstacle course with twists and turns and gates and jumps. In this case, the creative Tahoe crew decided a snowmobile served as a hardy substitute for real horsepower and it was interesting enough to attract a crowd.

"People liked to watch. It was such a novelty. It was like—Holy Cow! It's a whole new sport!'" Jim says.

When 1970 rolled around, Jim was a veteran snowmobile racer. He remembers, "Before races I would lay back on my snowmobile and meditate about the course. I would see myself winning. It was my way of collecting myself." Jim did his fair share of winning on top of making fun memories. "I ended up with hundreds of trophies. I have an instinct of knowing how to control those machines. I never crashed. I know how to push my limits just right."

Pre-race meditation

Jim also opened Schmit's Sports Sales to sell snowmobiles and other winter sporting equipment. Because snowmobiles were still a novelty in some ways, the shop would attract people who were just curious about the machines.

Tom confesses, "Jim got involved with the national race team for ArctiCat. He was a good driver...and would win. But I wondered why we were selling snowmobiles. Jim said if we sell snowmobiles people will stop. If they stop, we can talk about real estate," Tom pauses, "and it worked!"

Pretty soon, Jim had his friends and their friends, wives, and kids racing. Conveniently, under the World's Biggest Christmas Tree was the fully outfitted Schmit's Sport Sales with every item one needed for snowmobiling. Jim would sell the snowmobiles themselves for very little profit—and made most of the money selling the accessories for the sport: helmets, gloves, gas, trailers, and apparel.

Schmit's Sports Sales almost turned to embers when a snowmobile caught fire in the shop one day. Jim says, "I was in the shop and a snowmobile was being serviced and fueled. When it was started up, I guess the fuel line clamp wasn't put back correctly and it caught on fire. I grabbed it and pulled it out of the building and I think Bill Smith came out with a fire extinguisher. That could have been bad."

Snowmobiling wasn't all about racing or profits for Jim; he genuinely enjoyed introducing people to the sport and looking for good spots to kick up some snow. One day in the early 1970s, an older man in a dated, squeaky pickup truck dropped by Schmit's Sport Sales and was asking about snowmobiles. Jim remembers that he was a little reserved but seemed interested. Jim loved snowmobiling and would talk to anyone about it.

The fellow asked, "Do you rent snowmobiles?"

Jim said, "No, but I'd be happy to take you out on a ride—I know a great spot."

The older gentleman agreed.

In the next few days, the fellow returned as planned. He and Jim loaded up two snowmobiles and headed out to Charity Valley to ride on a beautiful expanse of land Jim had discovered. It had some nice wide-open fields and trails great for riding; the magnificent pine trees and mountain views were breathtaking.

Jim provided his usual instruction on how to operate the machine and started the tour nice and easy. Soon they were off racing around and enjoying the day, cruising past one of Jim's favorite landmarks, a log cabin on Red Lake.

After a quality amount of riding time, the pair loaded the snowmobiles back up on the trailer and returned to the shop. The man thanked Jim for everything and climbed into his tattered truck and headed on his way. Jim wasn't sure if his guest had enjoyed snowmobiling; the guy had a stoic personality that was hard to read. Regardless, Jim had fun and was glad he went.

A few days later, the gentleman revisited the snowmobile shop driving a Rolls Royce in place of the pickup truck. He found Jim and formally introduced himself as Loren Bamert. It turned out that Mr. Loren C. Bamert wasn't your average pickup-truck-driving man. He was the president of the American National Cattleman's Association and owned heaps of land south of Lake Tahoe and the Z-brand—the first cattle brand in the state of California. Bamert had so much land he could run cattle from Sacramento to the Kirkwood Meadows along Route 88. He had a lot of land and a lot of cattle.

Bamert told Jim that he had been to a handful of places in Nevada—places like Reno, Carson City, Minden, and Gardnerville—to see about renting a snowmobile, but nobody would give him the time of day until he met Jim. That day Bamert bought two snowmobiles and a trailer.

"Then he told me that the land we were riding on in Charity Valley was his land." Jim grimaced at this news, feeling a little bad about having trespassed on Mr. Bamert's land. But Bamert welcomed him to continue to ride there whenever he wanted.

"He also told me, 'That log cabin you like is mine too. You are welcome to stay there anytime you'd like,'" Jim pauses. "I'm always nice to people; it's just the way I am. But that was a good reminder to never judge a book by its cover. You never know who you are talking to."

Jim did not restrict his snowmobiling to racing and introductory tours. In his early snowmobiling days, he and friend Bill Smith, a former Marine and intense by nature, decided to do a back-country snowmobiling adventure. The plan was to take a day trip from South Lake Tahoe to Bear Valley, stay one night, and return the next day.

Jim says, "Bill was my pilot and he loved to snowmobile and he raced for Schmit Sports Sales. He and I came up with the idea of the trip. We had the route plotted to go along a series of mountain ridges until we found Highway 4, which is closed in the winter, and take that over to Bear Valley."

Four more well-known locals opted to join in the adventure. They called themselves the Six Musketeers and they all agreed on the plan heading out with the mantra—all for one, and one for all.

About 30 miles into the tour, riding along peaks and ridges, someone believed they spotted the snow-covered Highway 4 in the distance. However, it was not perfectly clear whether it was the highway or a snow-covered river or stream bed. "There was a doubting Thomas. The group took a vote, and most everyone believed the path we saw was Highway 4. So we headed that way," Jim says.

The group stuck with the musketeer mantra and started down off the ridge to Highway 4 in the valley as planned. The late afternoon sun was falling in the sky. Once they reached what they thought was their destination, they found themselves in a valley along a river; it was not Highway 4 after all. Despite multiple attempts to return to the ridge they came from, the snow on the steep incline would not cooperate. All they were doing was overheating themselves with sweat and frustration.

"It was a steep canyon. By this time the snow was soft because the sun had been on it. We couldn't get enough traction to get out of that valley and continue along the ridge to reroute and find Highway 4. We were stuck. We didn't have food and it was getting dark. Some of the guys seemed to get a little panicked. We were like the Donner Party," Jim teases.

Between his own logic and Bill's cool head and Marine Corps training, Jim had no doubt they could make it through the night. And if they were stuck a second night, for whatever reason, Jim figured a search party would be out before too long; there were too many big shots on the trip and people would notice they were missing. In the meantime, Jim started a fire and was building a shelter out of tree limbs while Bill went exploring.

Bill says. "We figured we were down in a streambed and if we followed it out it would intersect with the highway. As I was scouting a way out, I found a cabin."

The Six Musketeers were all pleased to get the news that they would be sheltering in a structure with actual walls. However, moving their snow-mobiles to the cabin was the hardest part. Bill remembers, "It wasn't easy getting out of there. We had to put ropes on the sleds so they wouldn't slide down the hill in some places. It was tough. It was one of the toughest rides I've been on."

The group stayed in the cabin overnight, huddling up for body warmth. Leaving early the next day, they managed to ride out of the valley and find Highway 4. The morning snow was frozen and easier to ride on, but it was still somewhat challenging terrain. Once on Highway 4 there were no more major peaks and valleys to face, so the threat of getting stuck was largely over. As the group continued along the highway to Bear Valley, the sun was shining and temperature warming.

Bill adds, amused, "I remember, when we broke off the road towards the end of our ride there was a guy all alone laying on a snowmobile sunning himself. It was the movie star Robert Conrad."

When they returned, a local news article was written about their trek calling them, 'The Six Men Against the Sierras'.

Chapter 16:

THE SPEAKER

Just five years after moving to Lake Tahoe, Jim was living a new lifestyle with unusual friendships and luxurious things. However, Jim is the first to say he credits a lot of his success to good partners and mentors. Unfortunately, several of Jim's business partnerships and mentorships would be cut short unexpectedly.

Jim remembers walking into Jim Wilson and Bob Watson's offices the first time being a big deal. "The next thing I know, every excuse or idea I had I would go talk to them. I picked their brains and remembered everything they said. They took time to talk to me, teach me, and share their knowledge. I considered both of them as mentors. I learned so much."

In particular, Jim remembers a few lessons he learned from Bob Watson. "Bob emphasized that it was important to make time for fun even when you were busy. He always encouraged creative thinking and taught me to never burn a bridge because you never know when you'll need to walk back over it. But mostly, I remember he was such a loving man and would say the word *love* a lot. It was a little different for me to hear. I clearly remember him telling me once that you should tell the people close to you that you love them because you never know what could happen."

Jim Schmit had the good fortune to get to know Jim Wilson better than most of his other colleagues at Tahoe Paradise. The two had a strong bond of respect and friendship in addition to being in business together.

Jim clearly recalls the time he accompanied Jim Wilson to Los Angeles for a business meeting. After their meeting, they both headed to the LAX airport and together they had a cocktail at an airport bar. Wilson was heading to Sacramento and Jim was going back to Lake Tahoe. They finished their drinks and parting ways said goodbye.

"We shook hands and I said—I love you. He looked at me, slightly surprised and said, 'Oh, I love you too.' Jim Wilson didn't use the word *love* as freely as Bob Watson." Jim pauses. "The next morning I got to the office at 8:00 a.m. and Jim Wilson's secretary came in an hour later. She told me he had had a heart attack and died the night before. I had just seen him. I'll never forget that. I was so glad I told him I loved him. Honestly, it scared me a bit. I didn't want to tell people I loved them and think they were going to die. But I got over that and since then, I've been telling my friends I love them every day."

In 1970, at the young age of 48, Jim Wilson passed away suddenly. He continues to be remembered as a respected and knowledgeable man, and the original developer of Meyers, California. Although irreplaceable, Mr. Wilson—who had founded Tahoe Paradise College—had left behind a student of his own in Jim Schmit. Jim highly valued and never forgot what he learned from one of his mentors and was capable of taking the baton to continue developing Meyers to meet Mr. Wilson's vision. Tahoe Paradise College, on the other hand, closed with the death of its founder, and when it did, Tom Fields decided to pursue real estate full-time.

Tom recalls the early full-time days of real estate. "For a brief period of time, Jim and I had a third partner named Bob Hanson. He unfortunately passed away not long after he joined our team. But I remember Bob saying, 'I figured if I followed Jim Schmit around for the rest of my life and picked up the change that fell out of his pocket, I would be a rich man.'"

A lot of other people felt the same way.

There are countless stories that come to mind when Tom reminisces about his early days in real estate with Jim. One day in the early 1970s, Tom remembers a couple stopped by the office in a beat-up old Volkswagen van wearing tie-die shirts and the sales attendants overlooked them, believing they couldn't afford any property and that talking to them would be a waste of time.

Tom says, "Jim walked over to talk to them. He talked with them for about an hour. By the end of it, Jim sold them two lots. Everyone else had assumed they didn't have any money, but one of those hippie kids had a wealthy grandmother."

It was another example of Jim's gift not only for property sales but having an open-minded approach to people—simply another experience confirming that you can't judge a book by its cover.

In the same vein, Jim tells a story of finding himself on the receiving end of stereotypes. He remembers, "It was one of my goals to buy a new Cadillac convertible when I had made it. It seemed like Jim Wilson would go buy one every year from Hubacher Cadillac, the dealer in Sacramento. I liked those Cadillacs."

In 1972, Jim was ready for his Cadillac. As chance would have it, Bill Smith was ready to trade in his Volkswagen and suggested that Jim take it over for him.

"Bill had this ugly Volkswagen station wagon thing he wanted to trade in. I had Tippy in the back seat and drove up to the car dealership and parked it under a tree, leaving Tippy there in the shade. I walked into the dealership and all the people were working in their cubicles and nobody helped me," Jim says.

The green convertible Cadillac sitting in the showroom immediately caught Jim's eye. Without anyone's help, he had decided that was the one he wanted. Then he waited. And waited. And waited a little more.

Finally, Jim asked if he could talk to Mr. Hubacher directly. An assistant asked for his name and he introduced himself saying Jim Wilson had recommended he buy his Cadillac here.

The assistant immediately went back to find Mr. Hubacher who came out promptly to talk with Jim and asked what he could do for him. Jim simply explained that he wanted to buy the green convertible Cadillac. Mr. Hubacher asked if the salespeople had helped and Jim said no, they had not.

"The car was around $6,800 [$55,000 in 2021 dollars]. I wrote Mr. Hubacher a check and put Tippy in the back of that Cadillac and we drove to Lake Tahoe with the top down listening to the music of Montavani on 8-track all the way home. I was so proud of that car," Jim says.

While stereotyping and making assumptions had never been a problem for Jim, it seemed to be an issue for so many others. "Mr. Hubacher asked me if I would come back and talk to his salespeople about customer service. I said sure and one day went back over there and told my story about unknowingly meeting the wealthy Loren Bamert. You just never know who you may be talking to."

Tom reflects on all the memorable stories of the time, "Every day was an adventure. I got in the habit of getting up at 6:00 a.m. because I was excited about the day and what it would bring. It made me realize that when you look forward, life is exciting, but if you look back, it can be hard to get out of bed. That's the way Jim works—always looking forward."

Chapter 17:

THE BOSS

Tom and Jim's continued real estate success required new talent to assist with the increasing workload. With additional salesmen to take on the fieldwork, Jim could run between the Lake Tahoe and San Francisco offices to motivate staff and expand business. Jim summarizes, "I ended up taking over all of the Tahoe Paradise real estate sales with Tom's help. The company owed me so much money, in the end they just turned all the sales and remaining properties to me and we considered it a buyout and I was paid off. I turned Tahoe Paradise into Yank's Reality with an office in the Market Campus Shopping Center. The name came from Yank Clement, a Tahoe pioneer. We had other Yank's offices too."

A young woman named Marty (Leatherbury) had moved to Tahoe in 1972 to enjoy her summer before starting graduate school that fall. When the fall arrived, though, she found she wasn't quite ready to leave and took a job as a bartender at Yank's Station near Yank's Realty—both owned by Jim, or Jimmy as Marty calls him. Marty was one of the first female bartenders in the area. Her plan was to work in the evening and ski during the day.

Marty details, "Jimmy would come in at 5:08 p.m. and have a drink at his bar. He would ask me what a girl with a good education was doing behind a bar. I told him, I'm skiing, Jimmy. He couldn't fathom it."

Marty remembers some drama from her early days as a bartender. She started working at Yank's Station with a guy named Dick who had been there a while. She recollects, "I was tending bar when money started disappearing from the drawer. Things weren't adding up. Jimmy didn't think it was Dick but approached him and Dick pointed at me. I didn't know it, but Jimmy watched me for a few days and eventually came up to me upset because he thought I was stealing from him."

Marty naturally explained that she was not stealing, because she wasn't. Then days later Dick disappeared along with a whole lot of money from Yank's Station.

"I thought it was Marty and it was Dick that took the money. He hit the road with several thousand dollars," Jim says.

"I remember Jimmy came back and told me the whole story and felt bad he had doubted me," says Marty.

The months ticked by and the option of graduate school resurfaced. Marty recollects, "I fell in love with skiing and Tahoe, and I wanted to stay. Jimmy suggested I go get my real estate license and go to work for him." Once Marty got her license, she switched from working at Yank's Station to working at Yank's Realty.

In November 1972, two young ski bums and recent graduates from the University of Wisconsin ventured into Jim's office. Dick Schwarte (not the crooked bartender Dick) had a desire to create and was on the brink of moving back to Wisconsin to pursue a graduate degree in architecture. Bob Novasel was less certain of his future, aside from knowing he liked the snow skiing out West and wasn't ready to leave. A friend of theirs had suggested to them the year before that if they wanted to make money, they should go into real estate.

With that tidbit of information, one day the two found themselves standing in front of Jim Schmit talking about real estate. The two kids started working for Jim and eventually bought three lots together. They, along with a few other 20-somethings, were known collectively as the Mod Squad, after a popular television drama in the late 1960s.

Business was growing. Tom and Jim had between 25 and 50 people selling for Tahoe Paradise in the 1970s. With more staff doing more work, Jim and Tom found themselves building a substantial real estate business. "We had about seven real estate offices in South Lake Tahoe. Jim's philosophy was if you have all the hot dog stands in town, you will sell all the hot dogs," Tom says.

Marty recalls, "Jimmy had a crew of people working for him. He and Tom had their offices and the rest of us had desks. Jimmy hired and fostered people to follow their dreams and do well. He just took you under his wing. He likes to open doors for people. We loved it," she laughs. "Jimmy was Mr. Yank's Station. Mr. Tahoe Paradise."

In those days, selling real estate was generally considered more of a part-time job, something on the side. Jim was encouraging his staff to be professionals and start to look at real estate as a full-time occupation. Dick remembers, "We would go into work on Mondays, and Jim would give these inspirational and interesting talks. Every day was different."

Marty adds, "Tom would come in and share the nuts and bolts of the business. Jimmy would come in and tell a colorful story about thinking outside of the box. He would sometimes hire a good speaker to come in and talk to us. Years later my mother came out to visit and Jimmy talked her into getting her real estate license too. Then she went to work for Yank's Realty."

There was a lot for the protégés to be excited about. They were afforded the chance to live among the mountains they loved, work under a successful boss who was open and excited to share his knowledge, and enjoy the flexibility and creativity to earn a good living. Bob Novasel credits his long-term friend Dick with the idea of drive-through realty. It was one of the many creative ideas they were allowed to pursue in their new jobs.

He and Jim also ran a free dinner program designed to compete with the timeshare market. Tom explains, "We hired a minister to give our free dinner talk in San Jose. Then we would take $25 reservations for people to come up and check out property."

The Mod Squad managed the Tahoe Paradise property and vacation rentals, and also dabbled in selling Impossible Cabins. Bob Novasel insists, "Jim was the best salesman there ever was without breaking the rules. He was inspirational. He's a big reason why Dick and I are still here working in Tahoe over 45 years later."

Dick says, "Jim and Tom taught us that you make money investing in real estate, not selling it. We learned to buy the good deals that came along." Advice they put into practice and that has paid off well.

In the late 1970s, Bob and Dick got into mortgage lending, which worked well for all of them. Jim and Tom now had two trustworthy lenders to recommend. It was another win-win.

On top of the knowledge and experience garnered under Jim and Tom's leadership, one of Marty's standout memories was Jim's fashionable leisure suits of the day.

"Jimmy always wore very nice, expensive clothes. He had this yellow pants suit, and at the time we would think—oh my goodness!" Marty laughs, reminiscing. "He had so much self-confidence, we were impressed. And he loved gold nugget jewelry. It was California in the '70s. It doesn't get much trendier than that."

Marty and Jim dressed up

Jim's success had opened up new doors for real estate sales and land development in other places. He found himself traveling throughout California and to Hawaii to manage offices, motivate staff, and make deals. He continued to invest in good opportunities when they popped up with partners new and old. The constant motion and investing suited him.

"I kept myself virtually broke. The only thing I gave myself was a good home and a nice car. I've always had a weakness for cars," Jim says.

One of the many investments that kept him cash poor was the purchase of a new lakefront property in Tahoe Keys. The Tahoe Keys is a development of peninsulas and lagoons dredged out of the Upper Truckee marsh and designed to maximize lakefront living in South Lake Tahoe. The nearly 1,600 lots carved out of 500 acres created 12 miles of shoreline for purchase. Lots started selling in 1957, with the majority of homes built in the 1960s and 70s. The development originally was intended for summer cabins, but condos and model homes proved more popular. In 1967, the price of a Tahoe Keys waterfront lot ran upwards of $11,500, or roughly $88,000 in 2021 money. Today, many of those properties are worth seven figures.

Jim's Tahoe Keys bachelor pad was decorated with Western antiques and collectibles, and had a Ferrari in the garage. Jim had also opened his doors to roommates, although he didn't necessarily need help with the housing costs. Like any clever, straight young man would be prone to do if given the choice, he was inclined to have smart and good-looking female roommates.

Jim met one of his roommates, Dina, through real estate connections. Dina remembers the evolution of she and her friend Nancy becoming Jim's roommates. "Nancy and I were getting divorced at the same time and Jim needed someone to take care of Tippy—he traveled a lot then. It was an offer we couldn't refuse. We were a happy family. I did the cooking and Nancy did the cleaning." It was a good living situation. The girls were good house guests taking care of everything and, Dina acknowledges, they paid super low rent. In time, Dina became the boss of the Mod Squad, where she met Dick Schwarte, whom she would later marry.

When the house next door to Jim's went up for sale, he called his friends Rick and Pam Barry to give them a heads-up. They purchased the home, which made Jim neighbors with a troop of four Barry boys and one Barry girl, a squad the size of a basketball team.

Pam remembers, "It wasn't very luxurious. There was no television. No insulation or double paned windows. It wasn't necessarily up to code. It needed work." She likened it to camping with walls. "Little by little, we made improvements."

More importantly, it was this basic structure that started a new tradition. "That house began the Tahoe days. I would take the kids up as soon as school was out," Pam says. Conveniently next door was Uncle Jim with fun toys and endless energy for entertaining.

Chapter 18:

THE COMPETITOR

Sailing with Scooter Barry

Lake Tahoe is a veritable summer camp for kids and adults alike. When there wasn't snow on the ground or a deal to be made, Jim could be found gliding on Lake Tahoe in a sailboat or revving up the engine of a fancy car. While he enjoyed the tranquility of a nice drive or an evening sail, he also dabbled in the competitive side of these hobbies.

Even when hosting friends or the Barry kids on his sailboat, he was conscious of practicing and improving his skills. His mind was never at rest, learning each day about how the wind funneled through a ravine near the lake or how the glare of the sun hit the water at a certain time of day. Jim was and remains present and observant of his surroundings despite a world of ever-increasing distractions.

Similar to snowmobiling, Jim enjoyed pushing the envelope with sailboats too. "I liked sailing on Lake Tahoe at night when the wind was up with a Catamaran on one hull. I've never dumped one. I know the water so well that it was relaxing and thrilling."

Jim learned to perfect his sailing while competing in the Lake Tahoe Wednesday night Beer Can Regatta sailboat races. His first race found him and his boat crew in last place. He admits he didn't know what he was doing at first, but learned fast. Soon thereafter, Jim would become a contender in those races always vying for a top finish. His Wednesday night boat of choice was a 35-foot Columbian Race Sailboat. The other not so competitive sailing excursions were often taken on a 35-foot regular sailboat called *My Pad*.

My Pad was owned by Ken Madsen, a successful businessman just a few years Jim's senior. He had started working at 18 years old and ran nine transportation companies simultaneously at the peak of his career. Ken Madsen and Jim shared an affinity for sailboats and fast cars, which made them instant friends.

Ken recollects, "I met Jim through a guy named Gary Eden. I bought my first Lake Tahoe condo from Gary. I went to go check out Gary's boat in Tahoe Keys and it was at Jim's house. When I met Jim, he had this Dino Ferrari in the garage, and he took me for a ride. I loved that car."

Jim's affinity for cars was not restricted to leisure. "Rick Barry started the Ferrari thing. I had a silver one," Jim says.

That purchase would be Jim's first and certainly not his last foray into buying fancy cars. The Dino was a Ferrari sports car available in 1968 and made to compete with the Porsche 911. Named after Enzo Ferrari's son, who designed the vehicle's V6 engine, the car was labeled only as Dino so as not to water down the high-end sports car brand. Nevertheless, the model is often referred to as the Dino Ferrari. In 1976, the Dino name was retired with future models adopting full Ferrari branding.

Ken recollects shortly after meeting Jim, he liked that Dino so much, he says, "I went to Reno to the Modern and Classic Motors and I bought my Dino Ferrari. I bought the Dino that Bill Harrah would let his star guests drive to and from Lake Tahoe and Reno. But it blew up on me."

Ken drove a substitute Ferrari in the meantime until the Modern and Classic Motors could repair his Dino. When he got his back, he painted it black. Ken had also bought a chocolate brown Rolls Royce as a birthday present for his wife Bonnie. Several years later, he bought the Strawberry Lodge for her too, but not on his own. His partner and half-owner in Strawberry Lodge was Jim Schmit.

Strawberry Lodge was built in 1858 and the lore is it was named after a common phrase used by the Pony Express riders when stopping through. They would ask the owner Irad Berry, "Got any straw, Berry?" Tucked in the pines just off Highway 50, Strawberry Lodge is southwest of Lake Tahoe and around nine miles west of Echo Summit. It is a picturesque alpine experience with Lover's Leap serving as part of the view.

Unfortunately, not long after Ken and Jim acquired the Lodge, Bonnie found comfort in the arms of a Lodge bartender who was regularly spotted driving her chocolate brown Rolls Royce around town. Needless to say, Ken's marriage to Bonnie eroded, only to lead him on the path to meet the love of his life. "Something good can always come from something bad." Jim says often. "Later on, Ken found the best lady and now he's very happy."

Across the street from the Lodge was a small building that became home to Jim and Ken's car museum. It would be the first of many museums Jim would manage, this one displaying his collection of beautiful, rare, and extraordinary cars.

"We had President Eisenhower's 1953 Eldorado Convertible—Serial #1 Presidential Cadillac. We had a couple of Model As, a Ferrari, and a rare Mertz car too. There were maybe 15 to 20 cars in there," Jim says.

For a short while in the late 1970s, Jim actually raced his Dino in a local racing circuit. After gaining experience in several nearby competitions, Jim won a race in Tahoe that earned him entry into a higher level race in Sacramento.

On race day, Jim was running abnormally behind schedule and arrived in Sacramento much later than planned. As a result, he hadn't had time to study the racecourse—to learn each turn, strategize, and visualize a win. Nonetheless, he hopped in his Dino when it was time to go and gave it a shot.

Jim recalls, "I had these regular tires on my Dino; they were not made for racing. When I went into a curve, the walls of the tires were not strong enough for the turn. The sides of the tires rolled under on the first curve. I spun out into a field barely missing a steel light pole. That was my last race." His auto racing days were fun, but short-lived.

On another occasion, Jim was not so fortunate to avoid an accident in his Dino. Early one morning, a 16-year-old kid driving drunk after a raucous night outran a red light and barreled into Jim's car as he was proceeding through the green light. The Dino ricocheted into several other stopped cars waiting at the intersection. "The doors were really thick and the driver's side door wrapped around my shoulder. The car was demolished," Jim pauses. "Tippy was in the passenger seat; I went to the hospital and she went to the vet. We both had the same problem—a broken right clavicle. I can still feel where I broke it. It overlaps a little."

Jim's hospital visit lasted merely hours because there was not much the doctors could do for a broken collarbone, but his recovery took considerable time.

Pam recalls, "Jim had a horrible car accident one morning. He came down to our house in Danville to recoup for a while. He went to the kids' games and stayed for about six weeks. That was fun because he got into the family routine."

Tippy and Jim recovered together. Later on, Jim would find out that his heart was temporarily dislodged because of the accident. Jim's heart would prove to be rather special, in more ways than one.

Chapter 19:

THE CUSTOMER

Like his taste for cars, Jim also had a taste for fine jewelry. "Once I started to make money, I decided I wanted a gold nugget watch. I think I started looking for that watch around 1969. I would look while I was in New York and Los Angeles, but I never found one."

Jim was searching for a watch similar to the one worn by the big tipper when he worked as a bellhop at The Waikikian in Hawaii. The watch represented more than an ostentatious accessory; it was a salute to the man that gave him the advice to move back to the mainland and start his career. It symbolized Jim's transition from receiving big tips to giving big tips. It also represented his silent dedication to passing on tips, as both money and advice, just like what was done for him. Jim's search for his gold nugget watch ended surprisingly close to home when he walked into The Jewelry Factory in Lake Tahoe.

Bob Lindner, Sr. opened The Jewelry Factory in Lake Tahoe around 1973. Years before, Mr. Lindner bought a jewelry store in downtown Sacramento. Unfortunately, a downtown construction project diminished their customer traffic and nearly put the store out of business, so they came up with the idea to relocate the business to Lake Tahoe, where they also had a cabin. After all, it was clearly a destination that attracted people with money to spend. Once Bob Linder, Jr. was done with school, the Lindners relocated to Lake Tahoe full-time and opened their store.

Bob Jr. remembers, "We were hungry for business. We didn't have the money to buy inventory so we started making our own jewelry."

The Jewelry Factory became well known in Lake Tahoe and amongst celebrities nationwide for their ability to make elaborate, custom jewelry. Bob Sr. was the salesman and he ran the shop, while Bob Jr. ran the design and manufacturing side of the business. Bob Jr. became a skilled craftsman, creating inimitable jewelry masterpieces difficult for even the most wealthy, flamboyant stars to imagine.

Bob Jr. recalls memories of Jim about town. "We knew who Jim was because he had a Golden Boy reputation in Lake Tahoe. He seemed to be successful at everything he tried. He lived down the street from my Dad in a cool house decorated with totem poles and boats." Bob adds, "Jim was well known and had a lot of girlfriends. He was like a nice Donald Trump."

Jim remembers, "Bob Sr. was very outgoing, a very colorful guy. He was the front man for the store. He would schmooze customers like Liberace and Engelbert Humperdinck. Bob Jr. was an introvert. He did the design and manufactured the jewelry."

Of Jim's gold nugget watch request, Bob Jr. says, "Jim had seen a picture of a gold nugget watch and asked if we could make it for him." Once Bob Jr. confirmed he was up to the task, the watch project began.

Jim remembers the day he got the watch he had waited for so long. It weighed about one pound in gold and was exactly as he had pictured it. The face of the watch was flush with diamonds and the gold nugget band had Jim's initials embedded in diamonds in the latch.

"The day I got it, Tom Jones' manager was staying at my house in one of my extra bedrooms and I was excited to show it to him. Later we went to Tom's show and he and Sammy Davis, Jr. saw it too."

Tom Jones and Jim wearing the latest fashion

Bob Jr. was so talented it only took the word getting out through a few celebrities to make The Jewelry Factory a recognized jewelry source for the wealthy and famous.

Lake Tahoe had become a well-established destination for the wealthy for myriad reasons. Through a combination of geography, politics, and unhappy relationships, Lake Tahoe gained a reputation as being a destination for the rich and the famous and a gathering place for promiscuous people with money and marital issues. Scott Lankford's book, *Tahoe Beneath the Surface,* elaborates on how Lake Tahoe became the hub of glitz and glamour and spurred a sexual revolution well before the 1960s—starting with a rollback of regulations as early as the 1930s. Lankford writes:

> By canceling all wealth taxes, legalizing gambling, and cutting
> the residency period for a quickie Nevada divorce down to

just six weeks, Nevada provided the nation with a fast track to freedom that ultimately proved irresistible.... Meanwhile, more than eighty of America's wealthiest families immediately relocated to Nevada to avoid taxes, the vast majority settling down on Tahoe's north shore along a strip of beach still known today as Millionaire's Row.

Back in 1931, one immediate result of Nevada's reforms was that the number of divorce cases filed there doubled the following year, filling Tahoe's plush hotels and dude ranches to overflowing with the eager (and often fabulously wealthy) divorced-to-be, soon to include Frank Sinatra—not to mention a fresh flood of gamblers.

Joseph P. Kennedy, Sr., father to President John F. Kennedy, was a powerful force in the Democratic Party and frequented Lake Tahoe starting in the 1920s to indulge in more ways than one. Years later, his sons would follow suit in both political ambitions and Lake Tahoe philandering. Rockefellers, Vanderbilts, and Roosevelts added to the long list of famous and wealthy names using Lake Tahoe as an escape. The Cal-Neva Lodge, located on the north end of Lake Tahoe and straddling the California-Nevada state line, was a center for these faces.

Casino performers were as attractive to tourists as the serene lake itself. Performers were paid top dollar for drawing and entertaining fans to Lake Tahoe, and several of them became consistent patrons at The Jewelry Factory. When Frank Sinatra came to Tahoe, the famous Rat Pack, including Mr. Sammy Davis, Jr. often came with him.

Bob Jr. explains, "Tahoe was glamorous before Vegas and the famous would come in and bring their friends. Harrah's and Harveys' Casinos had their own jets and would fly in high-rollers from all over the world. It was a fun time to be here."

By the time he started frequenting The Jewelry Factory, Sammy Davis, Jr. was a tenured performer in Lake Tahoe, having first arrived and performed there in the 1950s. But he had come from poverty and an era of racism. Jim says, "Sammy had a big part in racial integration. He was the first Black performer to entertain in the large showrooms in Las Vegas and Tahoe on equal footing with White entertainers. Frank Sinatra helped open doors for Sammy and was a huge supporter of integration."

Bob Jr. remembers, "I would be in the dressing room before a show, and Sammy would always ask what the count was. He always wanted a full house. I thought to myself: 'What are you worried about? You're Sammy Davis, Jr. You don't get much more famous than that!' Later on, after I read a few books about him, I realized how badly he had been treated before he was famous. He didn't want to relive those days. Sammy was always focused on making sure he sold out his crowds."

Jim's connection to celebrities was fun for him and good for The Jewelry Factory business. Jim sent the multi-platinum singer-entertainer Engelbert Humperdinck to The Jewelry Factory. After a while, the famous faces walking through The Jewelry Factory doors turned into the faces of regulars, and friendships emerged.

"We never asked for pictures, autographs, or favors from the celebrities. We treated them like friends and equals, which allowed us to be in the inner circle. Sammy Davis used to call us his Tahoe family. Sometimes he would come and hang out in the store to sneak away from security," Bob Jr. says. "Sammy was very generous and was always buying presents for his friends."

Sammy appreciated the jewelry and the people at The Jewelry Factory to the point where he happily promoted the store on television. He was never paid for The Jewelry Factory commercials; he provided his star power out of gratitude. Bob Jr. feels that Sammy appreciated their friendship and understood that he was never taken advantage of.

"We charged time and materials. We provided good service and we never asked for favors. If we needed to go repair some jewelry at 3:00 a.m., we would go do it. We were friends," Bob says.

The famous entertainer Liberace also volunteered to promote The Jewelry Factory. Liberace was a larger-than-life presence. Known for not only being a piano virtuoso and one of the highest paid performers in the world throughout the 1960s and 1970s, he lived at the pinnacle of excess and by the motto, "Too much of a good thing is wonderful!" To top off his extravagant costumes, Liberace required extravagant accessories.

"Bob made everything Liberace wore. I had a Tippy ring and Liberace had a Baby Boy ring," Jim smiles, reminiscing about both of their beloved dogs. Bob Jr. had crafted the likeness of Tippy lying in a bed of diamonds with diamond eyes.

Jim and Liberace at The Jewelry Factory

Bob Jr. recalls the time when The Jewelry Factory had a Liberace room, Bob Sr's idea. It was like a museum. Liberace agreed to the idea and the Lindners drove down to Liberace's Hollywood house to pick out a piano and other memorabilia for the room. After the room was completed, they decided it needed a proper opening.

"Liberace said he would show up for the opening, and he did! And Jim was the master of ceremonies. We got a lot of publicity out of it," Bob Jr. remembers.

"I said he was my boyfriend," Jim laughs. "I was kidding."

Although well received on this occasion, Jim's joke was generally a touchy subject for Liberace's career. The performer chose to never disclose his homosexuality, concerned it would upset a large portion of his fan base. Nevertheless, it was quite apparent to most that he was gay.

"Around us he never talked about being gay. He never mentioned it. But we knew he was gay," Bob Jr. says. Pausing, he adds, "Liberace was one of the nicest people you would ever meet. His personality on stage was exactly how he was in real life. He was a really classy guy. He was a great person, on the top of the list of people you would ever want to meet."

Bob Jr. made Liza Minnelli a necklace and a bicentennial ring for President Ford. He also designed for George Burns, Frank Sinatra, Rich Little, Bill Cosby, Tom Jones, Frankie Fanelli, Rip Taylor, and a lot of other great people. When asked if he ever made anything for Elvis, he replies, "I fixed a lot of his jewelry, but I never made anything for him. I did get to fly in his Learjet once."

Jim had his own encounter with Elvis—an evening involving professional football player Fred Biletnikoff, a boat, and eggs for breakfast.

Fred was a wide receiver for the Oakland Raiders for fourteen seasons from 1965 to 1978. He helped them get to two Super Bowls with his sure hands and was named the Super Bowl XI Most Valuable Player when the Raiders beat the Minnesota Vikings 32–14 on January 9, 1977. Jim explains, "Fred was a personal friend. When he injured his knee in his second year with the Raiders, he moved up to Lake Tahoe and worked for me while rehabilitating." After Fred's recovery, he and Jim remained good friends. Years later, Fred started what would be one of Jim's most memorable nights, in the spring of 1976.

"Fred was staying at my house when Elvis was in town performing. I thought it would be neat to meet Elvis. I knew he was a football fan, so I suggested Fred call the hotel where Elvis was staying and ask if he could meet him. Then I could tag along with Fred," Jim grins.

The call worked, and Fred was invited to the show with Jim as a tag-along. However, they chose to skip the show and simply meet the famous singer afterward. The casino had suggested Fred and Jim drive over to join the post-performance flotilla, sure to involve many lovely women. Instead, Jim requested that the boat simply swing by his house to pick them both up. Jim was certain that the boat captain knew where he lived—his was one of the few houses in Tahoe Keys. Besides, Jim was thinking strategically—if there were ladies onboard, they might remember him a little better if they knew he owned a nice house on the Lake. So, Fred and Jim, along with a few other select guests—yes, many of them beautiful ladies—joined Elvis on a boat after the show.

Several hours into their starry night cruise, it was so late it was early, and people started to think about breakfast. Elvis mentioned that he could cook a good breakfast and, according to Jim, one of the guests challenged him, saying, he bet Elvis had never cooked an egg in his life. To settle the matter, Jim suggested they all swing by his house for Elvis to prove his break-fast-making skills; and they did. The party moved to Jim's house, where Elvis cooked up a bunch of eggs for guests and crew, and they ate Elvis Presley eggs while the rest of Lake Tahoe was sleeping.

"I remember that avocado green stove I had at the time. I had all the top appliances in my house. Elvis cooked on that stove," Jim says.

The eggs were not memorable, but the night certainly was. Jim was having such a good time he drank rum and cokes to stay awake. Late nights were an abnormal occurrence for Jim as were the cocktails, but a night cruising Lake Tahoe with Elvis Presley and Fred Biletnikoff proved an appropriate exception.

In the end, Jim was extra fortunate to have met Elvis as it was his last performance in Lake Tahoe. A little over a year later on August 16, 1977, Elvis died in Memphis, Tennessee.

"Elvis was a great guy. I'm lucky I got to meet him," Jim says. "I wasn't very star-struck about celebrities because I was used to being around them a lot. It was easy for me to talk to them. I could kind of fit in. But Elvis was," Jim pauses, "...*Elvis!*"

Of course, in addition to the stars, Bob Jr. still made jewelry for the regular old millionaires out there like Jim. The gold nugget watch remains a treasure to Jim in its symbolism of a lifelong friendship with the Lindners. Along with that watch, Jim collected quite an assortment of rings, necklaces, bracelets, charms, and medallions from The Jewelry Factory, including a gold nugget ring he still wears daily.

Bob Jr. sums up that epoch of Tahoe: "Our timing was perfect. Jim's timing was perfect. Nevada had a lot going on. It was a hot place. It was glamorous and personable."

The range of The Jewelry Factory customers was vast and varied just like the range of characters finding purpose in Lake Tahoe. On one end of the spectrum were the famous that sought the spotlight—and on the other were the infamous that stayed in the shadows.

Chapter 20:

THE OUTSIDER

Mafia roots ran deep in Lake Tahoe's early days. The Cal-Neva Lodge & Casino, situated at the north end of Lake Tahoe and straddling the state boundaries, was a hub of underground activity—literally and figuratively. It was outfitted with a showroom, a helicopter pad, and secret tunnels used by famous musicians, actors, politicians, and criminals of the day.

Under Frank Sinatra's ownership, in the early 1960s, the Cal-Neva Lodge & Casino welcomed friends, guests, and members of the Rat Pack. The Rat Pack was a famous group of charismatic entertainers who cavorted together in the early 1960s, entertaining crowds as crooners and on the big screen. Frank Sinatra, Dean Martin, Peter Lawford, Joey Bishop, and Sammy Davis, Jr. were considered the core of the group. Some members of the Rat Pack contributed their celebrity to John F. Kennedy's successful presidential campaign; not surprising given that Peter Lawford was Kennedy's brother-in-law.

Today some believe the Cal-Neva Lodge & Casino is haunted by ghosts. Marilyn Monroe was a regular guest at the lodge and spent some of the last days of her life there in early August 1962, before returning to Los Angeles where she was found dead just days later. Her presence has been reported to have been felt in the cabin she regularly used.

Sinatra's ownership of the Cal-Neva Lodge & Casino was short-lived. About a year after Marilyn's final visit, he sold it under pressure from the

Nevada Gaming Commission after authorities identified a mob boss at the casino who had been blacklisted from gambling establishments. Sinatra's gaming license was revoked, and his casino-owning days were over.

Mafia connections were not exclusive to the Cal-Neva Lodge & Casino in the north of Lake Tahoe, nor did they disappear with Frank Sinatra. The mafia presence persisted in the Lake Tahoe area through the decades, and both Bob Jr. and Jim had their own encounters with mafiosos. Bob Jr. remembers: "In 1966, when I was 16 years old, I played drums for a topless show called Billy and The Beavers at The Nugget Casino owned by Sharky and [Richard] Chartrand. There were four of us in the band and two dancers. We lost our dancers and it was hard to find them in Lake Tahoe at the time. So my Dad and his friend, just helping us out, naively went to North Beach in San Francisco to hire some dancers. Before they knew it, they were being beaten up by the Mob. These Mob guys told them the next time they saw them in their territory, they would be floating in the Bay. Two years later, Chartrand was killed from a car bomb planted in his Cadillac. Some say that was the end of Mob influence in Tahoe. Either way, it was a sign of the times."

The Bonanno crime family had roots in New York and business dealings in gambling and narcotics. Joseph Bonanno was a dominant figure in the New York mafia, but when he unsuccessfully plotted against other mafia bosses, he disappeared for a few years in the mid-'60s, effectively splitting his family. As coined by the media, this *Banana Split* or *Banana War* led to half of the family remaining loyal to Joseph Bonanno and the other half supporting the new family boss, Gaspar DiGregorio. In 1968, Bonanno, after a short return to running the family, suffered a heart attack and retired.

With Jim's golden boy status and connections around Lake Tahoe, he mingled with celebrities on a regular basis. He would occasionally join Cher at the Midnight Mine after her shows. Of course, there were Sammy Davis Jr., Tom Jones, Liberace, and that night on a boat with Elvis. Jim also got to know lounge crooner Frankie Fanelli. "Frankie Fanelli and I were really good friends. He stayed at my house and we traveled some together."

Frankie Fanelli, also called the Pleasant Paisano, moved to Reno to pursue a singing career. He began by singing in the Reno clubs at night and driving a beer truck by day. Frankie spent time in the spotlight from the mid-'60s through the early '80s in Reno and Lake Tahoe and was known for his talent and great personality.

When Sinatra was ousted from Lake Tahoe, Fanelli stepped in as the next crooner. And like Sinatra, Fanelli had some connections to the local mafia scene. One night, Fanelli invited Jim to his show. Jim was led to a front row seat with a number of Fanelli's other friends, and after the show they were all invited backstage.

"Later, when we got back to my house, Frankie asked me if I knew who I was sitting with. I had no idea. He told me I had been sitting with members of the Bonanno crime family. I was sitting right in the middle of this gang. Their guards were lined up behind us and I didn't even realize it," Jim says.

Jim explains the depth of his mafia-savvy in one basic rule: "There is one thing I know you must never do—not that I ever would—you never mess with an Italian's wife. It doesn't matter if they have a few mistresses, the wife is off limits."

There was this whole other side to Lake Tahoe that Jim had never associated with and a casual interaction was enough for him. Despite the criminal contingent around Lake Tahoe and their mean guy reputations, Jim reflects about crossing paths with the Bonannos, "They were nice to me."

Chapter 21:

THE STATISTICIAN

By late 1974, Jim had worked himself into a tizzy. He took some time off in early 1975 and began the year traveling with the Golden State Warriors serving as a team statistician. His connection was his old friend Rick Barry. Rick was a basketball veteran by then, having spent nearly a decade perfecting his game. He had worn a number of different jerseys since his first year with the Golden State Warriors and he consistently put up incredible numbers on the court, including making nearly every underhanded free throw he tossed up. Rick found himself back on the west coast in a Golden State Warriors jersey in 1972.

As the Warriors 1974–75 season progressed, Jim was tallying up their points, assists, rebounds, steals, and every other statistic they requested. Jim would travel with the team for away games and be right in the mix. On the road, Jim would go out exploring while the team was practicing. "I couldn't just sit and watch practice. I never wanted to waste time. I would be a tourist. I had plenty of money so I would hire a cab for the day and have them show me around the area. I was interested in wherever I was."

On his outings, Jim always kept an eye out for property. His specialty, after all, was not basketball statistics; it was buying and selling real estate as well as developing housing and resorts. Jim always enjoyed touring the big town attractions. However, he took greater interest in exploring small places.

When it was game time, Jim was courtside on top of the action sitting center court to assist the announcer by providing stats for him. He remembers, "You know being in charge of the stats was not an easy thing. It's not like baseball where there is a lot of time between the action. Basketball is fast-paced. You have to have your wits about you."

Jim kept sharp stats and as the season and games ticked by, he realized that he was working for a special team. As luck would have it, Jim picked the optimal season to float around the country with the Golden State Warriors. The team ended regular season play taking the division crown and leading the Western conference with 48 wins. The Warriors then defeated the Seattle SuperSonics in six games and the Chicago Bulls in seven during the playoffs. They had made it to the championship series based on old-fashioned teamwork. It was a feat unpredicted by all sports fans, pundits, and critics. In the era of short shorts, tall socks, and big hair on the basketball court, it was all working for the Warriors.

By May of 1975, the Warriors were matched up with the impressive Washington Bullets, battling to win four out of the seven final playoff games for the Championship title. The Bullets had logged in 60 regular season wins and had beaten the Warriors in three of their four regular season matchups; they were highly favored to win the championship.

The Bullets would host the first game, in the Washington, D.C. metropolitan area. The Warriors were to host the following two games, but their home court had a scheduling conflict. So instead of hosting the Bullets at the Oakland Arena, the Warriors would use the Cow Palace near San Francisco as their home court.

Jim remembers, "They weren't expected to be in the finals and then they couldn't play where they normally played. They didn't even have home court advantage. They weren't supposed to win any of the games."

The series started out surprising when the Warriors made an epic second half comeback to win the first game over the Bullets, 101 to 95. The second and third games at the Cow Palace were combats to the end; the

Warriors won by a slim one point in the second game, with Rick contributing 36 points. The Warriors won by eight points in the third game, with Rick accounting for 38 points.

By the fourth game, back on the East Coast, the Bullets heavily targeted Rick, knowing he was an exceptionally dangerous threat. Rick was aggressively guarded from the first whistle. After he was violently fouled just minutes into the game, he reacted by shoving the Bullet defender who had fouled him. Warriors Head Coach Al Attles raged out onto the court in defense of Rick. As a result, Attles was ejected from the game, possibly in Rick's place. The remainder of the game was coached by assistant Joe Roberts, and the indignation of that foul only ignited the Warriors' game. They would outscore the Bullets in the three remaining quarters, despite boos from the Washington home crowd. The final game ended in with the Warriors beating the Bullets by one giant, series-ending point; the final score was 96 to 95.

Against great odds, the Golden State Warriors had swept the Washington Bullets to win the NBA Championship in four consecutive games. Celebrating was in order—it began on the court after the final buzzer and continued into the locker room. In an online archived video following the fourth game, Most Valuable Player Rick Barry reflected in the locker room:

> This has been such a fantasy year, I mean, the way we started out...we battled and scratched and fought our way to be world champions. It's a fitting climax, I think for one of the most unique teams in pro basketball history. A team that has guys who care about one another as individuals. Guys who will never quit; never give up. I don't know how many teams have come from as many games behind as we have to wind up becoming champions of the world and beating a team four-straight—that they were supposed to do that to us. It's the end to the most rewarding, fulfilling year of basketball in my life. I don't know how anything else could ever top it. The fans back home have

been fantastic. We love them. They were a big factor in our getting this far.

1975 NBA Finals Most Valuable Player, Rick Barry during his locker room interview with Jim at upper right

All the while, a shaggy-headed Jim can be seen bobbing around in the background just past Rick Barry's head grinning from ear to ear.

"They won the championship in Washington! It was amazing! Rick averaged 30 points a game for that year. He was shooting out by the three-point line, but he only got credit for two points. So now, with the three-point rule he might have easily averaged 40 points a game," Jim says.

The three-point line would be added in professional basketball at the start of the 1979–80 season, which would be Rick's last season playing ball. He concluded it with the Houston Rockets, setting a free throw percentage record with a 94.7 percent rate for the season, thanks to his famous and accurate underhanded shot.

Jim also recalls two particular friendships that originated from his statistician days. Doctor Albo was the team physician for the Warriors as well as the Oakland Raiders. "Doc was a striking presence. He was a powerful man with a great stature. The guy was brilliant. He was a very famous physician and also collected magic stuff. It was his hobby. Albo was a classy guy. A first-class dresser."

Before becoming a physician, Doctor Albo was a respected athlete in his own right. A 2011 *East Bay Times* article states, "He was one of UC Berkeley's finest two-sport athletes before spurning a Major League Baseball offer to attend medical school. He helped finance his education by doing magic shows. He later became an international authority on magic, writing 15 books on the subject."

Not only was Doctor Albo an all-around good guy and friend, but he would also become one of Jim's future investment partners.

Another friendship that exists thanks to that Warriors championship season is Jim's close connection with Clifford Ray. Jim says, "We just hit it off and befriended each other. Clifford is a very warm person with a deep, calm voice. He is so easy to talk to and he talks to everyone. The waitress, the bank teller, the whoever. He's very outgoing."

When Jim and Clifford Ray met that year, Clifford was new to the Warriors and played an important role in melding the team together. He was not only a tower of muscle at 6'9" and 230 lbs, but he was also the epitome of a team-oriented, selfless player. Clifford would focus on what he needed to do to help his team win by putting ego aside. His contributions were monumental; he led the Warriors in rebounds, and his strong defense and rebounding skills helped anchor their championship season.

Jim says of his friendship with Clifford, "We are quite a pair. He is a giant black guy and I'm a little white guy. People can't help but notice Clifford and then probably wonder—Who's the little guy with him?" Jim laughs, then adds, "He lives to fish."

Jim's time off as the Golden State Warriors' statistician ended in a championship and, more importantly, a couple of new and wonderful friends.

Chapter 22:

THE ENTERTAINER

Dotting the shores of Lake Tahoe are luxurious and elaborate estates built with fortunes dating back to when acquiring swaths of land along the shore-front was still possible. "I had planted a seed in my early Tahoe days that I wanted to own one of the famous lakeside estates," Jim says.

On the east side of Lake Tahoe sits the Thunderbird Lodge built by the eccentric playboy George Whittell, Jr. His vast wealth was credited to his clever immigrant grandparents laboring successfully through the Gold Rush and investing in San Francisco real estate. The fortune was enhanced as his parents continued investment in real estate and railroads.

George Jr., on the other hand, had a fondness for women, wild animals, and defying the wishes of his parents. After traveling with the Ringling Bros. and Barnum & Bailey Circus, serving a tour in World War I as an ambulance driver, and a decade of partying, George Jr. found comfort on the shores of Lake Tahoe. Construction on his Thunderbird Lodge began after he bought the land in 1935, which included plenty of houses: guest houses, a card house for poker games, a lighthouse, a gatehouse, a private zoo with an elephant house plus an atrium, and a boathouse with a 600 foot tunnel to the main house. The boathouse protected his lavish wooden speedboat, the gorgeous Thunderbird yacht, made for cruising around the lake. The Thunderbird yacht is still operational today and is considered a historic landmark. It is cared for by the Lake Tahoe Preservation Club and used for chartered cruises and special events.

One of Jim's favorite estates is found in the southwest corner of Lake Tahoe at the tip of Emerald Bay; the secluded Vikingsholm castle was one of the first summer homes on the lake. The land in Emerald Bay had been bought and sold a number of times until Lora Josephine Knight purchased it and built a Scandinavian-inspired summer home in 1929. The home boasts detailed Nordic carvings, multiple fireplaces, paintings on the ceilings and walls, and hand-crafted furniture. It also features a tea house on Fannette Island, which is a collection of granite rocks sitting in Emerald Bay and the only island in Lake Tahoe. The large home was built for hosting family, friends, and events in elegance and comfort amidst unmatched scenery. In its entertaining days, the house required a staff of nearly 15 with a caretaker manning the property year-round.

On Lake Tahoe's western shore is a small community called Homewood, nestled amongst the feathery green pines near the ski runs of Homewood Mountain Resort. The town was founded in the late 1800s and hosts some of the most luxurious old Tahoe estates on the Lake, including Henry J. Kaiser's retreat he called the Fleur du Lac or Flower of the Lake. Kaiser, along with several other partners, built 17 homes on the property plus a boathouse, guest cottages, and servants' quarters. The Kaiser estate is often referred to as the *Godfather* estate after being featured in the movie *The Godfather II*.

Two doors down from the Fleur du Lac sat the Douglas Oil estate, built from oil money accumulated by the Douglas family following World War II. The home was outfitted with a swimming pool, tennis courts, and private pier. It was a mountain-inspired home capturing old Tahoe extravagance—and exactly the type of estate Jim wanted to own.

Not long after the Warriors won their 1975 championship, Jim remembers, "I was having dinner with Doctor Albo and Charles Schulz at one of my favorite steakhouses in Oakland. Doc was friends with Charles Schulz, the Peanuts guy. Anyways, I got a call, and was told the Douglas Oil estate was going to be up for sale. I mentioned this to Doc and asked if he wanted to partner in the purchase. He said sure and we bought the mansion fully furnished."

Doc named the place Shangri-La, a nod to the tranquil paradise described in James Hilton's 1933 novel *Lost Horizon*. Shangri-La is a fictional mountain hideaway of unsurpassed beauty full of contented people sheltered from the chaos of the outside world. While Shangri-La is considered a mystical place, it also very much reflects Jim's mindset in any location: always content and sheltered from the misgivings of the rest of society.

Also nearby was the estate of David Packard, United States Secretary of Defense under President Nixon from 1969 to 1971, who had co-founded Hewlett-Packard in 1940. Several years before Jim and Doc invested in the estate in late 1975, the Watergate scandal in Washington, D.C. was filling the headlines. A thorough investigation took place, and President Richard Nixon denied involvement or knowledge of any clandestine activity. Yet on August 9, 1974, Nixon became the first and only United States president to resign from office.

He left in shame and disgrace. The events had taken a toll on the former president, and he retreated to recover in the ocean air and sunset-facing beaches of his home in San Clemente, California. Far from Washington, D.C., Nixon was working to mentally recover though his body began to physically fail. He needed to disappear; he needed a hideaway, a location where he, too, could be content and sheltered from the misgivings of the rest of society, possibly up near a mountain lake.

"Someone, and I can't remember if it was Packard or somebody else, told me that I was sleeping in the same bedroom Nixon had stayed in before I moved in. I remember thinking, oh that's really interesting. Of course, I can't really prove it, but it makes sense. Packard's estate was close by," Jim smiles.

Of the 14 bedrooms in the house, the *Nixon* bedroom was the one with the best view overlooking the lake and the pier. "There was this beautiful red bedspread in the master bedroom. It was strange to think that President Nixon may have slept under that bedspread," Jim says.

After Jim and his beloved dog, Tippy, moved in and occupied a tiny fraction of the mansion, Jim realized the home would be an ideal setting to host a special event. "I wasn't a party guy, but I wanted to host one super party—like you see a movie star host. So, I did it. I went all out!"

He was dating a gorgeous heiress of a retail giant based in Dallas, Texas, and decided her birthday was the perfect occasion for a party. Jim wanted to impress her. He spent around $15,000, or nearly $65,000 in 2021 dollars, to decorate and cater the event. He sent out invitations to 50 close friends and bigwigs, and decorated the house with flowers, including floating orchids in the pool. "Girls like flowers, so there were flowers everywhere," Jim explains.

Jim had arranged a Rolls Royce shuttle to pick up friends in South Lake Tahoe and welcomed others to boat over and tie up to the 200-foot long pier. The guests arrived in pressed suits and exquisite dresses for the party of the decade, enjoyed a catered sit-down dinner complete with wait staff in the formal dining room, and were serenaded by Frankie Fanelli.

Jim invited a lot of friends he worked with. Marty Leatherbury reminisces, "It was a beautiful night. Everything was decorated up and fancy— to the nines. Everybody who was somebody got invited and we got to go because we worked with Jimmy. I went with Bobby Novasel, and Dick and Dena Schwarte. We were stressing about what we were going to wear," she pauses. "That party meant a lot to him."

"I remember going to a party there. It was one of the old mountain-style estates on the West shore. It had tennis courts and a swimming pool," Bob Jr. remembers.

Jim was pleased with the turnout. Smiling, he says, "It was talked about for a long time."

After about a year, the hour-long commute back and forth to South Lake Tahoe from Homestead grew old. Jim felt his dream of owning, living in, and entertaining at a grand estate was fulfilled so he sold out his partial ownership to Doc without a single regret.

Chapter 23:

THE ENTREPRENEUR

Although known and respected as an incredible professional basketball player, Rick Barry had gained a reputation as having a bit of a salty attitude through his career, and as a result, endorsement opportunities did not readily flow his way. "I think it was unfair. In my opinion, whenever Rick made an argument or got upset on the court, it was for a good reason," says Jim.

In addition to playing basketball, Rick enjoyed experimenting with creative and prospective business ideas. Jim and Rick's first business partnership blossomed about the same time as the Golden State Warriors' memorable championship season in 1975. Jim says, "We had Rick Barry, a superstar, in our pocket, and he was game for a marketable product; he was ready to make money."

Jim, Rick, and Tom Fields had brainstormed an idea different from the typical big business endorsement deals handed out to professional athletes. They created the Rick Barry Top of the Line Club. The club encouraged card-carrying members to frequent certain restaurants, retailers, and businesses. Merchants paid $50 and received advertisement through the club and could post Rick Barry Top of the Line Club signs at their locations. Members paid $25 to join and received discounts and perks at the participating businesses. For instance, one restaurant provided a free bottle of wine to cardholders, while a small grocer gave a 5 percent discount. The Top of the

Line Club had real potential. Therefore, the three friends decided to invest their own capitol rather than recruiting investment partners.

"We didn't want to raise money from investors because it was such an unusual idea," Jim says. But that novelty also made it a challenging concept to sell in the 1970s.

"It was very innovative. This was before airline miles, bonus points, and all the other reward programs out there today. The only thing close to this idea was the gas stations and their green stamps program," Tom remembers.

The Green Stamps program is credited to the Sperry & Hutchison company, originally founded in 1896. Sperry & Hutchison owned supermarkets, department stores, and gas stations, and incentivized customer loyalty by giving customers green stamps when they checked out based on the total of the purchase. The stamps were pasted in free booklets and could be redeemed for housewares and other goods at a brick-and-mortar Green Stamps store or through a catalog. The idea generally lost popularity in the 1970s when customers found it more trouble than it was worth.

Today, rewards programs are ubiquitous. Despite the potential of the Rick Barry Top of the Line Club, Tom says, "It didn't get off the ground. It was too new and while everyone was positive about the idea, it fell under its own weight."

Jim says, "We used our own money to a point until we felt too much risk. Then we abandoned the idea."

"It was a great concept. We were ahead of our time," Rick concludes.

They regrouped and came up with another concept. Jim remembers, "The Pet Rock became a big thing in 1975. It was a rock sold in a box and it took off like crazy. We were looking for our Pet Rock idea!"

A Pet Rock cost $3.95, nearly $19.00 today, and came complete with a straw nest, a box with air holes, and a quip-filled owner's manual. As inventor and advertising copywriter Gary Dahl believed, it was arguably the best pet known to man because it required no feeding, walking, training, or cleaning, and it never died. The owner's manual, entitled *The Care and Training of Your Pet Rock,* was full of comical information and advice, including sections that cover rock pedigrees and training tips:

> There are hundreds of breeds of rocks. Of the hundreds of breeds of rocks known to man, only a few show the necessary aptitude required of a PET ROCK. The more important traits associated with genuine PET ROCKS are gentle disposition, eagerness to please, and a profound sense of responsibility. ...

> Fetch. To teach your PET ROCK to FETCH, throw a stick or a ball as far as you can. Next, throw your PET ROCK as far as you can. Rarely, if ever, will your PET ROCK return with the object, but that's the way it goes.

The concept originated in a bar and the genius was in the packaging. The Pet Rock became an American sensation for a few months. Sales were boosted thanks to an appearance on *The Tonight Show*, countless news articles, and availability just in time for Christmas. After the focus on Christmas turned to New Year's, the fad lost momentum, but not before approximately 1.5 million Pet Rocks were sold making Dahl a millionaire in mere months.

In seeking out a Pet Rock idea, Jim, Tom, and Rick came up with the Rick Barry Products Company. They developed about 20 ideas, and the one that gained the most momentum was the Flip Card Traffic Communicator. It was a small flip chart, 5" x 10" with around 10 pages. Each page had a message to communicate from one car to another well before cell phones were an option. The cards would say *Check Tire, Check Door*, or simply *Hi* or any other number of helpful or amusing things.

The Rick Barry Products Company took this idea all the way to Detroit hoping to get a car manufacturer to include it in each vehicle as a safety device. Jim and Rick even made it to see Gerald Ford in the White House and inform him of the Flip Card Traffic Communicator idea, but it was never picked up.

Jim brainstormed up other car-centric ideas to sell. He had noticed that on many mountain roads in the Lake Tahoe area, there were no reflectors on the roads to help guide drivers at night because the snowplows would simply pluck them right off the road in the winter. Jim began brainstorming a solution.

"My idea was to create a reflective disc that looked almost like the top of a tennis ball, and about that size too, and scoop out a small portion of the roadway to inset the reflective disc. I figured the snowplow could just go over the top of it and not knock it off the road. I proposed this idea to some highway guys, and they said it would not work because sand and debris would just get stuck in the hole and cover up the reflector."

Jim was convinced it was a good idea, and debated with them, but after getting negative feedback, he let it go. He had other things to do. "It seems like a year later or less, that's what they did. They embedded the reflectors in the mountain roads. That really bugged me for a while." Jim continues, "I also thought about having a green light in the back of cars to show when drivers were accelerating, like when a brake light shows when a driver is hitting the brakes. I thought it might make traffic flow better because drivers would know exactly what the person in front of them is doing—braking or accelerating. We tried different things. Unfortunately, none was very successful, but we had a lot of fun trying."

The inability to get their new company off the ground may have been a blessing in disguise for the three friends. Pet Rock inventor Gary Dahl expressed some regrets later in his life about the success of his wildly popular stone pet. For the rest of his life, individuals constantly inundated him seeking advice for their ideas. Dahl was quoted in an Associated Press article in 1988, saying, "There's a bizarre lunatic fringe who feel I owe them a living. Sometimes I look back and wonder if my life wouldn't have been simpler if I hadn't done it."

Like so many entrepreneurs, Jim and Tom experimented with countless new ideas, but they always returned to what they knew best: real estate.

Chapter 24:

THE RANCHER

Jim with the escaped buffalo

Rustic Fiddletown, California, was first home to Gold Rush miners in 1849, subsisting in tents and shacks awaiting their fortunes to flood in or providing services to those awaiting their fortunes to flood in. In the mid-1970s, Jim and his friend Dr. Peterson invested in a ranch near Fiddletown.

Jim had plans to develop land near the town with what he called *ranchettes*, or a 40-acre plot of land with a corral and a cabin. To get people's attention, Jim was up to his old marketing tricks. Jim recollects a song called *Ya Can't Roller Skate in a Buffalo Herd* that inspired an idea. It's a silly song that explains how some things are impossible to do, like taking a shower in a parakeet cage or fishing in a watermelon patch or roller skating in a buffalo herd—yet it inspired an idea.

"I decided to get a buffalo herd. I don't remember where I got them. It was only about six or eight buffalo. I kept them along Highway 49. It was a marketing ploy, a hook. I wanted people to stop and look at the buffaloes then maybe they would check out these ranchettes we were selling. It was a quick way to become a rancher."

To help his potential customers envision the ranch life and the size of the lot, he would place a section of three-rail white fencing at each of the four corners of the ranchette to help the potential buyers envision the size of the property. People stopped to look at the buffalo and, of course, some of them bought ranchettes.

Buffalo, or the American bison, is the national mammal of the United States. Excessive hunting by sportsmen lead to the near demise of buffaloes around 1900, leaving only hundreds left and pressure to repopulate the species. Since then, the buffalo population has revived some, but Jim's small herd was still novel enough to get the attention of people passing by.

Jim kept his buffaloes in a field with a high, heavy-duty fence to pen them in. Despite his containment efforts, a bull jumped the fence one day and disappeared.

"It was a buffalo rampage," Jim jokes.

There was a loose buffalo near Fiddletown, California, and the hunt was on. Jim knew of a man from near Placerville, California, by the name of Harvey Gross. He owned a big buffalo herd and kept it on his Harvey's James Canyon Ranch where he sold bison burgers at his casinos.

"I called him up and told him if he got that buffalo, he could have it for his herd. It was a big buffalo," Jim says.

Gross decided to hunt via a helicopter equipped with a tranquilizer dart gun. He found the massive beast, but in the end could not contain it.

So, Jim turned to another hunter, Donald Jack who had helped build the Impossible Cabins.

Jim says. "Jack tracked the buffalo out to the middle of nowhere and shot it. We had a buffalo barbeque that lasted over the weekend and into the next week. We gave away free buffalo burgers and steaks at Tahoe Paradise. And I had the head preserved—a full mount to the chest."

Along with buffaloes, there were chickens and, more importantly, sheep at Jim's ranch in Fiddletown. "That was the main reason I wanted the ranch. I missed my sheep."

Pam remembers, "Jim was really good with the kids in Fiddletown. We planted veggies and rode the tractor to town. It was a healthy exposure to a life they weren't living. They loved it."

It was a simple life. *Town* was a few buildings a couple miles from the ranch, or as Jim recalls, "just a little nothing country store." Yet Fiddletown was a comfortable place for him. It brought back the most pleasant fragment of his childhood, though he didn't spend a lot of his time there. He was busy doing all sorts of other stuff.

Fiddletown hayride with the Barry kids

Jim was once heading to Fiddletown on a snowy road in his new Land Cruiser when, "I went around a corner—and went off the road, over a hill, right around a bunch of trees, then came right back out up onto the road. I had steered right through the trees and come back on the highway."

His quick reflexes certainly aided in avoiding a serious accident. After thinking about it more, he was puzzled at how he was even alive. He decided to turn around. "I returned to the scene of the incident and realized that somehow I missed all those trees. I was wondering how I could do that. I should have been killed because I was going pretty fast. It was a miracle," he says.

His time spent at Fiddletown was typically lighthearted, enjoyable, and restful. There is one very somber occasion associated with Fiddletown; it became the resting place for Jim's best friend, Tippy.

Pam explains, "The kids and I were there when Tippy died. She was an incredibly devoted dog and would do whatever Jim asked. Tippy was Jim's shadow." Pam and her children were also there for Tippy's burial, placing flowers on her grave. A mournful day turned into a mournful night.

"Jim was an emotional wreck," Pam reflects, and pauses. "We calmed him down and everyone went to bed. But that night I woke up and had this feeling... I walked by his room, but he wasn't in there. I found him laying on top of Tippy's grave, crying. He didn't want to let her go. I couldn't get him to come into the house."

Like most people, Pam was accustomed to seeing a tireless Jim constantly on the go, positive in every regard, buzzing about and making things happen. Tippy's death stopped his world for a moment. There was no trip to hasten away on, there was no task to distract him, and for a night Jim lay motionless and aching. He was grieving over the hole that was left in his life with Tippy gone. It was difficult for the forward-thinking Jim to accept that Tippy was now a part of his past.

"It was so interesting for me to see this side of him. This grieving side; he was so attached," Pam says.

Jim admits, wholeheartedly, "I get attached to my dogs. I truly enjoy caring for them." Tippy would not be his last dog.

Chapter 25:

THE PATIENT

Whether it was a crew of young ski bums and snowmobilers or wealthy entertainers, Jim was comfortable mingling with everyone. Like all the other residents of Lake Tahoe, Jim lived in the epicenter of excess that was never short on parties, booze, and drugs. Aside from an occasional drink, Jim wasn't one to lose himself in that kind of revelry. Drugs never interested him.

"My younger co-workers would invite me to their parties and really want me to come. I didn't go often, but if I did, it was usually on the earlier side because I liked to go to bed at a reasonable hour. I never knew until much later that there were all sorts of drugs at these parties—I didn't even notice. I was told that they would hide them from me because they knew I didn't do that stuff. But the truth is, I really didn't mind and probably wouldn't have realized what they were doing anyway," says Jim.

Jim's aversion to drugs was quite simple. While most people indulge to escape their worries, problems, and concerns, Jim always wanted to be mindfully present. With a penchant towards a pleasant state of mind, it made no sense to escape his natural air of contentment and then suffer the backlash of a hangover when he was already perfectly happy. Jim had no need or desire to escape himself.

Jim stayed healthy thanks to his constant work schedule and occasional time for hobbies keeping him active. Aside from teaching gymnastics, snow-mobiling, and some hiking, Jim did not maintain a strict exercise regime in his early years. His innate strength and stamina impressed people, including his professional athlete friend Rick Barry.

Rick thought there was no way Jim could keep up with him on the five-mile runs he took to prepare for basketball training camp—but was promptly proven wrong. "He ran the whole five miles and wasn't breathing hard. I'm a world-class athlete, and he kept up with me. He's very athletic. He could do a standing front flip...impressively athletic."

At nearly a foot shorter than Rick, Jim was sure to have taken many more steps on that run, but never showed the effects of that handicap.

Similarly, Bob Lindner Jr. was instantly impressed with his older friend on a jog together with his wife, Sherri, when they were in their early twenties. Bob Jr. admits he wasn't much of a runner, but Sherri enjoyed it and so he decided to go with them. Bob Jr. remembers, "There I was huffing and puffing, and Jim was running next to us—jogging backwards!"

Bob Jr. also recalls a race Jim entered last-minute, where he beat all the teenagers in a pair of sneakers and shorts he had bought just before the start. "Jim's a freak of nature. He can do incredible feats," Bob Jr. says.

"I'm not sure why I entered that race. But I beat all those kids," Jim laughs.

Bob Jr. sums it up, "Jim's got a crazy-strong heart. But there is something about his heart...he has an enlarged heart."

"My heart is larger. It pumps more oxygen. I have the heart of a professional athlete," says Jim.

Later in life Jim had his heart tested and received results that put him in the bottom percentage of heart health in the nation. The doctors branded Jim as having a bad heart. However, despite the tests, categorizing, and comparisons, Jim still isn't worried about those test results.

"My heart rate is 48 beats per minute. When they did the stress test on me, they had me run on the treadmill. I maxed out the treadmill and couldn't get past 100 beats a minute."

The tests also revealed that he had a blockage in one of his arteries, but instead of having a heart attack and requiring bypass surgery, his heart had adapted. "Picture a river flowing along that gets plugged, then forms little streams around the obstacle. That's how my heart responded to the blockage. My heart builds veins around the problem." Jim laughs, "...And they think I have a bad heart. My heart is perfect!"

Jim's heart seems to mirror his mindset—he remains ever adaptable to any obstacles that come his way. Despite his athleticism, he has had his own unexpected health obstacles. It is the memories of those imperfect times that make him all the more appreciative of and dedicated to maintaining his health each day.

One day in early 1978, Jim discovered a lump near his groin. He called his friend Doctor Albo, who was in Mexico at the time, to ask about it. When Doc expressed some concern, Jim panicked a little. "This was about the time Rick Barry asked me to go to Monte Carlo with him because I was into auto racing, but I couldn't go. I thought I was going to die," Jim reflects.

This lump appeared at the same time Jim was suffering with painful gout, or arthritis caused by excessive uric acid collecting and crystalizing in his joints. Uric acid is a waste product from the body's natural breakdown of food. The pain can come in waves and also onset suddenly, ranging from warmth and swelling in the joints to limited mobility. Some suffer far worse than others.

"I had gout so bad in my shoulder and hips that I couldn't lift my foot to drive my sports car. It is so painful; it's hard to explain. You could have taken a saw and cut off my arm and it would have been the same amount of pain as gout," Jim says.

To manage the pain, he was getting cortisone shots, but now he had this mysterious lump to contend with. Jim was initially diagnosed with Hodgkin's Lymphoma, or cancer in the immune system. Following the initial tests, Jim was given the news that he wouldn't live to see 45, giving him only eight years left to live.

When Doc came back from Mexico, he removed the lump and sent it to the lab. Then Jim checked into the Mayo Clinic in Rochester, Minnesota, in May 1978.

"Verna Harrah, Bill Harrah's last wife, was a friend and she made arrangements for me to go there. You had to have clout to get into that clinic," Jim says.

Jim made an unexpected acquaintance as he prepared to start the battle for his life. June Carter Cash had also checked into the Mayo Clinic, with back problems, which interrupted her tour schedule with husband Johnny Cash. She spent the month of May recovering and Jim's stay overlapped with hers for a few days.

"We hung out for a couple of days. We were hospital friends. Just talking small talk," Jim recalls.

Meanwhile, Jim was the subject of many tests at the Mayo Clinic, poked and prodded in an attempt to identify and remedy his health issues. Miraculously, within days of checking into the clinic, his body took a turn for the better.

"Everything went away. Everything disappeared and I was so glad. There was no explanation for it. Everything vanished, the gout and everything, and I've never had a problem since."

His recovery was surprising to everyone, even positive-thinking Jim himself. He had a new lease on life and with it he decided to explore and do things he'd never done before.

"When I landed at the airport in Reno, I had a limo pick me up and take me to the Bunny Ranch. I had never been to a house of ill repute, but I had decided I needed to experience everything—so I went to a whore house," Jim reminisces.

The Moonlite Bunny Ranch, established in 1955, is a legal brothel located in Moundhouse, Nevada, just east of Carson City. As one of the most eligible bachelors in Lake Tahoe, Jim never had problems meeting pretty ladies and did not require nor take interest in the services offered at a brothel. Jim is also a man that greatly respects women. Needless to say, this was a rather unusual destination, but for Jim, that was precisely the point.

Jim describes his experience walking into the building and sitting at the bar while these pretty girls, with every hair color, walked out on parade and awaited selection. "There were all different makes and models."

Fellows then get to pick the lady they like and proceed back to a bedroom. "I'll never forget," Jim remembers after reaching the bedroom with the pretty girl he had selected. "They put on music and when the record was over you were out of there. That was your time." The record, Jim estimates, lasted about 30 minutes.

Instead of the usual activities that one partakes in at a whorehouse, Jim says, "I told her I just wanted to talk. She was confused. But I really just wanted to know about these ladies. And I asked her why she was doing this."

After a few more confused looks, the woman realized he sincerely wanted only to talk. And they talked. Her simple answer to his questions was *money*.

As explained in two articles: '25 Stimulating Facts About Moonlite Bunny Ranch, Nevada's Most Famous Brothel' and 'The Women of the Moonlite Bunny Ranch Brothel Answer Your Questions About Working as Legal Prostitutes,' women working at the Bunny Ranch could make $250,000 a year with the more popular ladies bringing in half a million annually. They work as independent contractors, receiving 1099 forms at tax time, and pay the brothel half their earnings. Several interviewed Moonlite Bunny Ranch employees explained they felt empowered and confident in the profession and because of it had become very skilled negotiators and marketers. The working girls range in age, size, and appearance, and most of them spend between three and five years selling intimacy. A few will make it a lifelong career, but most simply want to work long enough to pay off a home loan or college debt or make enough money to invest in their own businesses. Because it's a choice, these ladies see prostitution as an opportunity. It is one of the only industries, if you will, where women make more money than men do.

The Bunny Ranch's clients are 92 percent men, and 8 percent women and couples. Males who buy sex, or who admit to it, make up about 14 percent of the American male population, making selling sex a rather profitable endeavor in a country with over 160 million males.

Jim had plenty of money and no discount was necessary. His fee was $100 in 1978, no small change then at about $395 in 2021 dollars.

His Bunny Ranch experience was as that of an inquisitive man, not of a needy one. In the event Jim had decided to take the woman up on her offer, his heart, hips, and shoulder were painless and working just fine. Although, the Bunny Ranch girl would not be the last Bunny he encountered.

To this day, Jim remains focused on his health, drinking milk daily and every morning completing his exercise regimen: 25 minutes on an exercise bike, including three rounds of lifting dumbbells to the side, front, and overhead while cycling; 50 pushups; 30 squats; 120 crunches; and 120 seconds spent lying on his back and holding his feet six inches off the ground.

"I have good muscles. I am probably healthier now than I was in my 20s. People are amazed that I can move furniture by myself. I also haven't had a cold or been sick in ten years. But I'm very careful about germs," says Jim.

Chapter 26:

THE RESTAURATEUR

When Jim was back on track with his health and ready to get busy working again, he and Tom Fields decided to experiment further in the restaurant business. They had initially dabbled in this industry in the late 1960s, opening Tippy's Tavern, Yank's Station, and The Rough and Ready Room at the Market Campus Shopping Center where a beer was 25 cents and a hamburger was $1.

Even in the restaurant business, their underlying goal was always about investing in real estate. In fact, Tom and Jim once bought an empty restaurant because the property had a lot of potential. They ended up reopening that restaurant for less than a year, increasing the value of the land, and selling it for profit.

In the mid-1970s, Tom remembers getting a notice in the mail explaining that a lottery would be held in Sacramento for a coveted liquor license in El Dorado County, encompassing South Lake Tahoe and swaths of land to the south and west. In California, the number of liquor licenses available was determined by county population. As the population increased in El Dorado County, so did the number of available liquor licenses. There were two types of liquor licenses: year-round and seasonal. Jim and Tom put their names in for the lottery and surprisingly won a year-round liquor license, which they quickly put to use.

Jim and Tom agreed that a restaurant on the water would be ideal. Jim lived in Tahoe Keys and was familiar with the nearby marina. A decent-sized clapboard building with a rock base sat near the marina housing a boat supply, rental, and sales shop on the first floor. The owner of the marina, a man named Anton Schmidt, lived in the sizeable apartment on the second floor.

Jim inquired with Anton if he'd be willing to lease out that apartment space so they could put in a bar and restaurant, and he agreed. Jim and Tom began remodeling the second floor. The capital came from the pockets of the wealthy cattleman Loren Bamert and another wealthy fellow who owned a vineyard.

Tom remembers, "They had the money and we had the energy. It wasn't an investment for them; they just thought it would be fun."

The apartment walls were pulled down and the space reconfigured for upscale lake view dining. The decorations and furniture were bought from The National Hotel, which had become an antiques store, in Jackson, California, about two hours southwest of Lake Tahoe on Highway 49. Jim and Tom adorned the new eatery with mismatched antique chairs, tables, stools, rustic decorations, and a repurposed bedroom hutch for the back bar.

"It was an antiques store selling liquor. It was classic. People enjoyed coming," Tom explains.

When the Tahoe Keys Marina Bar and Restaurant opened around 1976, people came to enjoy the view, the food, the drinks, and the company. The restaurant also featured live music on the weekends, benefiting from a deal made with several other restaurants in the area to schedule local bands and musicians on a rotating basis. This meant the restaurants didn't have to compete for live entertainment, and the musicians had regularly scheduled performances.

In fair weather months, the place was busy. However, the gravel road to the restaurant was problematic to maintain in the winter; business suffered in the snowy months. Additionally, it was a lot to manage on top of their real estate business, which remained the top priority.

Jim and Tom's reign as the owners of Tahoe Keys Marina Bar and Restaurant would last two memorable years.

Tom says, "We were real estate guys, not restaurant guys. We liked to try different things, but when you diversify you lose a little control on the oversight of the business. We didn't start it to keep it. It was fun!"

When they sold the restaurant, they made more money on the antique furniture than on the bar items. They sold the liquor license separately, and just like that they were off to a new project.

A few years after Jim and Tom sold the Tahoe Keys Marina Bar and Restaurant, a man referred to as Mr. C bought the marina from Anton Schmidt around 1980. Jim had met and known Mr. C and had noticed he was an energetic guy working his way to success in town. "He knew how to run the boats; he ran the marina for a long time," Jim says. Jim could certainly respect a hardworking man and he liked that Mr. C planned to further develop the facility and marina.

Another of Jim's restaurant endeavors was later on in fast food with Bob's Burger Express. Back in 1955, Bob Corey opened Bob's Burger Express in Salem, Oregon. It was designed as a casual yet quality eatery selling 19-cent hamburgers featuring Bob's secret sauce. Unlike other fast food restaurants popping up around the nation, Bob's served fast food to customers not necessarily in a hurry to leave. It became the center of many a teenager's universe and the employees, some also teenagers, were treated well and appreciated by Mr. Corey.

Skipping ahead a few decades and after a successful 35 years of growing the business into a popular family dining destination in 17 locations, Bob Corey sold the business in 1990. Unfortunately for all of the Bob's customers, the next owner ran the eatery to the brink of failure. The restaurant was struggling, and the workers were starting to ditch their once-coveted jobs at Bob's to work for McDonald's because they could make more money. In order to recover the business, the new owner hired some advisors to help right the sinking ship.

Jim Schmit and Rick Barry were hired to salvage Bob's Burger Express. They focused on two key areas: marketing and improving employee satisfaction. They started with closing all the stores and holding a conference for all employees. They sought to encourage and motivate the staff and presented a new incentives program to show appreciation for their work.

"We explained to the kids that they were to bring in their report cards and if their grades went up a point or letter, they would get a $0.25 raise. We were pushing good grades—all the parents wanted their kids to work at Bob's," Jim says.

Along with Rick serving as a spokesperson, they also leveraged the networks of their existing employees to spread the word and bring in more customers. "Each employee had a number and was given passes to hand out to friends and family. If the person came to the store with that employee's pass, then they would get $0.25 added to their paycheck. They were walking advertisements. They were all behind it. And it worked! We got it up and running really well—the stores quadrupled their profit thanks to the employee incentives and marketing. We only lasted six months to a year as advisors though; after we got in business with the new owner, we realized we didn't like him much. He was an odd duck."

The rebound bought the company another 11 years of business, but the last Bob's Burger Express closed in 2001.

Chapter 27:

THE FRIEND

Jim values his friendships with four-legged and two-legged friends alike. Two of his best friends, Pam and Rick Barry, are particularly special to him. They were and still are endearing and kind people, ambitious and interesting. When Jim found time to play in Lake Tahoe, he would often include the Barry kids.

"Jim was great with the kids. He would take them fishing on Lake Tahoe, into town, or on the tractor in Fiddletown. He took Scooter fishing overnight once. He also took Brent, my most cautious son, out on the motorboat. Jim made a quick turn and scared Brent, so he had Brent drive the boat home," Pam recalls.

Pam tells a story from when her daughter was 13 months old: "She was a solid three-hour napper. We wanted to go water skiing so I asked Jim to watch her. She was sound asleep. We came back from skiing and Jim was standing on the dock. His face was green. Green! And he said, she had a messy diaper, and it was the most disgusting thing he had ever been involved with in his entire life."

"I remember that," says Jim, the man that can't remember the question he asked President Kennedy or the exact sequence of events that unfolded during the unplanned, overnight survival snowmobiling trip. Jim remembers that dirty diaper.

Rick mentions, "Jim was great to the kids. Always willing to help out."

Family time with all of the Barry's together ended in 1979 with Pam and Rick's divorce. Loving both of them, Jim had no other choice than to remain friends with Pam and Rick individually. This can be a tricky feat for any friend of a divorced couple. Fortunately, for Jim, Pam and Rick understood and have each stayed close to Jim, though their worlds diverged.

The divorce was difficult, as they tend to be, and Pam needed to escape. At the same time, Jim was going through a breakup and so were a few other friends. It was a period of limbo and recovery for this crew, so one friend suggested they all go to Europe—so they did.

While most people in the group were financially comfortable, they chose to travel on a shoestring budget. They traveled on trains at night to skip hotels and then sightsee during the day. If they did require a place to sleep, they stayed in hostels. The group would have one nice meal here and there, keeping it cheap the rest of the time.

Jim recollects, "There were funny things about the trip—just figuring out that you needed a coin to get water. That first night we checked into our accommodations, not realizing we were in a shared room, and waking up the next morning to all these strangers."

Pam says, "It took us a bit to learn the train schedules and knowing what direction and which track to stand near. Then we had to figure out how to get the tickets. And once you get the ticket you have to validate it and if you don't, they will throw you off the train." She laughs, "We'd all argue because everyone thought they knew what they were doing, but they didn't."

Jim adds, "The biggest thing about the trains that we eventually learned was the Express passes and trains were the slow ones—it took forever to get anywhere. It was the Rapido trains that we wanted. We didn't understand that until the last week of our trip."

Once they learned the train system and format, Pam says "We just kept getting on trains that were leaving. Then we'd get our books out and read about where in the world we were going."

The trip was especially effective in getting Pam's mind off of her divorce for a time. Yet while the goofy antics of traveling with friends was a beautiful distraction for each of them, it was a stop in Germany that left the greatest impact.

Straddling the Amper River in Bavaria is the small town of Dachau. Its history traces back to Celtic occupation in 1000 B.C., and its bucolic setting became a haven for artists in the late 1800s and early 1900s. This period of peace and beauty would be tarnished less than half a century later by the Nazi Party.

The Dachau Concentration Camp was considered the first concentration camp of the period, established in 1933. Located on a former munitions ground approximately 10 miles northwest of Munich, in the early years the concentration camp was used to detain German Communists, Nazi Party opponents, homosexuals, Gypsies, and others who were unfavorable in the eyes of the Nazi Party. As the years stretched into World War II, eventually thousands of Jews plus prisoners of war were held there and used for forced labor, including construction and weapons production. Those prisoners too weak to contribute were executed via firing squad or gallows or shipped off elsewhere. The massive ovens in the crematoria were used to dispose of the bodies. Dachau also served as a training location for concentration camp guards and its management was emulated by most of the other camps.

As Germany's eastern and western defenses began to deteriorate and the Allies pushed eastward, prisoners from other concentration camps near the front were relocated to Dachau, which quickly became overcrowded. On April 29, 1945, American forces liberated the nearly 60,000 prisoners at Dachau and other nearby detainment camps.

Pam vividly recalls, "The ovens were still there. The steam room where they poisoned them was still there in perfect order. There were photos of mountains of dead bodies. People had written their names in the bunk beds." She pauses, "I was shocked. I had never been that close to something so horrific. Very powerful. Unforgettable."

"I remember how tragic the setting was," Jim says.

It was not quite 35 years after the war when the friends visited Dachau, a short enough period of time that people still living in town remember the events around World War II.

"I was in disbelief that nobody in the town of Dachau knew what was going on…at least that's the perception I got from the people I talked to. I couldn't wrap my head around it. The men in the town of Dachau would kiss their wives and head to work like they were going to a factory job. But it was a factory for killing people. It puzzled me how much denial these people were in. They had to know," Jim remembers.

It has been said that the first country Hitler invaded was Germany. Living a life outside of a concentration camp did not necessarily equate to freedom in Nazi-ruled Germany. Ignorance and denial may have been a form of survival for the residents of Dachau.

The heaviness of Dachau lingered on the group for a while. "After spending a whole day there, we were all sort of in shock mode the next day. We hardly talked," Pam says.

Visiting Dachau did not completely take away the heartache the friends were working through, but it helped to put their life and pain in a bit of perspective. They were healthy, young people with the freedom and means to travel. In essence, they were strangely privileged to have the freedom of a broken heart.

After their sobering day, the group welcomed a lighter moment. "I remember going up to the Matterhorn. That was cool. We went up on the cog railroad in these tiny rail cars. It's real steep and you chug up the hill past all these houses along the route. People are tucked up in the side of the mountain in these homes. It's beautiful," Jim says.

Eventually their weeks of train-hopping came to an end and they returned home. Jim returned to his work, his generous habits, and the hunt for his next lovely girlfriend, while Pam began to build a new life of her own as she continued raising her sons and daughter.

When Jim learned that his friend Fred Swanson, the buddy who traveled with him to Hawaii during the bellhop era, was terminally ill with cancer in a Seattle hospital with just days to live, he scurried up there to check on him. In their younger years, Fred was a tall, good-looking blonde with an impossible shyness that limited his circle of friends. By the time Jim reached the hospital, Fred was weak and scrawny, a shell of his handsome self.

"I remember walking in the hospital room, and he was so happy to see me. He didn't have anybody real positive around him," Jim remembers.

The Swanson family had the means to make sure Fred was kept comfortable in his final days. But Jim's visit had inspired a new plan for Fred's remaining time, a grand finale instead of a gloomy demise. Never married, Fred's only ties to Seattle were his parents, so he and Jim decided to go on an adventure. The medical experts balked at Jim's plan to take their dying patient out of the hospital, explaining that his death would be sudden once he left. Disregarding the warning, the two old friends headed to a place with a view.

"I took him to Tahoe. He loved it there. I wanted to see him die happy," Jim recalls. He put Fred in his own bedroom with the best view, making him as comfortable as his ailing body would allow. "I was leery going to sleep that first night because I knew he was going to die."

Without the medical support and expertise provided by the hospital, Jim was prepared to find his friend gone by the morning. Jim eventually managed to fall asleep, and in the morning awoke wondering how he would find Fred. Jim peaked through the door with caution and there Fred was, wide awake with a little spark in his eye, asking, "What are we going to do today?"

Surprised by Fred's liveliness, Jim hosted Fred for another great day. Each subsequent morning Jim found Fred alive was a pleasant surprise. It seemed that Lake Tahoe and Jim's company equated to better medicine than what was served in a sterile hospital.

"He was so happy to be happy. He didn't need to be plugged into all that stuff. He had a reason to live and he had the will to live again," Jim says.

Despite his ongoing health challenges, Fred continued to be quite stable during his visit to Lake Tahoe. Jim arranged for his pilot to fly them in the Cessna Skymaster 337 push-pull, that Jim owned in partnership with Bob Lindner, up to Vancouver Island in Canada to visit the lovely Butchart Gardens. They arrived with Fred in good form and Jim rolled Fred around in his wheelchair amongst the flora that had long adorned a former limestone quarry thanks to creator Jennie Butchart starting in 1904. It was a clever idea by Mrs. Butchart to take the ruins left from the quarry that provided raw materials for her husband's cement business and turn it into a world-famous destination, filling a former dead space with color and life. Even today, the gardens remain a family enterprise and continue to bloom for the more than one million annual visitors.

On the edge of death, Fred found himself living good—flying to other countries, immersing himself in pollen and nature, and mingling in bars around other germy people. He was doing all the things he wasn't supposed to do.

"He wasn't supposed to drink, but I got him a rum and coke. And I got these two pretty ladies to come over and dance around his wheelchair. I explained that he was going to die any day, and those nice women came over and danced with him."

Jim kept entertaining Fred, and Fred kept waking up in the mornings.

Eventually, Jim had to face reality. "I had to go back to work. I didn't anticipate he would still be alive. I had to take him back to the hospital in Seattle and then he went downhill again. I felt bad about that. But I'll never forget him. He taught me a big lesson. He inspired me. Fred is why I believe that mind over matter is extremely powerful."

Fred never reached his fortieth birthday; he had withered away in the prime of his life. He did, however, succeed in having a few fantastic adventures in his final days with his good friend Jim Schmit. Fred's parents knew Jim was a close friend and entrusted him with Fred's ashes.

"I never met his parents, but they arranged for me to get the ashes. We sailed those ashes out on my boat and scattered them right at the inlet to Tahoe Keys."

Jim had never seen human ashes until he poured Fred's remains into Lake Tahoe. He was surprised at finding some sizeable bone fragments mixed in with the dusty pale grey ashes.

"For a long time when I'd take the boat out, I would look down for Fred and he was there," Jim says. The combination of the white bone fragments, clear water of Lake Tahoe, and minimal current at the inlet where Fred was scattered, left his remains visible for a long time. It seemed to Jim that Fred was still enjoying the view from the other side.

Chapter 28:

THE GUEST

As much as Jim liked to take care of his friends, many of his friends enjoyed reciprocating and inviting or hosting Jim on adventures as well. Ken Madsen once rented a plane to take a crew of friends to Hawaii for fun. "We had the most interesting people on that plane. I brought friends, employees, customers, Jim, and Pam," Ken remembers.

"That was the trip I thought I went blind," Jim laughs.

Once they reached Hawaii and the friends had dispersed to their own hotel rooms, Jim remembers, "I woke up in the middle of the night, and I couldn't see. It was pitch black. I looked over—I thought there was a window, but I couldn't see anything. There were no buildings or lights shining through that window. Somehow, I figured out that I wasn't blind; the power had simply gone out all over Hawaii. It was incredibly dark."

Jim found himself on another private jet headed to Las Vegas one day. Together, Jim and pilot friend Bill Smith flew to Oakland in Jim's Cessna Skymaster, then hopped out and blended in with the large entourage boarding one of the two 737 planes owned by Adnan Khashoggi.

"We got an invite on the plane because Bill knew one of the pilots," Jim says.

They all took a short flight from Oakland to Las Vegas for a certain-to-be-fabulous Khashoggi party. For the man marketing himself as one of the world's wealthiest individuals, excess and extravagance were par for the course, and as a result, the myth was easy to believe. Born in 1935 in Saudi Arabia, Khashoggi spent his youth in Alexandria, Egypt, and later enrolled at Chico State College in California, introducing him to the United States. Khashoggi found he had a knack for brokering deals between Western companies and Middle Eastern interests, making approximately $150,000 selling $3 million worth of American trucks to Egypt in his first big business transaction, according to his obituary in the *New York Times*. Through this newfound skill, he would make millions in commissions and never saw the need to finish college.

Khashoggi spent his handsome fortune generously, acquiring a bundle of international homes, several mega-yachts, helicopters, and three Boeing 727 jets, plus investments on five continents through Triad International. He helped fund both of Nixon's presidential campaigns and donated millions to American University, among countless other endeavors.

Khashoggi strategically navigated the upper echelon social circuits of the world, with charm being one of his greatest assets. He hosted legendary parties, welcoming guests from royalty to world leaders to Hollywood starlets. By the time Jim found himself on one of Khashoggi's personal jets, marked with the Roman number III on its tail for Triad International, it was rumored that the man spent $250,000 daily to maintain his lavish lifestyle.

Jim remembers, "You wouldn't believe this plane. There was real gold everywhere. I remember clicking my seatbelt and the buckle was gold. We weren't allowed to take pictures, but I took a few. I wish I still had them."

Jim had his fair share of being around wealth greater than his own, but the opulence of the Khashoggi airplanes dumbfounded him.

"The two jets flew in formation to Vegas. And we played Triopoly on the way; it was just like Monopoly, but the board had a Roman numeral III in the center, was full of Khashoggi's properties, and his family was pictured on the money," Jim says.

In Las Vegas, Khashoggi had leased the entire restaurant at the top of the Sands Casino and had a villa built in the parking lot because he preferred not to stay in the actual hotel.

"There weren't many of us there at dinner, like 20 people. I remember meeting him and thinking, this guy is *really rich*," Jim says. "Friends make life really great! I got to do things money can't buy because of my friends."

Not too many years later Khashoggi was in dire financial straits, yet he still hosted inconceivably over-the-top parties. In 1987, Triad International filed for bankruptcy. The Khashoggi fallout is an epic of its own.

Jim's close friend Rick Barry, with his celebrity passport, was one of the most generous about inviting Jim to various exclusive events. "He came with me to the Bing Crosby Golf Tournament in Salem, North Carolina, and a lot of other charity events. I would joke that he was my bodyguard. A deadly black belt," says Rick.

"I got to meet President Ford because of Rick Barry. They didn't give a rip about me; they wanted to meet Rick Barry," Jim laughs. "Bob Lindner made Ford a Bicentennial ring, and Rick and I delivered it to him. I remember waiting in the Rose Garden and Ford was late because he had a meeting with King Hussein of Jordan. Don't ask me how I remember that."

Jim adds, his mind wandering, "I've met five presidents, come to think of it. I met President Kennedy when I was young and then Ford in 1976 when we gave him the ring. I met Jimmy Carter on an airplane when I was traveling to China once. I met George W. Bush briefly while he was president, and Trump, before he was president. I'll never forget what Trump said to me…you should either own your real estate free and clear or have the biggest mortgage in the world."

Jim's thoughts return to Rick: "I got to meet a *lot* of people because of Rick Barry. He has been a very big part of my life."

"Jim was always so appreciative of the things I invited him to. He doesn't expect much. He was always looking out for me. I liked to do the same for him," Rick explains.

While Jim met a lot of interesting people through his basketball connections to Rick Barry and Clifford Ray, Clifford says, "I've met a lot of interesting people with Jim. We've shared a lot of goodness."

Clifford enjoyed Jim's stories and how Jim was always doing something, but maybe most of all that Jim knew some things about fishing. He almost always had a house on a lake or river and was generous in sharing his home with friends like Clifford.

Clifford reminisces, "He had a cabin I loved—just what I would have scripted out my life as an older man—I could sit on the porch and fish."

The pair once took a two-week road trip together from Portland, Oregon, to Yellowstone, Montana, to Yakima and Seattle, Washington, and then back to Portland. On the agenda for the trip was fishing.

Clifford remembers, "We were in this little Jaguar with Jimmy's little dog and there was a lot of room. You'd be surprised! Jim had knowledge of everywhere we went. In Montana, we got a place on the Madison River and got to fly fish. We also stopped and fished in Cliff's Lake. I remember because it's my first name. We caught trout and had fish and potatoes for dinner."

"Clifford is the nicest guy and he'll talk to anyone. Everyone likes him," Jim says.

"Being around Jim, I realized what you do in life is important—how you live; what you do for people. He's always had a positive outlook. Being around Jimmy has always been fun," Clifford says.

Chapter 29:

THE EYEWITNESS

The year 1980 ushered in a new decade of hope and promise as well as new concerns and issues. Jim was flying high. He had lots of money and enjoyed spending it, and he continued to bounce around from location to location, house to house, and project to project. That suited him perfectly; he found comfort in being on the move.

Tom Field relays, "We called him the Energizer Bunny."

Although never afraid to set out on long drives to meet his demanding and geographically diverse schedule, Jim sometimes opted to arrange for transportation in the Cessna Skymaster 337 when a pilot was available.

In one instance, Jim, his girlfriend, and her daughter and mother, were on their way back from Victoria, Canada, in the Skymaster after visiting the Butchart Gardens and staying in the Empress Hotel. The six-seater was a noisy little plane powered by two engines—one in the front on the nose and one in the back towards the tail. They had stopped in Renton, Washington, for customs and were destined for Carson City, Nevada. It was a beautiful, clear day to fly, and on the way back Jim asked the pilot, David Barkley, to fly over Mount St. Helens.

On this early Sunday morning, May 18, 1980, the small plane and passengers breached the *no-fly* zone to swing by the majestic Mount St. Helens, standing proud at roughly 9,700 feet. Mount St. Helens, considered a stratovolcano due to its steep conical profile and proclivity to explosive eruptions, had been moody for the past few months. It had been quaking, spitting, spouting, and huffing and puffing after a 120-plus-year dormant spell. The mountain had awakened and become so unpredictable that by early April, Washington State's governor established a *red zone* around the volcano. The consequences for those caught in this zone without a special pass was either a $500 fine or six months in jail. This zone even shut out property owners and required some evacuations.

A few days after the *red zone* was put in place, Mount St. Helens had grown a noticeable bulge. Geologists kept a curious eye on the flexing mountain and were predicting major destruction if the mountain were to erupt. Through April and early May, it rumbled and moaned with 10,000 recorded earthquakes and visible, smoky eruptions. Then the mountain seemed to fall asleep again in mid-May. This lull in danger, along with significant public pressure, influenced officials to allow property owners into the *red zone* on Saturday, May 17, to collect belongings and once again evacuate. Another *red zone* run was planned for the next day, but the volcano had other plans.

At 8:32 a.m., a 5.1 magnitude earthquake shook the mountain from its core and dislodged the north side of the slope. A destructive river of volcanic mudflows created an avalanche of debris, flowing miles and miles from the mountain and forever changing the local topography. The explosive eruption coughed up thick ash reaching upwards of 16 miles into the atmosphere and blotting out the sky. The ash and dust would eventually settle across 11 states.

The explosion had blasted nearly 1,300 feet off the top of Mount St. Helens, reducing its peak to its current day height of 8,363 feet. Worst of all was the brutal tally of destruction left in its wake, possibly worse than the geologists had feared. The 1980 eruption of Mount St. Helens was responsible for the deaths of 57 people and the destruction of a significant amount of property, including structures, bridges, roads, and railroads.

Meanwhile, circling around up in the sky was a Cessna Skymaster 337 with five people on board witnessing the ascension of the ominous, smoky column from the center of the Saint. They saw lightning bolts and then the sky turned black. Under all the ash, lava began rushing out of the mountain, like water pouring from a cup.

"I thought we were going to die," Jim says, snapping what he thought might be his last pictures capturing a shot during and after the eruption. Then ash filled the air and consumed them in darkness.

Someone questioned, "Why are you taking pictures? We are never going to land."

Jim and the passengers were scared and disoriented, but the pilot had work to do. "David was a good pilot. He had flown around the world twice by himself in a single engine plane," Jim says.

Mount Saint Helens before and after eruption

David Barkley was an instrument-rated pilot and poised under pressure. He kept the plane level and flying, but as they continued to fly through the thick ash, the oil pressure gauges began to drop quickly. The ash was like sandpaper, going through the engines and eating up the pistons.

"For a second I thought we were going to fly until we ran out of gas. I really thought the world had ended," Jim admits. Then they flew out of the ash into blue sky again, a reminder that there was still solid ground on which they needed to land—as soon as possible. They got to the ground safely and David put in some heavy, thick oil so they could continue on to Carson City. They made it without an issue.

Jim says, "That was the last time I was in that plane. I sold it for $10,000. That was all it was worth. The engines were shot." He adds, "I didn't show those pictures to anyone for years because David could have lost his license. We were not supposed to be as close as we were; for good reason, obviously." As for the girlfriend? "She broke up with me after that," Jim shrugs his shoulders.

The loss of the Cessna presented a good time to upgrade. Jim's next plane was a Learjet. "I just wanted a Learjet. I could afford it so I got one." Jim says.

Plane travel was second nature to Jim, and so it seems, was witnessing plane mishaps.

The Lake Tahoe Airport, opened in the summer of 1959, had been planned to accommodate the growing number of visitors and residents to the region. The 5,900-foot runway, later lengthened to approximately 8,500 feet, parallels Highway 50 and today provides convenient access to South Lake Tahoe and nearby ski resorts for charters and private planes.

Years before, in the 1970s, the Lake Tahoe Airport was abuzz with commuter and commercial plane arrivals and departures. During this time, those buying property near the airport typically hesitated, concerned with air traffic noise. Jim was often successful at showing people the bright side of anything and was known to sell lots near the airport rather well. He specifically remembers taking a couple to see a lot off of Pioneer Trail in South Lake Tahoe one day.

"They were concerned about the airport located nearby, but I explained to them that the airplanes wouldn't be a problem. That they usually take off in the other direction into the wind." He walked the clients around the lot and continued with some small talk to show the potential of the purchase. At some point during their discussion, Jim heard an engine, some unnatural rumbling, and clapping growing louder each second. Right then a plane skidded out of the woods and into the open for-sale lot, its wings snapped off from crashing through the trees.

"That plane crashed right on the lot I was trying to sell. It was unbelievable," Jim says. Jim went over to check on the plane's occupants; they had all miraculously survived. "I think there were three passengers in the plane. It was crazy," At some point, Jim says, "I turned around and my clients were gone. I didn't sell the lot that day and I didn't have a ride back to the office."

Jim used the airport regularly for his travels and drove by it daily when in Lake Tahoe. He shakes his head, "Back then the rules were a little different. You would see the same pilots day in and day out. You would see them in the airport bar drinking right before they were going to fly." He adds, "I also remember a time I was going hunting with some friends, and we would carry our loaded rifles and shotguns right on the plane. My friend was asking about my gun and wanted to see it, so I got up, took it out of overhead storage, pulled it out of the case, and he had a good look at the gun—in the aisle, in the middle of our flight. That doesn't happen anymore."

Rain, snow, or sunshine, the planes would be landing and taking off day and night during the 1960s and 70s. On one slushy day, Jim watched a commercial plane sitting on the runway, waiting.

"The pilot must have been doing a pre-flight check at the time, but I was curious to see if they were going to take off. Having lived in the area for years and knowing snow conditions really well, I thought it was way too slushy and thick for that plane to be taking off. The runway hadn't been cleared well," Jim says.

Jim sat there and watched the airplane attempt to increase speed down the runway, but hindered by the thick snow, the plane wouldn't go airborne and skidded straight off the end of the runway.

"Nobody was hurt, but I couldn't believe the pilot actually tried to take off in those conditions. It must have been a pilot that had visited the airport bar before he got in the cockpit."

The worst plane crash at that airport took place just before Jim had moved to Lake Tahoe. Nobody witnessed it; the flight simply went missing. In March of 1964, it was found that a Paradise Airlines flight en route from the Bay Area struck the 8,675-foot Genoa Peak after aborting a first landing approach at the airport due to heavy snow decreasing visibility. All 85 individuals onboard, passengers and crew, perished. The investigation revealed that the pilot would have cleared Mount Genoa with an extra 300 feet of elevation.

Surprisingly, these Lake Tahoe airplane accidents were not the first Jim had witnessed. When he was a kid, he had found a rare opportunity to sneak away from farm work and chores for gaffing salmon on a tributary of the Puyallup River in Washington State with his buddy.

"It was illegal, but we were kids and didn't see the harm in it," Jim explains about gaffing salmon. "We were there on the river, far away from any roads, and I heard this engine. It was getting louder and louder, so I thought it was the game warden."

Nervous about getting caught, the boys wrapped up their fishing and headed out. They were trekking across an open field as the engine grew even louder. They kept looking around, but there was no game warden in sight. Jim eventually looked up and saw it was a plane flying too low with a missing wing. Jim states, "The plane kept going down and down and down, and we watched it crash right into the ground. It was an open cockpit plane with one pilot on board and it burst into flames. I ran over to see if there was anything I could do, but I think I knew the pilot was already dead. I got to the plane and all I could see was his arm sticking out of the flames in his leather flight coat. I pulled and pulled and yanked his arm right off. There I was holding this pilot's arm. It was all that was left of him. My friend was yelling at me to get away from the plane because he thought it was going to blow up. I'll never forget that."

The year 1980 wrapped up with two more shocking events. In an attempt to extort $3 million from Harvey's Resort Hotel in Stateline, Nevada, a deranged man looking to get his $750,000 in losses back and then some, placed a monstrous bomb with nearly 1,000lbs of dynamite at the hotel that August. The hotel was evacuated and the gas main shut off while the FBI worked to disarm the well-built bomb because it was too difficult to move. The attempt to disarm the device would fail, and the bomb was accidentally detonated destroying much of the hotel and also damaging Harrah's Casino nearby. Fortunately, no one was injured.

The 1980s also highlighted things to come. In California, environmental sensitivities led to increased regulations in Lake Tahoe, which slowed land development opportunities. Ever adaptable, Jim began considering other locations for real estate investing and land development. He kept Lake Tahoe as a base, but found himself spending more and more of his time in Oregon.

Chapter 30:

THE CATCH

Jim was always diligent with professional business, until one day he realized it was time to pause and take care of some personal business. Jim had never quite recovered from the loss of his first love. He had dated beautiful ladies, but seemed unable to fully open his heart to them. Sharon Belmont, his very first girlfriend from Olympic College, still had a hold on him.

Through the years, Jim had kept in touch with Sharon's mother, who informed him one day that Sharon was divorced and living in southern California. Jim got her number, gave her a call, and winged off in his Learjet to meet her. He landed in a small airport somewhere in Los Angeles, the steps of the jet folded down, and Jim walked across a red carpet on his way to the waiting room. Jim had vivid memories of his first love, her beautiful brunette hair, and her unique half-Cherokee and half-French features.

He anxiously walked into the waiting room and this pretty girl walked up. "Here comes this blonde with a nice figure. It took me a second and I realized the blonde was Sharon. Her being blonde was simply shocking; it wasn't the same. The spark was gone."

While he knew immediately that his days of pining over his first love were over, he followed through with the date. They flew to the south shore of Lake Tahoe in his jet, then drove his Rolls Royce to a beautiful house on Lake Tahoe for an evening together. All the time Jim was wondering what she was thinking.

"There was no romance. There was no hugging or kissing at all. She stayed overnight in her own room and the next day I asked her if she wanted to go back to Los Angeles or to Bremerton, Washington. She picked Bremerton and my pilots flew her there. I never saw her again."

All this time Jim had had a stubborn longing for this one brunette he had put on a pedestal. The one who had broken his heart. The one who had dumped him for a sailor in a '57 Chevy. The one who was now blonde. The one that would not be on Jim's mind any longer. He had found his closure with Sharon Belmont.

"It was the best thing I could have done. Deep down I was comparing other ladies to the Sharon I remembered from college. Now I could move on." He adds with a giggle, "I could have owned one-hundred '57 Chevys at that time."

Not too terribly long after Sharon whiplashed through Jim's life, on one seemingly normal day, a 40-year-old single Jim returned to Tahoe from Fiddletown with five dozen eggs produced from his own chickens. "I walked into the Jewelry Factory saying, 'Eggs, eggs for sale,' as a joke. I would always bring back some eggs to Tahoe and give them away."

It was just after Christmas in 1981, when a petite blonde named Vicki accompanied a friend to The Jewelry Factory to exchange a Christmas gift. Vicki distinctly recalls the moment she first saw Jim. She realized in a moment, without even seeing his face, "Gosh, I'm going to marry that guy. I had the weirdest feeling, and I just knew I was going to marry him. I was so relieved he was cute when he turned around."

But it wasn't that simple. At the time, Vicki was married to the father of her two daughters, although they had been separated for several years. She had decided to move to Lake Tahoe from Salt Lake City, Utah, and had found a job as the executive secretary at Caesar's Palace. Vicki and her separated husband were both moving on with their lives, and they had made agreeable arrangements for sharing custody of their girls. Vicki found a place to stay in Tahoe Paradise, had started seeing another man, and bought a Porsche with her newfound income.

She remembers after getting settled in Lake Tahoe, "I was finally ready to get the divorce. Meeting somebody new was not at all on my mind."

When she saw Jim, she decided to buy some eggs as an excuse to talk to her future husband.

"How much are the eggs?" She asked.

"One dollar," Jim answered.

"I wrote him a check for $1 because it had my phone number on it. I figured he would call."

"I sold her eggs. That's how we met," Jim laughs. "She was classy without a doubt. And very confident and friendly."

Marty, Jim's roommate at the time, explains, "Jimmy came in and said, I just met this girl and she is so amazing. She thinks I'm an egg salesman. Look, I have her check and I have her number."

Jim set Vicki's check down by the phone in the kitchen, but before he knew it, he was off and running on a few more business trips.

After their first encounter, Vicki remembers her girlfriend saying, "Do you know who that is? That's Jim Schmit. He has a girlfriend in every state. There's no way that guy is getting married."

Vicki's friend was right about one state at least, New York. Jim had been seeing a beautiful girl, a model, living in New York City.

"She was a real wealthy girl. Wait, maybe she was a Playboy Bunny," Jim shakes his head, "Yes. I think she was a Playboy Bunny. She was very pretty. I met her about the time I bought my favorite car, the Doval Shadow."

Weeks later when he came home, he was greeted by a basket of chocolate chip cookies from Vicki, and her check was still sitting patiently by the phone.

"I called her and asked her if she needed some eggs," Jim says. Jim and Vicki's friendship began.

"Jim and I did a lot together, but nothing romantic at first. He would stop by the house I was staying in on his way to work in the mornings. I knew he had girlfriends. I knew he had a girlfriend in New York. I called her Miss New York," Vicki remembers.

Jim reminiscences, "Vicki called me up and asked me if I could teach her how to drive her new Porsche in the snow." She was good at finding ways to keep his company.

During this time, Miss New York invited Jim to Studio 54, the famous New York City nightclub that opened in April 1977. It was an exclusive late-night haunt for A-list celebrities and others with connections. Fame or not, you had to be glamorous enough to get in. Its 2,000-person capacity was outrageously large, but with such a high demand to get through the door, the owners could be highly selective on who was allowed in and still easily fill the massive space. It is said that Frank Sinatra was once turned away.

"It was the *in* place. You either had to know someone to get in or be really wealthy," Jim says.

Being a Playboy Bunny, Jim's girlfriend had pull at the door. Once inside there was a smorgasbord of pleasure-seeking opportunities, legal and illegal alike. The crowd was the most diverse and interesting group of people anywhere around, and the bond that had brought everyone together was extravagant and unlimited fun. Those passing the velvet ropes joined an exclusive society. A visit to Studio 54 was unforgettable…except, for Jim Schmit.

"I remember the girl I was dating asked me what I was going to wear. I told her about my favorite suit. But she said I couldn't wear that suit because the lapels were too big—I guess the West Coast and East Coast styles were different. I had to go buy a new suit to go to Studio 54. That's the main thing I remember about Studio 54—I had to buy a new suit," Jim says.

Following Jim's not-so-memorable Studio 54 visit, the days passed by and winter turned to spring. Jim resumed his busy schedule based out of Lake Tahoe and when the snow melted, Miss New York came out to spend the summer with him.

Vicki explains, "When Miss New York arrived, I went to a friend's house who lived across the lake from him and we used the telescope to see my competition." She figured after months of friendliness it was her turn to get to know Jim better. Vicki devised a plan.

"One morning when he stopped by to see me on his way to work, I had my suitcase and filled it up like I was leaving. I told him I was going on a weekend trip with the guy I was dating." Vicki pauses, "Within an hour, he sent Miss New York home and realized he wanted to date me."

Jim now had a Miss California, Vicki, to ride with him in his beautiful, new Doval Shadow.

Chapter 31:

THE FAMILY MAN

The Doval Shadow

A convertible built for two, the Doval Shadow showcases American ingenuity in its neoclassical tuxedo exterior. Built over several years in the late 1970s, the long nose, chrome side pipes, individual fenders, and boat tail make it a piece of art capable of turning anyone's h00ead. One could easily envision Bruce Wayne driving it to Wayne Enterprises in Gotham City on the rare occasions he actually goes to work.

The Doval is powered by a V8 engine set on a Ford-reinforced chassis dressed in a hand-beaten aluminum body. It is covered in 34 coats of lacquer with 24-karat gold leaf pinstriping details and safeguarded by steel bumpers. The driver and passenger are surrounded by plush Connally leather, English walnut dash and details, and a sewn mohair convertible top.

"Only 18 were made. I have number 18," Jim says.

Jim acquired the rare car by paying $50,000, plus the Auburn Speedster he rarely drove, to a contractor in Sacramento. The contractor had put down a deposit on the Doval and subsequently fallen on hard times. He had been looking for another car enthusiast to buy him out of the Doval Shadow he had ordered. Jim got word of the opportunity and happily jumped on it.

"I will have that car until I die! It's my favorite car. Nobody else drives one," Jim says matter-of-factly. "Everyone is infatuated with that car. It's fun to drive because no matter where you go, everybody talks to you about it. There is something about it that makes people happy. It's a conversation piece and I love conversation."

Occasionally he'll get an inquiry from a potential buyer, yet he never entertains a sell. In many ways, the Doval exemplifies the pinnacle of Jim's career. He had made it to the very top. When he wasn't being flown around on his Learjet, he was driving his automotive masterpiece from one place to another.

During one of Jim and Vicki's Doval-driving adventures, they stumbled upon the small town of Lakeview, Oregon, on their way up to Flathead Lake, Montana.

"Vicki was navigating and we ended up accidentally on the wrong road and in Lakeview. I thought it was a pretty town. We drove around some and went and looked at a ranch. I think I bought that ranch that same day," says Jim.

As Vicki simply states, "We never left."

"We were on the wrong road, and it ended up being a good thing," Jim says.

Named for its expansive view of Goose Lake, Lakeview is five hours due north of Lake Tahoe. At an altitude of nearly 4,800 feet, it is referred to as the *Tallest Town in Oregon* and is the county seat of Lake County. Lakeview has mountain views to the east and an open valley on the west.

The modest town is situated on US-395, a thoroughfare funneling drivers south to Reno and north to open country. Its roots come from the frontier days; the community developed as a business center for surrounding sheep and cattle ranchers in the mid-1800s and evolved into an official, established town in 1876. The population of Lakeview in 1980 summed up to a grand total of about 2,700 people.

A few weeks after Jim and Vicki discovered their new town and bought a ranch with a fixer-upper house on the property, Vicki moved her two daughters to Lakeview where they all began to settle into a domestic life.

Life in Lakeview was small-town living. Before long, Jim, Vicki, and the girls knew almost everyone in town. Vicki found a flexible job and the family eased into the community and she and Jim fixed up their new house. The girls attended school, Jeni in fourth grade and Aspen in kindergarten, spending the school year in Lakeview and summers with their dad in Utah.

Jim now considered his home base to be out of Lakeview instead of Lake Tahoe, although he kept a house in Tahoe. When he was at home in Lakeview with his family, he enjoyed spending time with the girls and working on various hometown projects.

"Half the things were closed in town; I opened a dry cleaner business and restored the golf course," Jim says. He also purchased the old, abandoned movie theater in late 1985. "Inside it looked like it was 1940. It had red velvet seats. I cleaned it up and the first movie we showed was *Top Gun*."

"Jim bought a gas station and mini-mart. It was known for making the biggest sandwiches in Oregon. They were so big you couldn't get your mouth around it and people came from near and far to eat them. They were *giant* sandwiches," Vicki laughs.

"I enjoyed making that town a better place and the people really appreciated it," Jim says. In recognition of his influence, Jim was asked to be the high school graduation commencement speaker.

Between Lakeview projects, Jim kept traveling to buy and sell property in Lake Tahoe, Los Angeles, San Francisco, Hawaii, and Arizona. He stayed mobile, a comfortable and effective habit of his since the mid-1960s. Another habit he established was buying homes in locations he particularly liked. For years, Jim hopped around between as many as seven homes scattered around the West Coast, rarely sleeping two nights in the same place.

In Lakeview, Vicki worked as an accountant for a local attorney a schedule that fit perfectly with the girls' school. She didn't need to work but had a lot of energy and enjoyed working. Jim, however, had other plans.

"Jim knew the attorney and walked in and quit my job for me," Vicki recalls. Instead of work, her days were filled with other adventures. "We did a ton of snowmobiling back then. The kids would be in school and we would wrap up some hotdogs and place them on the engine, and ride around and the hot dogs would cook. We would stop, have a picnic lunch, then go pick up the girls from school."

At 93 lbs., Vicki was a tiny woman managing a heavy machine. With Jim's coaching, she became an adept snowmobiler. Jim and Vicki arranged a winter snowmobiling trip to Yellowstone with another couple. The group toured around, each on their own snowmobile, spotting wildlife and revving their engines. "The guys would go so fast. My friend and I stopped and hid from them just to see how long it would take for them to miss us. It didn't take long," says Vicki.

Jim and Vicki's time in Lakeview together was also riddled with silly memories of simple living. Vicki recounts, "Jim was having trouble with his tractor, so I was towing him into Lakeview. I was being careful not to drive too fast, but I looked out the window and he was passing me by. Ends up the brakes weren't working on the tractor either. I was driving too slow."

Jim never tried to substitute as the girls' father; they already had a father. He simply enjoyed time with them, as well as having the chance to contribute to their childhood and raise them in a good town. Jim was committed to making sure they got through high school and attended good colleges. He was also very sensitive and considerate of them. Jim would take Aspen for drives in Lakeview, get her pizza and candy, and help her with gymnastics.

Aspen remembers, "Jeni was into horses and I was into gymnastics and dance. I would go outside and practice my gymnastics in the yard, and he would come out and practice with me. He would help me with my back walkovers and show me front handsprings. Now that I'm an adult, I can't believe he could do that stuff. Most adult bodies don't bend that way."

Aspen took a keen interest in Jim's success and joined him on one business trip, to Seattle. She decided to interview him and received three tips from Jim:

1. Follow the news daily and stay current so you can have intelligent conversations and spot opportunities;

2. Play golf, because a lot of business is done on the golf course; and

3. Learn to dance and how to conduct yourself etiquette-wise.

"Jim told me that there are many times when business deals happen outside of the boardroom and not just in formal meetings. In these times and places when you have the ear of the right people—you have to be prepared," Aspen recalls.

Aspen credits Jim as being a big part of her pleasant childhood. "For Jeni and I not being his biological children, he did so much to support us. He would come to our games and events. I know he had business dealings, but when he was there, he was present."

In many ways they were a traditional family unit, including a dog named Pepsi and another named Cola. Pepsi was an unusual little poodle, having been born with three rows of teeth. Jim took her to Sacramento for dental surgery. As Pepsi aged, she would become known as the *Hairless Wonder* and the *Bionic Dog*.

"Pepsi was Jim's go-to dog; she went everywhere with him. She had this leg that would pop out of socket sometimes when she jumped off the bed. Before we had Pepsi there was Harry. Harry was awesome," Aspen says.

Tom Fields with Jim and Pepsi at The Fantastic Museum

Like every family, they had ups and downs too. Jim recalls a day when Aspen told him in tears that she wasn't allowed to play with her friend Autumn anymore because Vicki wasn't married to Jim. It bothered him that Aspen was being punished for something out of her control and it stuck with him.

On September 23, 1983, Jim and Vicki were in Lake Tahoe picking up an antique fire truck, a 1931 Model A Hook and Ladder, when Vicki brought up marriage. They had been together over two years and the subject had come up before. Jim simply hadn't given it much thought, but this time was different.

This time Vicki suggested, "I tell you what, if you marry me and after one year you are not happy, you don't owe me one dollar." Jim wasn't thinking about the money; he was thinking about Aspen and them as a family.

As they were driving down into Carson City hauling the fire truck back to Lakeview, he saw a wedding chapel sign. He pulled over and walked right in and said, "We want to get married."

The man running the chapel explained that they had to go to the courthouse to get a marriage certificate and then come back for the ceremony. They did just that, and upon returning to the chapel were asked if they had a witness. Vicki and Jim looked at each other and said no. The man walked to the back room and found a lady to come witness their wedding.

Vicki and Jim returned to Lakeview married, which meant Aspen could play with Autumn again. It was more than that though—they were a good couple. They cared for each other and they made a good family.

Vicki became Jim's second wife. Jim was briefly married on December 3, 1966, to Rosemary Watkins, from Los Angeles, California. He claims to have felt the pressure to fall into a routine American life like his mentor Jim Wilson. One day he spotted a pretty girl and after courting for a short period they married. However, his first marriage was annulled shortly after it started. Marriage simply didn't suit him at the time. He helped to put Rosemary through college and bought her a car. He took pride in having the ability to continue to provide for her even after the relationship had ceased.

When Jim and Vicki married, Jeni was 11 and Aspen six. Lakeview would be their childhood home with unforgettable memories.

Aspen remembers, "We had a ton of freedom. We could go to stores and we had tabs. My mom and Jim would just get a bill. Jim bought Jeni and I a dinghy rowboat. I can't believe we got to do that at such a young age." About their home life, she says, "I loved the freedom that he and my mom gave me when I wanted to make recipes. I would just make things up for dinner. He would eat anything and not complain, as long as it was not tomatoes. I appreciated the latitude to figure things out on my own."

Jim smiles, "Vicki was positively engaged with the girls. They were good kids. They had total respect for me, in a good way. I never had to raise my voice; all I had to do was look at them and they knew I was serious when I needed to be."

Chapter 32:

THE COLLECTOR

In the 16th century, a *cabinet of curiosities* was a room prized by scholars and gentiles to showcase their unusual items. It was a hobby enjoyed by those with means and academic interest in examining and studying artifacts from other parts of the world at a time when great exploration was underway. Over the next few hundred years, collecting evolved from gathering unusual items to classifying and preserving items, even common items. Preserving came naturally to Jim; even the preservation of some of the most unusual things.

The ranch and house Jim purchased upon arrival in Lakeview encompassed about 100 acres with a little barn plus an old, crooked outhouse with a half-moon carved in the door. The boards were old and weathered, but the structure was intact. When Jim was made aware that the outhouse was not included in the sale, "I told them I didn't want the property without the outhouse. I loved that old outhouse."

Jim eventually moved the outhouse to Five Corners, a spot just a couple miles outside of Lakeview near a little store and gas station. Then someone else told him they had an outhouse on their property they would give to him. He took it. More people surfaced with more hidden outhouses, which began to assemble on what Jim would call Privy Lane at Five Corners. The word was out about Jim's new outhouse collection, and at some point, it spread nationwide.

"I would get calls from people in other states wanting to sell their outhouses to me. I even got a call from Hawaii."

In the grand scheme of history, it wasn't that long ago that Americans lived without running water and sewer systems. Early American settlers managed trash, of all types, by disposing of it in streams, fields, and forests. Then, similar to their European counterparts, colonialists would simply throw garbage, including that which was caught in a chamber pot, out the front door for consumption by pigs and other scavenger animals.

The creation of the outhouse allowed for some privacy and comfort for one to do their business in a structure separate from the main house. Outhouse doors traditionally had half-moon cutouts or stars that provided much-needed ventilation in addition to a little lighting.

With the advent of plumbing and sewage systems, outhouses lost their purpose and became artifacts of a bygone era left in the corners of farms and ranches scattered across America. Though, quite a few of these forgotten structures found their way to Lakeview for keeps under Jim's stewardship.

When one inquired as to how much Jim would pay for these peculiar structures, he decided to price outhouses by the hole—$25 a hole. Most outhouses have one hole. Jim had acquired several one-hole and two-hole outhouses. "Some outhouses have four holes for multiple people to do their business. Did you know that? It all started as kind of a joke. I mean, who collects outhouses?" Jim asks.

About the time the outhouse collection was gaining momentum, Jim purchased Hunter's Hot Springs, a piece of land planned for use as a health resort and club by the original owner, Harry Hunter. In an attempt to develop the land, Mr. Hunter had three wells drilled on his 40-acre property in 1923. Instead of retrieving water, the wells consistently spit and spewed their way into man-made geysers. While two of the geysers have died down, Old Perpetual remains a marketed tourist destination and is still known to flamboyantly erupt depending on the water table.

Under Jim's ownership, Hunter's Hot Springs was outfitted with an RV park, teepees for campers, and a 7,000-square-foot building. Soon enough, Hunter's Hot Springs was not only known for Old Perpetual but for being the home of the odd and ever-increasing collection of outhouses standing together proudly on display in solidarity instead of tucked away in shame.

Jim moved his Privy Lane outhouse collection to Hunter's Hot Springs, where it would grow to nearly 100 wooden structures exhibited along US-395 in an eye-catchingly abnormal display. Like the buffalo, the collection of antique potties was successful at grabbing the attention of passers-by to make them slow down and sometimes stay in Lakeview, if just for a short time. Outhouses, along with old-fashioned farm equipment, however, were only the beginning of Jim's Lakeview-era collecting.

As a young man, Jim had an atypical appreciation for the past. It wasn't until he had the means and the space to store collectibles that he began to build a cache of antiques—and a reputation as a collector. The items symbolized purpose and utility, and Jim enjoyed being surrounded by the past. It comforted and intrigued him.

"I started collecting Tahoe stuff, wagons and buggies, and logging equipment. I liked the old-fashioned ship lanterns, wine barrels, totem poles, ice cream parlor chairs, and antique furniture. I liked preserving the local history and would decorate my homes and businesses with these antiques and unusual things."

Jim takes pride in salvaging, protecting, and honoring vintage items, and has a distinct appreciation for those who toiled with them. He would consider the stories behind the objects he owned, like how many dresses were sewn at an old sewing machine or who sat in the ice cream parlor chairs.

He began collecting in his early Tahoe days after observing and inquiring about an old wagon nestled in the weeds on one man's property in Lake Tahoe. Jim stopped, talked to the owner, and offered to buy it. Once the word was out that Jim was interested in items from the Wild West days, and soon thereafter antique cars, people began to call him. Sometimes he would buy items he had no place for and donate them to museums, such as the old logging carts with solid wooden wheels, which he bought and donated to the Historical Society of Lake Tahoe.

Jim also had a knack for neatly displaying and arranging his collectibles, some just for decoration and some he actually used, like the furniture he would restore and reupholster. "My house in Lake Tahoe was a museum," he says, then points out, "but my first actual museum was a car museum across from the Strawberry Lodge."

Jim had always had an eye for cars and transportation-related items, and he continued this pursuit in Lakeview. "I had a double-decker London bus. I would drive it around and take people to a winery or kids to a party. It was Lakeview, Oregon. There wasn't much to do so we drove around in a double-decker bus," says Jim.

"He had buggies, a Model T, Model A, '34' Dodge, JFK's 1938 Ford sedan. And he would drive them too," Vicki shares.

Bob Jr. remembers, "I knew about Jim before I ever met him. He had the cool house down the street from my dad that was decorated with totem poles and boats. He would often drive by in his Ferrari."

Marty adds, "He loves Americana. There was one time I was in Alabama and Jim flew out to shop for antiques in the South. We filled up a truck with antiques and Jim, my mother, and I all drove back to Lake Tahoe. He always liked to drive."

"One of the nights I remember the most," Marty continues, recollecting when she and Jim were roommates, "was when Jim and I were watching the news. He was drinking a glass of milk, and it came on that someone had discovered a gauge off the Hindenburg. He got so excited he jumped up and said he needed that. He booked a flight and went and got it. He is one of the most spontaneous people. With the hint or a whisper of anything that interested him, he would pursue it."

Jim was absolutely certain he needed to own the gauge from the ill-fated Hindenburg airship. It was a piece of American history beckoning him. He recalls, "I went to Reno and got on a red-eye flight to Lakehurst, New Jersey."

The first airship, Luftschiff Zeppelin 1 or LZ-1, was completed by Count Ferdinand von Zeppelin and took its maiden voyage in 1900. The airship was an oversized structured balloon filled with hydrogen for lift, while gas engines powered the propellers for direction and a sliding weight along the bottom provided pitch. The Count continued to refine his concept and eventually improved control, power, speed, and range of the airship. By 1908, the Zeppelin caught the attention of the German government, which proclaimed to fund future development if the airships could complete a 24-hour flight. Unfortunately, during a 24-hour prototype test, a surprise storm whipped through and tossed the anchored ship around. The ship went down in hydrogen flames, leaving behind only a bent interior frame. Instead of taking this catastrophe as a sign to abort airship development, Count Zeppelin was met with a surge of money that came pouring in to support his efforts to evolve the airship into a viable means of passenger transportation.

The Hindenburg, or LZ-129, was a luxury airship that began passenger service in March 1936 and completed 17 transatlantic flights in its inaugural year. On the evening of May 6, 1937, the Hindenburg was reaching its final destination in Lakehurst, New Jersey, after a multiple-day voyage over the Atlantic Ocean that had begun in Frankfurt, Germany. The captain of the Hindenburg was concerned about the weather conditions in Lakehurst and the decision was made to wait out the weather along the coast and return to Lakehurst when the weather cleared in a few hours. Once the weather cleared, the captain piloted the airship back to Lakehurst, believing he had a calm weather window for landing.

Amidst challenges with the ballast and shifting winds, the captain and crew skillfully steered the balloon to the mooring mast. Minutes after the Hindenburg came in nose first toward its mooring mast, or tower used for docking, flames emerged toward the rear of the Zeppelin, the fire spread rapidly, and the tail began to lunge to the ground. The fire destroyed the airship in less than a minute. Passengers onboard were either tossed around or trapped, while some opted to jump to the ground a great distance below. The 1937 disaster killed 36 people, including one person on the ground. Many of the 62 survivors were severely injured.

The Hindenburg's fiery plummet to the ground in Lakehurst, New Jersey, is believed to have resulted from a spark that ignited some leaking hydrogen. The highly visible and dramatic tragedy along with competing air transportation options brought the glamorous airship era to an end. The invention succumbed to advanced technology and now belonged to American history, a piece of which Jim Schmit was excited to own and preserve.

The Hindenburg gauge was originally found by a security guard stationed nearby the crash scene. It later ended up in a museum in Lakehurst and when the original owner died, it was willed to his son, who was mentioned in the news report Jim and Marty were watching.

Jim says, "I called the kid and told him I was interested in buying it. I arrived in Lakehurst at 10:00 a.m. the next day and knocked on his door."

During the flight, Jim had decided he was willing to pay $50,000 for the gauge. But when the door opened, a kid dressed in hippie attire came out.

Jim introduced himself and asked, "How much do you want for the gauge?"

The hippie asked how much Jim would pay. Jim offered $4,000. The kid countered with $5,000. Jim stuck his hand out for a handshake and became the rightful owner of the only surviving Hindenburg gauge for $5,000.

Most often, though, Jim found items through word of mouth and auctions. Sometimes he was looking for specific items to add to existing collections; other times he would simply purchase something that interested him.

"It was fun to go to auctions with him," Vicki says. "He bought the remnants of a boat that crashed on Lake Tahoe when trying to break the sound barrier. He had a vest worn by Eliot Ness." Ness was a key player in bringing down the infamous Chicago gangster Al Capone in the 1930s.

Sometimes it worked the other way around, and interesting things would find Jim. The film *Cleopatra*, starring Elizabeth Taylor and Richard Burton, was released in 1963 and grossly overbudgeted for a number of reasons—one of many may have been Taylor and Burton's highly publicized affair during its filming. The movie studio, 20th Century Fox, was so financially strained by the overblown budget that it sold almost 300 acres of Los Angeles land to cover the expenses. When that wasn't enough, the company sought out other solutions.

"*Cleopatra* almost broke 20th Century Fox," Jim says.

Because of the extravagant delays, the studio very badly needed to finish the film. The idea behind the trailer was to keep Taylor's head more focused on the movie and less focused on her affair with Burton. The 36-foot dressing trailer was built and decorated as if she was on the set of *Cleopatra* costing $75,000—nearly $650,000 in 2021 dollars.

"The studio called up Mr. ZX Ranch, I can't remember his name… he was a billionaire that lived in New York City. He bailed out the movie." Bordering the tiny nook of Paisley, Oregon, populated with not quite 250 people, was the massive ZX Ranch, owned by Nicolas Salgo, best known for developing the Watergate Complex in Washington, D.C. The ZX Ranch, long believed to be one of the largest contiguous land cattle operations in the United States, has access to over 1.3 million acres of public and private land for grazing livestock.

"Mr. ZX Ranch said he wanted that trailer when the movie wrapped," Jim pointed out. The studio made good on their agreement and handed over the Elizabeth Taylor trailer to Mr. Salgo, once the filming was done. He used that trailer as a guest house at his ranch. Guests would come and stay in Elizabeth Taylor's trailer. "It was like the Lincoln bedroom," Jim says.

The ZX Ranch bordered part of Jim's Rivers End Ranch, a tiny 30,000 acres in comparison. The two owners had become friendly neighbors and Mr. Salgo was aware of Jim's collecting habit. Years went by and Mr. Salgo decided to sell ZX Ranch, around 1980. Before Salgo sold the ranch, he offered to give Jim the Elizabeth Taylor trailer for his collection; he was happy to take it.

Somehow though, there was miscommunication about the ownership rights of the trailer. Salgo had a daughter who believed she owned the trailer and she had offered it to the City of Lakeview. Jim remembers, "The city called me looking for the trailer. They told me the daughter had donated the trailer to Lakeview. It was a mix-up, so I offered to buy it for $10,000. The city was thrilled."

Jim parked the trailer inside his evolving museum. It was in pristine condition, as if Taylor had walked out the door and hour before and was on set filming at that moment. Jim displayed it so that when you looked into the door of the trailer, the movie *Cleopatra* was playing on a little TV, on a loop. The trailer had found a good home.

The allure and mysticism of relics and historical artifacts can connect us to another world by providing a glimpse of what it was like to live in another place and time or in another social class, culture, or mindset. Collectors have a fever for finding and holding the power harnessed in an object. "I like to preserve things and I like to see people laugh. Collecting was also my retirement plan. I figured that if I ever needed to, I could sell collectibles and live off of that money, month to month. Kind of like an insurance policy. Everything is for sale at a price," Jim smirks.

Chapter 33:

THE CURATOR

Jim enjoyed acquiring unique items such as the Hindenburg gauge and Elizabeth Taylor's custom-made trailer, but he also enjoyed collections in bulk. The collection that fascinated him the most was the Doc Jones Fantastic Museum that he happened upon during the 1962 Seattle World's Fair. "I went into the museum and remember seeing Olaf the Giant. The penny arcade stuff was cool. A full-sized, real-looking mechanized elephant."

The Doc Jones Fantastic Museum, with its own roaming vampire, left an indelible impression on Jim, more so than the actual World's Fair. The owner, Walter H. Doc Jones, was as eccentric as his collection. As a boy growing up in remote Ketchikan, Alaska, Doc treasured the traveling circuses and carnivals that only rarely made their way to town. When interviewed in by the Northshore Citizen Newspaper 1963, Doc said, "I still recall arriving in town just moments too late to ride on a steam-driven merry-go-round that was touring the Alaskan seaport towns.... I was heartbroken, and I suppose recollections like this provided the impetus for my present shows."

Before The Doc Jones Fantastic Museum days began, Doc was constantly collecting and building unusual attractions meant entirely for amusement. His hobby eventually expanded beyond the capacity of his and wife Dorothy's home near Lynnwood, Washington, north of Seattle. They expanded and bought a few acres that held the remnants of an old log cabin, sparking Doc's new hobby, building ghost towns. On these acres, the fictitious town of Rusty Gulch was outfitted with a barbershop, saloon, jail, and general store. For a finishing touch, there was whiskey hidden in the woods behind the town.

Their curious neighbors inspired the opening of an actual museum. Much of the ghost town of Rusty Gulch was relocated into a more modern and public building in 1959 named the Jones' Fantastic Museum. Several years later, as Seattle prepared for its worldwide showcase in 1962, The Doc Jones Fantastic Museum relocated to Seattle where Jim found it.

In his heyday, Doc explained, "I'm just trying to bring back some of the glamour, illusion, and fakery of the old-time medicine man shows and carnival sideshows." Upon Doc Jones' death in the early 1970s, the unconventional collection was inherited by his heirs. The museum was downsized and relocated but continued to entertain Seattle residents and visitors until 1980 when it closed. For nearly two years the collection sat forgotten in a storage space in Seattle, missing the giggles and gasps elicited from visitors.

As requested in Doc's will, The Seattle Children's Hospital received the extraordinary donation in 1982 with the stipulation that the collection not be broken up; and if sold it had to be sold as a package. The Hospital began searching for a buyer in 1984. It would take a unique collector to want a massive bundle of bizarre items.

About a year after Jim and his family settled in Lakeview, a museum broker tasked with selling the strange collection contacted Jim. Intrigued by the opportunity, Jim's interest transformed into action. With friend and successful Baltimore businessman Ralph Bothne on board, the two purchased the collection for around $400,000 in 1985, or approximately $950,000 in 2021. The massive Jones' Fantastic Museum was heading to Lakeview, Oregon.

A collection of this magnitude required extensive space and well-planned logistics to transport it the 500-plus miles to its new home. As usual, Jim came up with a transport plan as unique as the collection. He had estimated that it would cost around $25,000 to have it professionally moved. Instead, he recruited Lakeview friends and residents to volunteer a weekend to move the eccentric items at his expense. Between gas, meals, and hotels for the volunteers, it cost a fraction of the expense of a professional mover and created a unique small-town memory for those who pitched in.

In mid-October of 1985, a convoy of 30 trucks and trailers pulled into Lakeview to deliver most of the contents of the new Lakeview Fantastic Museum to its new space at Hunter's Hot Springs. The parade of flatbed trucks, hay rigs, and cattle trailers driven by teachers, ranchers, and neighbors arrived towing countless freakish and wonderful treasures: the four-legged lady, the two-headed lady, the laughing lady, and the abominable snow woman, carved wooden Indians, a bicycle air conditioner, Captain Hook's hook, musical monkeys, antique toys, an armored motorcycle, fun house mirrors, circus side show relics, and myriad other strange things—all guarded by a large mechanical elephant reigning over the procession.

There were several standout pieces in this treasure trove but in one of those trailers, tucked away in a glass coffin, quietly laid Olaf Stor-Bjorn. Olaf, the Giant Viking, was born in approximately 1335, making him over 675 years old. Originally found in a peat bog in Norway in 1888, Olaf's petrified remains measure nine feet tall were he standing upright. He has been considered to be part of what lends credence to the legend of Bigfoot. Accompanied by a large painted canvas, much like Jim, Olaf is somewhat of a traveling man. Before being acquired by Jim, Olaf toured with circuses and carnivals for years.

Jim remembers his first peek at Olaf at the World's Fair when he was in his early twenties and penniless. He remembers the allure and excitement he felt when he discovered Olaf while wandering through the Jones' Fantastic Museum. Miraculously, in a whirlwind of two decades, Jim was now in the position to provide that experience to others. Now the shriveled and dusty mummy could be found in Lakeview, awaiting a new generation of awestruck faces. This was the beginning of Jim's long and enduring relationship with his petrified buddy.

The Lakeview locals parked their museum loads in front of the 7,000-square-foot building at Hunter's Hot Springs, alongside the old farm relics from years past. Then began the arduous task of unloading the goods. Upon seeing his friends and neighbors pull up to the new building, Jim got tears in his eyes; he had never seen people who were so happy to do something.

In some ways, the hard work was just beginning for Jim. He now had to sort through and display the collection. There was so much stuff that not all of it could be shown at once. Jim decided he would simply rotate items to keep it interesting. Organizing and exhibiting all of these whacky and wonderful intrigues was time-consuming and physically demanding. Fortunately, Jim's endless energy was perfectly suited for such a task. "Jim is very talented at displaying and showcasing his stuff," Vicki says.

Items had to be shelved, hung, or stacked to keep everything in order. Once ready, the museum was opened to curious visitors free of charge on weekends all year long and every day from June through October. The Lakeview Fantastic Museum from then on became a part of Jim's and his family's daily lives. It was a labor of love for Jim, who was constantly accompanied by his poodle, Boomer.

Aspen remembers, "Jim included me on the museum, and I helped make decisions about concessions. I took great pride in running the museum entry counter through my teenage years. He taught me a lot on profits and how much things cost. That's probably why I have a business degree."

Vicki shares, "One time I wanted a couple of items from the museum and I forgot to turn the building alarm off when I arrived. The police came out to check on the alarm and found me reaching for whatever I was getting while on top of the fat lady that wiggles, shakes, and sings when she is plugged in. We all couldn't help but laugh."

Jim was always adding to the collection as well. "I bought stuff every day back then. I like history. I don't care if it's just old skis."

There was one particular item that was very much a part of Jim's personal history. Jim kept on display an extraordinarily large taxidermy buffalo head to guard his museum with its shaggy mane and brooding eyes. It was the buffalo that rampaged Fiddletown years prior, whose end resulted in a community feast. "He was huge. I had him preserved. He's been part of my collection since then," Jim laughs.

Jim would drive his Rolls Royce around in cowboy boots, not realizing he had become the Loren Bamert of Lakeview. He relished his ability to contribute to the small town in both grand and tiny gestures. His contributions even made national headlines. An Associated Press article entitled, 'Moves In, Invests $2 million: Millionaire Adopts Small Oregon Town' sums up Jim's contributions to Lakeview:

> Since his nationwide search for a small town to call home ended in Lakeview five years ago, the purposeful newcomer has, by his accounting, plunked something like $2 million into this town without expecting any immediate return. He's taken in more than 20 of the locals as partners in a dozen business ventures that he has acquired or launched. Those who sit the fence and keep score say that most of this town of 3,000, maybe 90%, seem to think Schmit is doing just fine, even if it doesn't understand exactly why he is here.

While the museum and town projects were moving along successfully, Jim and Vicki quietly ended their marriage. Vicki and Jim loved and respected each other, but something was missing in their relationship, and they affably agreed to divorce. Vicki was concerned about the girls having to deal with the stress of a divorce in a small town, and Jim understood. He was amenable to Vicki's request that he delay getting into another relationship until the girls were out of high school.

Aspen, Jeni, Vicki, and Jim with Pepsi celebrating Jeni's Graduation

Jim simply says, "When you really, truly love somebody, you want the best for them." In wanting the best for Vicki and the girls he honored her request.

"We had a good relationship, but I wasn't marriage material at the time. I was too busy doing business. It wasn't fair to her and the kids. I missed a lot and felt guilty about not being there but at the same time, I had to keep doing business," Jim reflects.

Jim and Vicki managed to maintain a normal married front for many years, an impressive feat in a small town. The family of four simply continued on as they had been. Jim still traveled. Vicki still took care of the girls. They continued their adventures together and making a positive impact on Lakeview. They were a good team, and time would transition their romance into a strong friendship. Jim is not one to walk away from good people.

"Vicki is the best. They don't get any better!" Jim says.

Chapter 34:

THE OREGON DEVELOPER

After the damming of Drews Creek in 1911 for local irrigation purposes, Drews Reservoir was formed 15 miles to the west of Lakeview with a reflective baby blue surface. Jim discovered a piece of land near Drews Reservoir that had been approved for a subdivision development. He saw potential in this affordable piece of property because of its proximity to the reservoir and waterfront views. He called a few friends to join in on the purchase, including Rick Barry and Tom Fields.

"I bought the land, put the roads in, and started selling the five-acre parcels," Jim remembers. Then it was off to the next project.

Whenever Jim traveled, he not only enjoyed the passing scenery, he studied it. He was always looking for new real estate opportunities. On a road trip to visit family in his childhood home of Puyallup, Jim passed through the small community of Redmond, Oregon, about three hours northwest of Lakeview. Redmond caught his eye enough to make him slow down, stop, and seek out a realtor.

Redmond was officially incorporated in 1910 with a population of 216. The town's pioneers were schoolteachers Frank and Josephine Redmond, who settled amongst the rocks and sagebrush on a homestead in Central Oregon's High Desert. The population grew after canals and a railroad were built through the community and continued to grow through the twentieth century largely thanks to improved irrigation systems. Lumber and potatoes were a thriving industry from the 1930s and into the 1980s. By 1990, Redmond's population had reached 7,165 residents. However, the viability of lumber production and potato farming was starting to waver by the end of the twentieth century. After three lumber mills closed, many Redmond residents were left jobless and with few opportunities for employment. As a result, housing prices were cheap. Additionally, increases in California state taxes began pushing out industries and businesses. California's neighbor to the north—Oregon—stood to benefit from these tax hikes.

Jim's intuition told him that Redmond was ripe for development. In 1988, Oregon had sponsored an Enterprise Zone in Redmond, a government-approved incentive program for drawing in business investments and creating job opportunities. These Zones are usually designated and supported by the State in locations where local economies are struggling. As a result of this government funding, Redmond could provide new businesses with waivers and discounts on permits, fees, and water and sewage services, among other benefits. Jim accurately anticipated that when the new businesses started arriving, the demand for housing would go up. He was able to rally some other investors to consider the idea.

Around the same time this idea gained momentum, Tom Fields was going through a divorce and ready for a change. After Tom and Jim sold two of their real estate offices in Lake Tahoe, Tom relocated to Oregon in 1990 to run the Redmond development project.

The original crew of Redmond investors organized through Jim had each agreed to contribute $10,000. With that capital, they were able to buy a large portion of properties in town for around $50,000. Their plan was to build homes for $60,000 each, rent them for a few years, and then sell them for $59,500 with no competition.

Tom recalls, "We developed a 100-lot subdivision in Redmond, starting with five spec homes across the street from Redmond High School, located in the middle of town. We had envisioned building a golf course on the 33 acres along this canyon but couldn't get it approved." While the city had stated security concerns, in truth, the city was doing its best to acquire that same plot of land for a greenbelt park. They didn't want a golf course.

As homes were being built and sold in the new development, and debate about the golf course continued, Jim came up with a new idea: If the city wouldn't approve their golf course plan, they would deed the open space to the homeowners so they could enjoy a nice green space and a five-acre lake. They created a homeowners' association and deeded the land to the homeowners. To this day, the open space is owned by the property owners.

The development proved to be a quick success. Jim, Tom, and the other partners ended up selling the land to another developer a handful of years later. "We came out very good. I still own a home on that green space in Redmond. I rent it out," Tom says.

Despite a change in business geography, both Jim and Tom kept close ties with the Lake Tahoe area. They owned homes and a motel there, and it remained a regular destination in their travel circuit.

Chapter 35:

THE VISIONARY

With his projects in Central Oregon growing in momentum, Jim felt a pull to spend more time in Redmond. While Jim still visited Vicki's daughters— teenagers now—when he was traveling through Lakeview, he found a new home base in Redmond.

In June 1991, Jim found 17,000 square feet of space in an old factory just south of downtown Redmond. It would serve as the new location of The World Famous Fantastic Museum. The museum façade depicted an old Western town, with a saloon, a hotel, and a country store from a bygone era. Plus, Jim exhibited his usual assortment of old wagons, buggies, cars, and Elizabeth Taylor's dressing trailer, among other attractions near the building. He set up the museum and hired a local girl to work the cash register.

Marty remembers, "He had a girl that worked the cash register with her feet. She had no arms. It blew my mind. You didn't want to stare, but it was so fascinating."

When asked about the woman, Jim jokingly replies, "Which one? I know a lot of girls with no arms." Then adds, "I don't really remember that. It's kind of a blur."

However, there was another woman in Redmond that Jim remembers very well. Her name was Jade. She had fair skin, auburn hair, and freckles that peppered her nose. She was living in Redmond and had been dating a fellow who introduced her to Jim. Little did he know that he was introducing Jim to his future girlfriend. Jade caught Jim's eye immediately.

"She was, and still is, a beautiful redhead. And she was very outgoing and happy-go-lucky. I sold a piece of property right next to the museum to the guy she was dating," Jim says.

Jade remembers, "Jim invited me and my boyfriend to Lake Tahoe and we decided to go. We went to Bob Lindner's Beach House. My boyfriend had other stuff to do so I hung out with Jim most of the time."

Bob Lindner's beach house is also referred to by his friends as *Bob's at The Beach*. Lindner's luxurious, 7,000-square-foot house was featured on Robin Leach's television show *Lifestyles of the Rich and Famous*. In addition to its prime location—on a peninsula with access to a private boat dock on the Tahoe Keys Lagoon and direct access to the expansive Lake Tahoe—the house also had a private beach, four bedrooms, 6.5 bathrooms, an indoor pool with a two-story waterfall, an outdoor hot tub, a dance floor, a gym, seven decks, and a pizza oven in the kitchen.

Back in Redmond, Jim began to ask Jade to join him on casual outings.

Jade says, "Before I knew it, I was dating Jim. He was much more fun than the other guy who was telling people around town that Jim came in and swooped me away."

Jim says he believes Jade and her boyfriend ended up breaking up six months after he met Jade. They hit it off and became an item for a short time.

One time, on a road trip to Yellowstone with Jim and her friend, Jade remembers that Jim started flirting with her friend. This upset her so much she broke up with him shortly thereafter.

Jim says, "I guess I flirted with her friend. I have a tendency to compliment people and it could be perceived as flirting. If I think an 800-pound lady at the bank has pretty eyes, I'll tell her she has pretty eyes. I like to make people feel good and I've always thought complimenting is a nice way to do that."

In addition to being a generous giver of compliments, Jim continued collecting. By this time, Jim had collected so many interesting items that he established a South Lake Tahoe branch of his museum and called it True Wonders, Museum of the Fantastic. It was located at the corner of U.S. Highway 50 and Park Avenue, just west of the California-Nevada state line.

"The Lake Tahoe museum was pretty big. It was by the casinos and run by Doug Higley. He was a disc jockey in Lake Tahoe and had a real deep voice. But the museum didn't go over well. You had to walk upstairs to view it," says Jim. The visitors that climbed up the stairs were treated to a vast toy collection and the extraordinary Olaf, among many, many other items.

Chapter 36:

THE EMPLOYER

A fellow by the name of David Chips McAllister moved to Redmond in 1990 to partner with a rancher in starting a horse and carriage company. Chips was a screen cowboy by profession in the 1970s serving as a stuntman in Western movies. He fit the image of a Western cowboy so perfectly that he was recruited by Marlboro cigarettes to serve as their Marlboro Man in 1979. Though the stunt work left his body battered, his Christian faith ran deep and he liked to work.

At the same time Jim was preparing to open his museum in Redmond, Chips was planning on make a living trying to stay on top of horses and in carriages instead of tumbling out of them in elaborate stunts. When Chips discovered that his friend's ranch was near The World Famous Fantastic Museum and saw the Old West-themed outdoor display, he stopped in to feed his curiosity. Chips quickly found himself in a partnership with Jim.

"We immediately struck up a friendship. I started the horse and carriage company on Jim's property," says Chips. He agreed to pay Jim 10 percent of his profits to cover rent for the property with one caveat; Jim explained that if Chips didn't turn a profit, he didn't have to pay anything. While it was a new venture—and there were known risks—Chips was excited to give it a go.

Chips recalls, "The first year went well, but the second year I was struggling. Jim said I didn't need to pay him anything. Jim's word is as good as a handshake, which are both better than a written contract. Jim honored the verbal deal he had made with me."

When Chips decided to let go of the horse and carriage company, Jim decided he needed a public relations manager for The World Famous Fantastic Museum.

"He invented a job for me. He gave me a BMW to drive around and promote the museum. It was a great car, but I had a bad back and it killed me to drive it. I gave the BMW back to Jim, and he tried to pay me for it but I said, no way," say Chips.

Early on in their friendship, Chips remembers Jim saying, "Chips, you're not motivated by money. But maybe you have the right idea. I've got all this money and all these problems."

Instead of the BMW, Chips found himself at the helm of Jim's latest purchase, a 40-foot antique tour bus. "I believe he bought it from the Kentucky Headhunters. I got about a 15-minute lesson on how to drive it. It was a great piece of machinery," Chips says.

When Jim purchased the bus, he was told that it had been Elvis' tour bus in 1976 and 1977. With Chips navigating, this bus turned into its own universe. The bus was both Jim's own tour bus and a tourist attraction. Chips and Jim rented out the bus for parties and charged $375 a day, or $2 to walk on and look around. Chips made nearly $1,500 on one particularly busy day from walk-ons alone. Jim and Chips shared the profits from this joint venture.

In their time off the tourist circuit, Chips and Jim scooted around the western United States in the bus with their friends in tow. At times there were unusual people on board heading to unusual destinations. Chips remembers driving the bus with the Chinese Red Army Basketball team on board. He also remembers white knuckling it down the winding, narrow road to Shelter Cove, California, after getting only a vague description from Jim that it would be kind of tricky to drive down there.

Shelter Cove is located in the King Range National Conservation Area of northern California along what is known as the Lost Coast. The small town remains secluded because of the challenging vehicular access, although there is air and sea access as well. Along the Lost Coast of California, State Route 1 veers inland away from the coastline because the rugged terrain was found to be exceptionally challenging and costly for building the road. In the light of day, driving a car down to Shelter Cove is a bit chilling, which means driving a bus down to Shelter Cove in the dark was an even mind-boggling.

"It was the middle of the night and the fog was like pea soup," Chips recollects. "It was a two-lane road with lots of switch-backs and a history of people dying in car accidents. I was using both lanes in first gear all the way down. When we got down Jim said to me, 'Chips, you have a couple of medals coming for driving a bus.'" After making two trips down to Shelter Cove in that bus, Chips decided it was enough.

If driving a bus down this road seems challenging, consider the logistical feat of bringing the *Blue Boy* down to Shelter Cove. Built in 1928, the *Blue Boy* yacht was used in Southern California as a rum runner during the Prohibition era. *Blue Boy* was once owned by William Randolph Hearst, the American businessman and newspaper publisher who hosted some of Hollywood's biggest names aboard the yacht while it was docked in San Simeon, California, before loaning it to the U.S. Navy during WWII. It has even been said that Robert Kennedy and Marilyn Monroe rendezvoused on the *Blue Boy* a few times. The boat is made from elegant teak wood and has brass railings and beautiful woodwork throughout.

"Carpenters would tell me how impressive and lovely the woodwork was on that boat. I can't even remember who I bought it from. I paid a lot of money. I took it out on the water a few times but it was a lot of upkeep," Jim says.

The Blue Boy makes it to Shelter Cove

Jim had taken a liking to Shelter Cove and had bought a large home on the cliffs in the late 1980s. Jim decided the *Blue Boy* would be a perfect addition to his home in Shelter Cove, serving as a guesthouse. The boat was mounted on a cradle by Jim's house and guests could sleep aboard the *Blue Boy* without worrying about seasickness. Getting the *Blue Boy* to Shelter Cove was another matter; Jim eventually hired a driver to haul the 67-foot yacht down the winding, little road.

Chips says, "The driver's wife was with him and bailed out of the truck. She was nervous…she couldn't watch. They did get the boat down there. Jim gets these wild ideas and he makes them work."

Chapter 37:

THE CARNIE

The next wild idea Jim concocted was turning the museum into an amusement and theme park with rides, batting cages, miniature golf, go-carts, bumper boats, a Ferris wheel, and other rides and games. After acquiring a Ferris wheel, which stood tall and bright next to the museum, he was now on the hunt for a Space Ball—a one-person rollercoaster ride that twists and turns like a gyroscope.

"I always wanted a Ferris wheel. I bought quite a large one from back east somewhere. There was this big, colorful Ferris wheel when you drove into this old country town of Redmond. ...I'm kind of a carnie," says Jim.

Jim's search for a space ball began and ended with Eric Elkaim. Eric, owner of Los Angeles Party Works, was good at tracking down fun things. Eric remembers, "It's a small industry, I found one within a week. Jim offered a reward. He insisted on getting my address and sending me a $5,000 check. I refused it. I couldn't accept it."

Eric felt he was simply doing his job. That $5,000 may have been the best money he never had because Jim took a liking to Eric after a handful of phone calls. Eric was professional and delivered on his word. Jim called Eric up and told him that he wanted to meet him, offering to buy him a plane ticket so he could fly to Oregon from Los Angeles.

Eric agreed to the trip. Jim and Chips picked him up at the airport in the bus and took him on a small tour to show him their development projects, the museum, and all the other good sights.

"We became quick friends. And I love his stories," Eric says.

Like Doctor Albo, Eric was into magic. Jim says, "He's a great magician. We were at a party once and he'd take watches off people in a second. They had no idea. Then Eric would hand me the watch, and I would walk up to them and ask if they were missing anything. I would pretend I had taken their watch and then give it back to them. They were so confused. We did that a few times. We had fun with it."

After his short stay, Eric returned back to Southern California, but he remained in regular contact with Jim. "Jim helped me buy property up in Oregon. It was raw land that I sat on for a while and eventually made $250,000 on it," Eric says.

Unfortunately, Jim's theme park wasn't fun for the Redmond locals for long. "The town didn't want it, so I took it down," Jim says. Although short-lived, the theme park was another wild example of an idea Jim made come alive. Around 1996, Jim closed the museum in Redmond and decided to move on. He didn't feel despondent about his decision to close the museum because he already had his sights set on the next museum location: Sisters, Oregon.

Chips remembers of the museum in Redmond before it closed, "My pastor lived right next to the museum. His kids were a little rowdy and wild and one night they vandalized Jim's Doval," says Chips. "Jim didn't press charges and didn't charge the pastor near what it cost to have it all fixed."

Through this experience, the pastor got to know Jim. Chips remains intrigued and puzzled by Jim's beliefs. "Jim seems to put the Lord second, but for some reason the Lord is okay with that. I believe he's absolutely blessed by the Lord," says Chips.

Another one of Jim's friends, Del Matthews, says, "Jim uses Christian principles in his life without practicing or pretending to be Christian."

Del met Jim after Del and his family stopped to visit the museum in Redmond. "I couldn't believe it," Del says, describing his experience walking into the museum. "There was a Picasso painting, button collection, and a violin collection.... I asked for the owner and that's when I met Jim."

Del Matthews had grown up in Nevada in the middle of nowhere. In his youth, he helped his parents run a garbage dump, went to school in a one-room schoolhouse, and lived 160 miles from the nearest town. "We lived 40 miles down a dirt road. My dad wanted to get away from people. My mother cried when we moved out there; we were just little kids."

Because of his strong and sturdy build, he became an accomplished high school wrestler. Jim says of Del, "When I met him, he was a human forklift; strong in all ways—both mentally and physically."

Del left home when he was 15 years old and moved to Ellensburg, Washington, where he discovered the auction business in the mid-1970s. His proclivity to collect and sell items came naturally, and his usual process was to go to the Midwest, buy antiques, and then sell them in auctions. He taught himself to be an auctioneer and after making a little money, Del went into real estate. He did well, quite well.

Del always appeared a bit disheveled and unassuming, not like someone who managed a real estate portfolio worth eight figures.

Jim and Del's friendship began the day they met as a result of their shared love of collecting. Del collected antique toys and when he learned that Jim owned a very large Disney toy collection, he told Jim about a massive toy collection for sale he saw sitting in a warehouse in Santa Rosa, California. Jim immediately insisted they go buy it. Del dismissed the seriousness of Jim's suggestion. He was in Redmond as part of a long-awaited family vacation; their final destination was Reno. Del's wife had previously been in treatment in Nashville, Tennessee, recovering from a malignant brain tumor and she was happy to be out and moving again.

Jim called Del repeatedly that next week. "He blew my phone up he was calling me so much," Del says. Jim was eager to see the toy collection in California that Del had mentioned.

Jim explains, "I believe there are thinkers and there are doers. I'm a doer. I always have been and always will be. I remember wanting to go see that collection. I didn't have a plane at the time, so I told Del I would rent a plane and come pick him up in Reno, then we could fly down to Los Angeles to see the collection."

Jim could sense Del's hesitation; when Del expressed concern about leaving his family, Jim suggested he bring them along. After a considerable amount of convincing, Jim finally persuaded Del to fly down to Los Angeles to see the collection and he chartered a larger plan so his family could all come.

"If I'm interested in something, I make it happen. That's how impulsive I am. I know this is why I have been successful; while everyone else is analyzing and deciding, I've already acted," Jim says. "I follow my gut feeling. And when I know it's a good deal, I make an offer. Of course, deals don't always go through. Making an early offer, even if you don't buy, can give you the upper hand."

It took them two hours to walk through the entire collection, which was over twice as long as it took to walk through Jim's collection. After giving it a little thought, Jim made a $1.5-million cash offer. However, the deal ended up falling through because the owner signed a contract with an auction company. Although Jim and Del left empty-handed, they had their new friendship and a good memory.

In addition to their shared love of collecting, Del and Jim both also had successful backgrounds in real estate. Del was a broker in Yakima, Washington, and owned a large footprint of properties near the old downtown. These two real estate dynamos had more than just toys in their collections; they had lots of properties as well.

At the same time that Jim and Del's friendship was beginning to flourish, an old friend of Jim's reentered the picture. Not too long after Jade and

Jim broke up, she had a daughter with another man. About nine months into motherhood, the father left Jade and her baby for another woman. Jim ended up helping Jade through the tumultuous time. He provided moral support and had an unwavering positive attitude when she needed him—when they needed him. Jim comforted Jade and enjoyed her sweet daughter to the extent that he could between travels. "We mostly saw him when he came through town," Jade says.

Jim and Del's first partnership was a land purchase in Madras, Oregon, 26 miles north of Redmond. They thought it was a good opportunity and purchased 100 two-acre lots. They named the development Canyon View Estates.

"There was a time when I would buy things I knew were a good deal, a good opportunity, and then bring in partners after the purchase. I might not have necessarily been interested in managing the project, but I couldn't pass up a good deal, so I would buy it and let someone else manage it," says Jim.

Jim transferred the management of Canyon View Estates to Del, wrote up the contract, and signed his interest in the subdivision directly over to Del.

"I owed Jim $350,000 to take over his contract once we closed the deal and made the purchase on the subdivision. Of course, I planned to pay Jim, but he told me to put the money in my pocket. To pay him some time later," Del shakes his head. "I realized then and there—this guy is strange. I was of the world, but I thought mostly about me. Jim thinks of other people to a fault, much more than he thinks of himself. Jim changed my mind about how to treat people...of how to look at the world."

Jim says, "Del is salt of the Earth. He's a good ole boy; he's really, really smart. He owned half of Yakima when I met him. He started Yesterday's Village, one of the biggest antique malls in America."

Yesterday's Village was 125,000 square feet of building space filled with several hundred vendors. Once Jim got a look at Del's monstrous antique mall, he started considering how to expand and make money on the concept. "I wrote a business plan to take this antique mall concept nationwide, combining brick-and-mortar stores and virtual stores," says Jim. Jim had realized the Internet—still revolutionary at that time—as a ripe marketplace. "The plan was to have products in stores and online too. By the time I had put the idea together, the dot coms were exploding and already making this happen. We missed the window."

Nevertheless, Yesterday's Village in Yakima continued to be a success. For Del and Jim, it was merely the beginning of countless partnerships.

"I don't remember half of it. I've done so many things that I can't remember them all," Jim explains.

Chapter 38:

THE BALLER

It was the mid-1990s—Bill Clinton was the President of the United States, O.J. Simpson had just been found not guilty for the murders of Nicole Brown Simpson and Ron Goldman, and the federally mandated 55-mile-per-hour speed limit ended, which resulted in many states increasing their speed limits. Jim could drive his nice cars between different towns faster. He regularly burned up the roads in central Oregon, where he was beginning a development in the town of Sisters, Oregon, and where he opened up his next museum. Not everything fit in the building he acquired for his museum in Sisters, so he sent a lot of museum items up to a storage space in Yakima, Washington. The remainder of his collection was sent to California.

"We made a deal with the City of Eureka, California, to move some museum pieces there for display. I moved thousands of items there, but there was a big storm that ruined a bunch of my stuff. I had taken the Instruments of Surrender there, too, and it was stolen," Jim says.

Around the time Jim lost a portion of his collection to weather and thievery, he gained one of his most beloved properties: Suttle Lake Resort. Surrounded by Ponderosa Pine and Douglas Fir trees, Suttle Lake is in the Deschutes National Forest, located 13 miles west of Sisters, Oregon. The shores of Suttle Lake have hosted campsites and lodges since the 1920s. However, the U.S. National Forest Service permits only a limited number of buildings in the surrounding area in order to preserve the peaceful hideaway. Therefore, any structures built adjacent to the lake were rare commodities.

Several years before, while he was living in Redmond, Jim came across Suttle Lake and discovered a log cabin he had to have. "I bought Suttle Lake Resort just to get this old, dilapidated cabin on the lake," says Jim. He found a guy to manage the resort, rent out the other handful of cabins, maintain the grounds, and keep an eye on things. He told the fellow that whatever he earned he could keep. "It wasn't an investment. It was just something I wanted to do."

Jim's primary goal was to fix up the old cabin for a retreat. "I loved the setting. It reminded me of the movie *On Golden Pond*. So that's what I named my cabin." In the back of his head, he also had plans to build something bigger.

Since Jim had spent his formative years in a humble log cabin, he had developed a special affinity for them. These rustic structures always caught his eye. Much like his collectibles, the log structures made him wonder about the people that had used them in the past. For Jim, log cabins were a symbol of America, a country that had been built on hard work and ingenuity, two things that he valued in his own life. Log cabins were a source of pride and nostalgia, and a place to tuck away and call home. Jim appreciated cozy log cabins and grand lodges equally.

"I used to stay in lodges, like in West Yellowstone and other places. One day I decided I needed to build a lodge. I knew it would be at Suttle Lake," Jim says. Suttle Lake would remain a work in progress and require considerable patience in order to wait for a permit approval for building a grand lodge.

Then Jim's old friend Rick Barry called about another piece of land just southwest of Suttle Lake. Located along the McKenzie River in the rolling green hills of the Willamette National Forest was a plot of 46 serene acres that was framed in proud pines and wrapped in fresh air. As business partners, Bruce O'Neil and Wilt Chamberlin decided this location would be an idyllic spot to open the United States Basketball Academy, or USBA.

Bruce O'Neil is a poised and confident man who played college basketball at the University of Hawaii. He graduated in 1969 and then coached there for several years. He lived in Hawaii for 16 years, and started a family before moving to Oregon, his home state. Bruce had wanted to transition into real estate. However, it was around the same time that the real estate market took a dip in the early 1980s. Instead, Bruce defaulted to what he knew best—basketball.

At 7 feet 1 inch tall, Wilt Chamberlain was seven inches taller than Bruce. Bruce and Wilt had been introduced to each other when Bruce was working at a new branch of the NBA focused on video development. This experience had opened Bruce's eyes to the demand for instructional videos for sports coaches when video production technology was still in its infancy. Bruce was the founder of a successful sports video company, Westcom Productions, Inc., based in Eugene, Oregon.

"We had a common theme and script on how to teach kids about sports. We would have celebrated coaches talk on tape and walk through the fundamentals, like John Wooden for basketball, Jerry Kindall for baseball, and Bob Gansler for soccer," Bruce explains. "There was the idea to work with ESPN and develop tapes and programming for the network. It took the video company up a big level."

When Bruce noticed a trend in Asian countries having a high demand for these videos and tapes, he decided to explore this opportunity more. "I realized there must be something going on here, so I took a trip to China and realized there was a lot of potential in that market."

Wilt was a great supporter of the USBA. Considered by some to be one of the greatest professional basketball players ever, Chamberlain began his 15-year career playing professional basketball in 1959 with the San Francisco Warriors. After shattering some scoring and rebounding records, he was inducted into the Naismith Hall of Fame in 1978, and in 1996, he was included on a list of the 50 Greatest Players in NBA History. Unfortunately, his passing in 1999 meant that his time involved with the USBA was short. However, his contribution in terms of developing the vision of the business was long-lasting.

Bruce and Wilt believed that the remote location of the USBA would provide players and coaches with some relief from their normal, everyday distractions, and an opportunity to focus on basketball skills, education, and teamwork. It could be an escape, a camp, a workshop, or school—any forum that coaches and players needed. Bruce also imagined the USBA as a destination for international athletes looking to expand their basketball knowledge.

They planned on building a number of dorms, cabins, a great hall, weight room, and indoor and outdoor basketball courts, and sprinkling them throughout the quiet forest. Bruce and Wilt's vision for building the USBA was supported by a number of different partners, including Rick Barry. However, they were struggling to make it a reality. While the partners knew a lot about basketball, they were less knowledgeable about how to build a destination. They needed someone who was skilled at managing partnerships and knowledgeable about land development. They also needed more financial backing. They needed Jim Schmit.

When Rick Barry remarried in the early 1990s, both Jim and Tom Fields attended the wedding. "I met Jim at Rick's wedding where he was the best man. We were looking for USBA investors, and Jim said it sounded interesting," Bruce says.

Jim and Tom were intrigued about this basketball camp opportunity. Luckily, they were also both living nearby.

"I introduced Bruce to Jim, and Jim salvaged the United States Basketball Academy," says Rick. "Jim is very much responsible for it becoming a viable entity. It's a cool place."

Bruce adds, "Jim stayed behind the USBA every step of the way. Every time we had a shortfall or needed some capital, Jim would help out, writing a check on the spot."

"I mostly did it for Rick." Jim says. "It sounded interesting. I put the deal together, brought in a few more investors, co-signed the loans, and used my construction crews to finish the buildings."

Some of the other investors Jim brought in for the USBA were Tom Fields, Eric Elkaim, plus a fellow named Rex Leatherbury. Rex Leatherbury married Marty, one of Jim's friends from his early Lake Tahoe days. After she lived in Lake Tahoe for about a decade, Marty moved to New Orleans where she met Rex, fell in love, they married, and started a family. When Rex met Jim, and they eased into their friendship effortlessly. In fact, today Jim considers Rex to be one of his closest friends.

Due to his Alabama roots, Rex speaks with a gentlemanly, Southern drawl, saying, "I was conceived under an azalea tree." Rex has a penchant for adventure and business—much like Jim.

Rex recalls, "I guess I've known Jimmy about 20-plus years. I had talked to him on the phone. He had a deal going in Lake Tahoe, an investment in a hotel he planned to turn into a Senior Living Center. I was in San Francisco and I decided to drive up and see him about the project."

At the Market Campus Shopping Center, Jim, Del, and Tom Fields met and decided to lease the big hotel to a firm that did senior assisted living. Each porch had a view of a golf course and there was an off-site recreation center—like a senior center—and casinos nearby. Along with Rex, the partners remodeled the building for this purpose. The new tenant moved in and started running the old hotel as an assisted living facility with approximately 30 rooms for rent. Unfortunately, due to miscommunication and issues related to the California's licensing process for assisted living facilities, the State of California shut down the facility.

"We had only five days to get the people out of our assisted living building. We gave them money to help them afford another place," Tom says. It was a frustrating project, and now that people were being displaced and inconvenienced, it was even more frustrating.

Once the tenants of the assisted living facility had all found new homes, Jim had an idea about how to fill the empty hotel. He had heard that the California Conservation Corps—a division of the U.S. Forest Service that employs young adults ages 18 to 25—was using an old ski lodge as a place to house its workers. They found themselves in a bind when the lodge did not pass its state inspection test. The California Conservation Corps had 30 days to relocate to an amenable accommodation; Jim suggested the Corps move into the hotel temporarily until they were able to build and move into their new facility. The agreement was made and the California Conservation Corps were able to house all of their workers and employees in the old hotel.

"Jim is a problem solver," Tom says.

Chapter 39:

THE FUNDRAISER

Jim and friend Arvydas

Jim's decision to invest in the USBA brought about more interesting opportunities and even more tall friends. Jim met Arvydas Sabonis, the behemoth Lithuanian center for the Portland Trail Blazers who was 7 feet 3 inches tall. "I got to know Arvydas pretty well. I got to meet a lot of ball players because of the USBA," Jim says.

Although Arvydas had been selected by the Portland Trail Blazers in the first round of the 1986 NBA draft, he did not play his first NBA game until nine years later because of a series of injuries, Olympics appearances in 1988 and 1992, and his time spent playing basketball internationally. Eventually, he played his rookie year in the NBA for the Trail Blazers in 1995 and soon thereafter, he met Jim. Even though it was the busiest time of Jim's life, he still managed to make time for basketball. Through Arvydas, Jim also got to know some of the other players for the Trail Blazers.

On August 10, 1996, Jim turned on the television to see a different kind of trailblazer. Smith Rock State Park, located nine miles northeast of Redmond, had caught fire as a result of sparks from a welding project. Nearly 200 acres of the park was wiped out, including a small pedestrian bridge over the Crooked River. The topography of Smith Rock State Park makes it a playground for rock climbers of all abilities and by the 1980s, it had become a premier rock-climbing destination. The bridge was a key access point for visitors to get to trails and routes for rock climbing. Now the park and the bridge were in ashes.

As he watched the news reporter interview the park's supervisor, Jim wondered about how much it would cost to rebuild the bridge. "I called the supervisor I saw on the news and volunteered to have it rebuilt. He estimated it would cost $50,000. I wrote him a personal check for $10,000 and decided to raise the rest of the money."

While Jim could have afforded to write a $50,000 check to cover the entire cost of the bridge, he decided to use this experience to create a unique opportunity for the town of Redmond. He called up a few of his famous Portland Trail Blazer friends and asked if they would help raise the rest of the money. Several players were happy to oblige as long as it didn't interfere with their game schedule.

Jim arranged to have a few of the players come to Redmond for a meet-and-greet at the Redmond High School. Donations for rebuilding the bridge were encouraged for a chance to get pictures and autographs with the players. The planning took several months, but the event was finally scheduled for noon on Monday, November 25, 1996, one day before the Trail Blazers were scheduled to play the Houston Rockets in Texas.

Jim remembers, "The local newspaper sportswriter thought it was a sham. I guess the guy assumed that there was no way several of the Trail Blazers could make it to Redmond, and then get to Houston for their game the next evening. The writer didn't know I had arranged a jet to transport them back and forth. We would have had twice as many people if the newspaper had published the right information."

Between that event and other donations, the money was raised and the structure was rebuilt. Donors who contributed to the project are memorialized on the *Wall of Flame* plaque at the park.

On a whim, Jim decided to hop on the plane he'd arranged for the Trail Blazers and head to Texas to watch their game against the Houston Rockets. On Tuesday, November 26, 1996, Houston squeaked out a one-point victory in overtime to win the game. Following the game, some of the players and Jim headed over to the house of Mildred Barrett—not an unusual after-game routine for a few of the Houston players.

Mildred Barrett was the mother of three; one of her sons was a devoted Houston Rockets fan and also close friends with one of the player's younger brothers. Mildred was a beautiful, strong woman doing her best to raise her three children the way she had been raised. She was also adjusting to her newfound independence and enjoying freedom from her ex-husband, whom she had discovered was unfaithful and unkind.

Mildred was born and raised in a small Mississippi town by kind and loving parents who respected and supported each other. For 35 years, her father made a living as a country lawyer and ran cattle as a hobby. Mildred's brother followed in their father's footsteps, becoming a successful lawyer. In one of his cases, he challenged the tobacco industry and worked on the first case to get a verdict against this powerful industry. Mildred and her siblings grew up in a home where they were undeniably loved and supported.

Mildred was a capable and adventurous young woman. After returning from a trip to Hawaii during her college years, she met her future husband, Don McGill. Mildred's father and brother were representing Don in a lawsuit at that time; Don and his business partners owned car dealerships in Houston. Brimming with Southern charm and intellect, Mildred quickly caught Don's eye, and he offered her a job in Houston.

After completing college, she accepted the job offer and moved to Houston with a few of her friends. It didn't take long before Mildred and Don began dating. At this time, Mildred's father advised that she should not date anybody she worked for and encouraged her to return home. Mildred had a great deal of respect for her father, so she did as she was advised. However, Don continued to court her and eventually won over Mildred's family. They married and had three children.

Unfortunately, after the marriage was consummated, Mildred found herself in the clutches of Don's control. His true essence unfolded bit-by-ugly-bit and the days ticked by. Twenty years later, the marriage would fully unravel and end in divorce. "It was a dysfunctional relationship. I was emotionally and verbally abused. He wasn't around much, so I raised the kids on my own. I was already a single mom in many respects," Mildred reflects.

While they were married, and after the birth of their third child, Mildred had a tubal ligation procedure to prevent future pregnancies. The couple chose to have embryos made and stored, from Mildred's eggs and Don's sperm, in case they ever wanted a fourth child.

At the age of 41, Mildred made a choice based on her personal values and implanted the last embryos. Mildred and Don had shared custody of their first three children, and she felt comfort in knowing she could raise this fourth child without the stress of an unhealthy marriage and an absent father. Plus, Don had informed her that he wanted no relationship with any future child or children from these embryos. Needless to say, the year 1996 had been unusual for Mildred and she found reprieve in hosting a crew of her son's friends, which happened to include a few NBA basketball players and, on one particular night, Jim Schmit.

Mildred had an enormous home fit with an Olympic-sized pool and indoor and outdoor basketball courts. It was a playground for sports enthusiasts of all kinds, even snowmobilers. Jim had never met Mildred when he found himself at her house with some of the basketball players.

"I think I was sitting in the corner of her big house in her big living room when she came up to me and asked me what I did for a living. I told her I raced snowmobiles. She mentioned how she would like to ride a snowmobile. I gave her my phone number and told her to give me a call." Jim adds, "She was very pretty."

"I remember talking about snowmobiles. We had mutual friends. Rick Barry and Clifford Ray both knew him. There was a little spark between us," says Mildred.

Mildred didn't give the spark a whole lot of additional thought. Dating a man who lived in another state did not easily fit into the equation of being a single mom with three children. Plus, Mildred was newly pregnant the night she met Jim.

Chapter 40:

THE GENTLEMAN

"We started talking on the phone," Jim says, describing his long-distance romance with Mildred. The first time she visited Jim, they stayed in Jim's log cabin at Suttle Lake and they went snowmobiling. Their relationship quickly developed and the equation became more complex.

In June 1997, Mildred gave birth to her fourth child, a healthy and happy baby girl. Her daughter was a true blessing. Shortly after having her daughter, Mildred flew out to meet Jim with her newborn and a nurse to help. "Jim and Chips picked us up in the limo and we had a wonderful time. We went to Suttle Lake. I remember getting sick after drinking a strawberry daiquiri—I never drink. They had to rush me to the hospital. Jim took care of me," says Mildred.

Jim remembers, "Suttle Lake was a big part of my life. I remember taking Mildred there when we first met. I had her fly out there to stay. It was an exciting time. I had a lot going on— then I met Mildred. She is a beautiful lady."

Being around Jim reminded Mildred about the importance of living simply, honestly, and with kindness. His presence was peaceful and comforting. His world in Oregon was full of blue sky, clear lakes, cozy cabins, and chirping birds. He was respectful, gentle, and liked taking care of her and her children. "He had a place outside of Redmond in a nice community on a golf course. There was a river running nearby and deer would walk up in the backyard. We would walk out the door and go for hikes. Sometimes it is the simple things that are the most profound," says Mildred.

Undeterred by the untraditional circumstances surrounding the schedule of a newborn baby, Mildred and Jim began dating. Mildred found herself happy with Jim—actually happy! Life was simple and enjoyable. Jim was pleased to have a lady by his side and he had the means and the heart to welcome her and all of her children openly into his life. Their courtship was cut short only by their decision to get married.

"When Jim and I decided to get married, my ex-husband had not seen or met my daughter. He knew about her and everything had been fine. Because Jim is sweet and respectful, he invited Don to lunch to assure him that he knew Don was the biological father," says Mildred.

While Don had not expressed any interest in Mildred's life since their divorce, he now decided he was very interested in the lives of his ex-wife and all four of his children. He also decided he was not happy with Jim's presence whatsoever. Whatever lack of interest Don had shown towards Mildred prior seemed to change immediately after that lunch. Nevertheless, Jim and Mildred loved each other, and they decided to get married. Conveniently, there was a brand new event space nearby at the recently finished USBA campus, called Jim Schmit Great Hall.

The Jim Schmit Great Hall stood at the center of the USBA facility, a 9,000-square-foot barn-style cabin with an immense open room. It had a kitchen facility capable of serving hordes of hungry athletes three times a day or wedding guests once. The largest structure at the USBA site was named after Jim to commemorate his key role in making the USBA possible. The other dozen lodging cabins were named after well-known basketball coaches.

The opening of the USBA was scheduled for Saturday, September 26, 1997, with an itinerary that included a free clinic with two famous coaches: John Wooden and Pete Newell. The opening weekend also included property tours, meals, and a last-minute wedding.

"We had a wedding for Jim and Mildred at the USBA. Mildred and Jim were both friends with a number of athletes that were already planning to be at the USBA opening. They simply invited other guests too," Bruce recalls.

"It made sense. Everyone was going to be together for the USBA opening, so we just decided to get married there, too. My minister came out to perform the ceremony and baptized my daughter at the same time," Mildred explains.

Jim and Mildred said their *I-dos* and started their life together wearing wedding rings made by Bob Lindner, Jr. Rex remembers attending Jim and Mildred's wedding. "They were having some big meeting at the USBA. Only a few of us knew Jim and Mildred were planning to get married that weekend. It was a surprise." He continues, "I remember Jim and Mildred stopped by when they were dating and we met her for the first time. She was really pretty, Southern, and sweet…perfect for Jim. We were all on board for that relationship. It was very encouraging."

Their nuptials marked the beginning of two new adventures for Jim: life with Mildred and her children and traveling for the USBA.

His life with Mildred started in an ideal way. She was smart, pleasant, and a wonderful mother. She was happy, plus, between the two of them, money would never be a concern. "We had cooks for the cooks. It was a bit strange for me not to be the main provider. I believe Mildred had more money than me," Jim says.

Jim and Mildred settled into a house in Eagle Crest located on a golf course in Redmond, Oregon. The boys stayed in Houston because of Mildred and Don's shared custody agreement.

Jim continued his nomadic routine of wandering between the various locations of his businesses: the museum, cattle ranch, his projects in Oregon and Yakima, and USBA, including trips to China with Bruce O'Neil to support the USBA. He also made time to be around his new family and children.

Tom says, "Jim was spending most of his time on the USBA project, while I was working on the Redmond projects."

As usual, Jim was buying, dealing, and preserving interesting things. Jim also managed to find the perfect person to take care of the *Blue Boy* yacht he was neglecting back in Shelter Cove. Mildred's brother was interested in the boat and Jim sold it to him for only $1 on the condition that he had to move it out of Shelter Cover and transport it to Lexington, Mississippi, where Mildred's brother wanted to house it. "I didn't need that boat. And now it's used as a guest house and beautifully displayed near a lake in Mississippi," says Jim.

In between traveling, working, buying, and selling, there was also a home life for Jim. Unfortunately for both Mildred and Jim, their dreamy marriage would morph into somewhat of a nightmare.

"My marriage to Jim triggered Don's sudden interest in my fourth child. He told me if I married Jim, he would sue for custody," Mildred says.

Don's newfound interest in Jim turned into an obsession. At the lunch that Jim had arranged in the hopes of extending an olive branch to Don, Don had threatened to make Jim's life miserable if he married Mildred. The first threats just seemed excessive, fed by jealousy and anger. Mildred and Jim hoped that the outrageous emotions fueling these threats from a man living thousands of miles away would soon subside. Unfortunately, the threats did not diminish and instead increased in intensity. Then they became real. One of Don's threats from the beginning was that he would buy the house next to Mildred and Jim in Redmond, Oregon, in order to keep an eye on them.

He did!

Don had also said on several occasions—including during that fated lunch—that he would never harm the mother of his children. Jim wondered, *If he is saying he wouldn't harm Mildred, is he implying that he would harm me?*

After Don became their dreadful neighbor, Jim and Mildred came home after a trip one evening to find all of the telephone wires cut out of the house and neatly wrapped up and set in the middle of the bed in the master bedroom. "It was certainly intended to scare me. And it absolutely did. I had no idea what I had gotten myself into," Jim remembers.

"This was a very ominous time for Jim. Don had people harassing Jim to buy his businesses," says Mildred.

Jim says, "He would spread rumors about me being a child molester."

While he chose to harass Jim relentlessly with scare tactics and reputation sabotage, he decided to go after Mildred legally. "When I married Jim, Don had married the mistress from the last ten years of our marriage. They sued me for sole custody of my daughter. It was pure sabotage," Mildred says.

The anxiety of the situation was greatly affecting Jim. He was being hunted and haunted because he loved a lovely woman. Mildred reflects, "I couldn't watch Jim be killed by the stress of it all. I knew I was in it, because I shared children with Don, but Jim did not need this. Jim didn't deserve this, he's too nice. There was no future for us, not like this."

Shy of their one-year wedding anniversary, Mildred left Oregon and moved back to Mississippi. Her custody battle with Don continued and became a bitter, expensive feud of *he said* and *she said* legal bickering.

"Jim and I got along great then, and still do. It wasn't anything between us," Mildred says of her and Jim's divorce on April 6, 1999. "I wasn't allowed to have a life then but knew Jim could and should have one.... It has been very friendly between us."

In a snap, Mildred was back to being a single mother, like she felt she was all those years she was married to Don. This era of single motherhood now also included a vicious legal battle. She was a world away from Jim, a world she had hoped to be living in calmly with her daughter. Her life was preoccupied with massive legal bills, verbal abuse, bold-faced lies, stalking detectives, and finally, new eerie Mississippi neighbors, who again turned out to be Don and his mistress wife. The story of Mildred and Don's custody battle was so outrageous it was featured on the television show *48 Hours*.

Chapter 41:

THE HOST

In 1999, the U.S. was all abuzz anticipating the Year 2000 Problem (also called Y2K), or the widespread concern that computer and automatic systems would crash due to the use of two-digit year numbers resetting the year 2000 back to 1900. Bill Clinton was nearing the end of his term as the 42nd President of the United States, and the Los Angeles Lakers won the NBA Championship after beating the Indiana Pacers. Thanks to USBA connections, Jim found himself immersed in a whirlwind of international travel.

When Jim was back in the States, he started taking care of Jade and her daughter. They had reconnected for the third time when Jade's little girl turned five years old. Jade was going through a custody battle with the father and there were geographical boundaries. "I wanted to move as far away as I could in the state. Jim let me stay at a house in Manzanita at the coast. The custody battle was a real mess, but Jim really helped us get through that," says Jade.

"That was a big, huge house…like 10,000 square feet. I guess I was looking at real estate there and bought it," Jim says.

It took time adjusting to the small community of Manzanita. Jade's daughter was enrolled in a small Christian school with 11 other children. Her first day of school started with a special entrance. "I think we rode with Chips to drop Jim off at the airport then we took her to school. She did not want to be dropped off in a limo," Jade says.

They stayed in Manzanita for a short time—just six months—yet Jim made his usual contributions to the community. "Jim would donate basketballs and do a lot for that little school," Jade says.

After Manzanita, Jade and her daughter moved to a remodeled cabin at Suttle Lake. Jim felt that their third time together could be the charm, and he hung a special ornament on the Christmas tree that winter. When Jade opened the special ornament, an engagement ring blinked back at her. She looked at Jim and said YES!

"Bob Lindner helped me find a beautiful white diamond. It was a nice diamond ring," Jim says.

Jade wanted to set a proper example for her young daughter and so she requested they not live together until they were officially married. Jim understood and accommodated her wish. Jim rebuilt the upstairs of a Suttle Lake cabin, added a bathroom, and Jade remodeled the kitchen. He also put a bar up in a doorway for Jade's daughter to practice gymnastics. "She practiced nonstop. Jim encouraged gymnastics and she eventually went to level 10 [the highest level]," Jade says.

When she wasn't driving her daughter to school in Sisters or gymnastics in Bend, Jade and her daughter enjoyed the seasons at Suttle Lake. They experienced a cozy, snowy Christmas, lots of snowmobiling, and an Easter egg hunt in the snow. In the warmer months, they loved sailing and boating in the lake and hiking or bicycling around it. It was a genuine experience for all ages. They would also occasionally accompany Jim to the USBA campus nearby and watch tryouts.

"I loved it when people came to visit. Jim would cater to our every need and bring us cocktails and food," says Jade. Even though Jade loved the natural beauty of Suttle Lake and the visitors they would host, the days could get long and a bit lonely. Jim was still on the road a lot for business and now found himself adding some international travel to his schedule as well.

Meanwhile, Bruce developed strong relationships with some business partners in China through the USBA. They began gravitating towards developing online training courses for Chinese coaches, a market that was showing lots of potential. For Bruce, travel to China became more common. Given his connections to the USBA, Jim began traveling to China on a regular basis as well.

Rick recalls, "We took trips to China with the USBA. Bruce is well connected there and was a second father to the son of a powerful man in China."

Bruce enjoyed having Jim along. "We've traveled all over and have gone to China on numerous occasions. He thrives to accommodate people on tours," Bruce says.

When Jim traveled to China, he either accompanied Bruce on business, or served as the host for a team or group of players. He would also bring along friends to enjoy the experience. Tom Fields says, "I went with Jim to China with a team from the USBA. Rick Barry was coaching. The American team played several games against the Chinese team and their star player Yao Ming." Every seat in the house was full. The purpose of the trip was two-fold: basketball and business.

"About 25 businessmen went on a trip to meet Chinese officials in Beijing. It was an opportunity for these American businessmen to get a foot into China, which was hard to do back then. These meetings opened a lot of doors. Jim and I went and bought suits in China, and we sat in on the meetings and tours because there was extra space. We went to the embassies, met interesting people, and then came home with a few gifts too—a big deal in China," Tom says.

As had been the case in the past, Jim's travels presented challenges in his relationship with Jade. "We were about to go to China and then I broke up with him. I felt so isolated. Jim is so comfortable moving and I need to be grounded," Jade says.

Jim understood that Jade was getting cabin fever at Suttle Lake and offered to move her and her daughter down to Newport Beach. "It was his last-ditch effort to keep us together," she says.

Jim and Jade decided to split up for the third and final time. In addition to letting Jade and her daughter go, Jim also had to face the possibility of letting his dog Buddy go. While they were still a family, Jim had bought a little Yorkshire Terrier dog and named him Buddy. Jade's daughter loved Buddy. Jim decided he wanted to keep Buddy after the breakup. To make up for it, he took Jade's daughter to buy a new dog. She picked out her new Yorkshire Terrier from the breeder and named it Buddy too. Now there was Buddy One and Buddy Two.

Following their final breakup, Jim decided to keep his home base a lovely house near the McKenzie River, where Buddy One went missing on day. "I remember that well; I was supposed to fly out to Florida for a huge real estate transaction—it was really important that I be in Miami. I called them and said I can't come because my little dog is missing," Jim says.

He posted flyers and ran a newspaper ad promising a $1,000 reward. The search for his Buddy was in full swing. After the third day of Buddy's absence, Jim raised the reward to $5,000 and updated his advertisements. Another few days passed. Jim went to the Register Guard newspaper offices in Eugene, Oregon, where he made arrangements for a full-page advertisement announcing a $10,000 reward for the return of Buddy One.

Jim recalls, "That ad was going to cost a lot. As I was in there and they were writing up the ad my cell phone rings. A guy said he thought he might have my dog. He described it and it was Buddy."

The fellow who had found Buddy One worked on a Christmas tree farm about three miles away from Jim's McKenzie River house. Jim drove out there and was reunited with Buddy amongst the Christmas trees as if he were a little gift. The man claimed to have found Buddy on the tree farm shivering and cold. It's possible Buddy ran away, though Jim had his doubts. A little piece of him believes Buddy was taken. Regardless, Jim says, "I gave him $5,000 and got Buddy back. I was so happy I didn't even question him."

As for Jade, a Southern gentleman courted her successfully into marriage when her daughter was seven. "I thought he was my white picket fence guy. The guy that was going to be around. After we married, I found out he lied about owning a house. He lied about so many things. I was shocked," says Jade.

Jim would check in on Jade and her daughter regularly. He kept them on his mind and dropped by to see them after returning from a trip to China. "Jim came over to bring us gifts from China and I literally started bawling my eyes out," says Jade.

Jade's marriage was falling apart, and money was challenging. Jade was preparing to live on a tight budget because her new husband had lied about finances. This meant there would be no gymnastics classes for her daughter. It broke her heart. She told Jim the whole story, and without even blinking or hesitating, Jim offered to help.

Jim and Del bought an old indoor tennis complex in Eugene, Oregon, and remodeled it. They put in basketball and indoor soccer courts, exercise equipment, a gymnastics center, and a food court. "It was first class. Del and I put in $12 million to make it a state-of-the-art sports complex. One of the reasons I built the gymnastics center was for Jade's daughter. I paid for her to have the best coach," Jim reflects.

Jade and Jordan ended up relocating from Bend to Eugene and starting a new life away from her ex-husband and his lies. Her daughter continued gymnastics and they settled into a more stable routine.

"Jim was always there for me. And he still is. I can tell him anything. I love Jim's positive attitude about everything. He's always been there as a good friend," Jade says.

Chapter 42:

THE TRAVELER

Fortunately for Jim, he was not traveling on September 11, 2001. "I remember exactly where I was. I was at Suttle Lake in the little cabin watching the news and saw it happen. There were a few girls camping at the resort, so I walked out and told them. I asked if they wanted to come see it on my T.V. and they said, no, it's okay. I was so surprised; they didn't even react," Jim explains.

On any given normal day, when planes were in the air, Jim was known to invite friends to travel to China with him. He liked hosting them and showing them around. Among these friends was his new love interest, Margaret, whom he met in late 2001. She had a worldly upbringing; she was raised by a German mother and Hungarian father, had lived in Brazil, and had lots of international neighbors and friends. She was a petite woman with a head full of brunette waves that framed her dark, curious eyes. While Margaret has always been more of a listener than a talker, she can speak German, Portuguese, and Spanish, in addition to English.

Jim met Margaret through her daughter Gina and Gina's husband Angelo. Jim had previously met Gina and Angelo through a mutual friend. Angelo recalls, "My friend Joe and I were going to invest in a restaurant in Huntington Beach, and Joe invited me up to Lake Tahoe to meet his buddy. We flew up there and met Jim at his house. He talked us out of going into the restaurant business."

"All I remember was him pulling up in a limo with his dog at our first beauty supply store location in Huntington Beach. Chips was driving, and we ended up in the limo. I probably knew Jim about a year before introducing him to my mother," Gina says.

Jim and Margaret first met near Christmastime at a house party. Margaret remembers, "We hit it off. He asked if I wanted to have dinner the next weekend. We did."

Jim went back and forth to Oregon for business and so their initial dating started slowly. Meanwhile, Margaret was working for the J.C. Penny executive offices. She was a dedicated employee and had never taken a day off in 12 years. "I never got sick. That is the German side of me," Margaret says.

Margaret lived in Huntington Beach near her daughter's family, when she met Jim. As their interest for each other grew, Jim's traveling started to make it difficult for them to be together. "I quit work because Jim asked me too," says Margaret. "It was too hard to go back and forth from California to Oregon." Margaret started traveling with Jim.

In 2006, for Margaret's 55th birthday, Jim took her on a long road trip to Idaho. They headed out in Jim's black 2002 Ford Thunderbird, or T-Bird; this new model was a far cry, and many years removed, from the red, 1955 T-Bird Jim traded in for the pink and white Jeep when he headed to Hawaii in his youth. "Those T-Birds were hard to get when they first came back out. I called around and found one. I had to have one of those," Jim remembers. He had enjoyed his T-Bird plenty.

Unbeknownst to Margaret, they were headed to a car dealership in Idaho. "We drove up to the dealership and walked over to the Corvettes. Jim looked at me and said, pick one. I had always wanted a Corvette...I picked the black one," says Margaret. They traded in the T-Bird and drove home in Margaret's brand-new black Corvette.

Jim loves to give gifts and surprises. Margaret had always struggled with her vision. "Jim treated me to eye implants. He gave me my eyesight," says Margaret as she blinks with extra clear vision.

When they were not road-tripping, they were flying to China. Angelo, Margaret's son-in-law, recalls a time when he took a trip to China with Jim and an American team scheduled to play the Chinese National Team. The most famous player on the Chinese National Team was Yao Ming, a player Jim had met at the USBA and knew quite well.

"He's a very warm and friendly guy. He's easy to be around, very accommodating, and appreciative. He was also pretty private," Jim says.

Yao Ming started playing basketball at the age of nine, deciding to follow in the footsteps of his parents who were both former professional basketball players—who were over 6 feet tall. Yao was offered a position playing for the Shanghai Sharks junior basketball team. After four years, he began playing for the senior team. By his third season with the Shanghai Sharks senior team, Yao averaged nearly 40 points and 20 rebounds a game. With his help, the Sharks won the Chinese Basketball Association championship.

While the 2002 season was Jim's good friend Arvydas Sabonis' last season in the NBA, it was Yao Ming's first. Yao was the first overall pick of the draft by the Houston Rockets, though he played in the 2002 China FIBA World Championships instead of participating in the Rockets' preseason training, which led to lingering questions about how he would compete in the NBA. However, by the end of his rookie year, he was unanimously selected for the NBA All-Rookie First Team. That year began his decade-long career of playing in the NBA.

Whenever Yao and Jim found themselves under the same roof, whether in the United States or China, they always spoke and checked in with each other.

Jim with Yao Ming and friends

On another trip, when Jim took Angelo to China with a U.S. team in a traveling tournament, they found themselves under the same roof as Yao for each game. Throughout the tournament, Jim and Angelo wore suits and sat on the bench with the American team. The games were televised nationwide in China, and the tour traveled through several cities.

Angelo remembers, "We get to the first game and Jim and I are on the court shucking balls at the players. Then Jim invited me to come out and stand with the team during the national anthem. By the third game we were playing bigger venues. When we pulled up in the bus, there was a sea of people as far as you could see. They were moving like a wave and the police had to escort the team by making an arm-in-arm human shield. You feel like a real celebrity."

Angelo also had the chance to meet and briefly chat with Yao. "I asked Yao for an autograph and photo. He had been hit in the head and had a bandage. He was nice and people were taking pictures of us. I remember thinking, there's 1.3 billion people in China and I'm sitting by their number one athlete. His fan base is something you can't even fathom."

In China, anyone associated with Yao Ming became intriguing to his fans. This ended up being the case for Angelo, too. Following one of the games in the tournament, Jim and Angelo were sitting courtside by the players and fans came up to ask for their autographs. Although they had no idea who Jim and Angelo were, they were part of the U.S. team and looked important in their suits. Jim had gotten used to this mild form of celebrity by association, so he signed a few autographs. Angelo was surprised and confused.

Jim remembers, "Angelo was there with me and people started asking him for his autograph. He had never autographed anything and said—Jim, I can't sign autographs. I told him; they want your autograph. Angelo started signing his autograph on whatever the fans brought up."

As a guy that owned a few beauty supply stores in southern California with his wife Gina, he never suspected he would be signing autographs in China one day. Life is certainly full of surprises, but especially in the company of Jim.

"What are the odds of an average person getting a chance to feel like a celebrity?" Jim says. Jim accepted this elevation in his status after a number of trips to China. "I used to guest- speak on some of the trips. I was a real good motivational and business speaker. People thought I was something in China."

Del remembers a trip to China when a business meeting was running late. "We were presenting, and I was looking at my watch because we had to be on a plane in 45 minutes. There was no way we would make our plane; the airport was too far away. Someone in China closed some roads for us and our driver drove 100 mph to get to the airport on time." They made their flight.

For Jim, it was fun to be treated as if he were a celebrity for a moment, before returning home to a quiet, comfortable life outside the limelight. He enjoyed the perks of temporary celebrity without any of the hassle of being a true public figure. It was a role he had become quite adept at playing, especially as Rick Barry's close friend.

Jim's friends enjoyed his company as much as the celebrity treatment they sometimes received in his presence. Marty says, "Rex loves traveling with Jim. They made a few trips to China together."

"One thing about Jimmy," Rex says, "he just loves to get out and see and experience everything. Every morning we would get up and go walk for an hour or more so we could see the city. I love street food…Schmit was appalled at that."

These initial trips to China ended up turning into something unexpected for Marty and Rex Leatherbury. "Marty would come back to the States and people would buy the jewelry off her neck. After the third time this happened, she figured she was on to something with her jewelry, and she turned it into a business." Rex adds, "We liked it over there so much that my wife and I moved there, and we ran the USBA office in Beijing."

They moved to Beijing in 2003 to live there full-time for three years and off and on two years after that. At first, they were surrounded by tight alleys, crowded with bicycles leaning against tiny structures and *hutongs* that housed generations of families. While they spoke and understood little of the Mandarin language and met only Chinese locals on their daily adventures, it was an extraordinarily exciting and fulfilling time for them both. They spent their leisure time perusing the jewelry markets and discovering and purchasing Chinese antiques. This interest came naturally for Marty, an interior designer by then. Their regular trips to the Pearl Market turned into a new hobby—and then a business—as Marty began designing and making jewelry.

Rex recalls, "When we first moved to Beijing, we did a two-week tour with the U.S. women's team. We traveled around China watching them play the Chinese National Team. Jimmy was with us. He loved watching basketball."

Jim vividly recounts one memory of watching the American women's team of 10 players practice, including athletes from both the Women's NBA and college teams. They were participating in a tournament of about six games across China. Jim enjoyed a fun challenge, so he offered to pay $100 to any player who could make a half-court shot in one try. All 10 girls, ranging from tall and lanky to tiny and strong, lined up for a try. Jim is not one to make a bet that he will not win, and he felt confident that he was safe on this bet. In the end, three out of the ten girls successfully made the half-court shot. Jim pulled out three $100 bills and paid the girls on the court. The women on the team didn't get paid that much to play and in China you could buy a lot of stuff for $100. The winners were pretty happy about their extra spending money.

The next morning the women asked Jim if he would make the same deal again. Jim remembers telling them, "No way! That cost me $300." Upon further consideration, he told the women that if they all made it from half-court, he would give each of them $100. The deal was that they *all* had to make it in one try each. Jim believed this was impossible; there was no way they could do that.

The first girl tossed up her shot and *swoosh*. The girls all laughed. The second and third girls made the shot. Four balls went in, then five for five, and then six for six. Jim was still very confident that his $1,000 was safe. There was no way they could all make it. He wasn't concerned about the bet. The seventh shot went in for seven, and the eighth ball for eight. The tension began to build. The girls were hoping to get spending money, and Jim was hoping to keep his money. Then, unbelievably, the ninth shot fell in the hoop: nine half-court baskets in a row from nine different players. The team was one shot away from the goal.

Jim says, "The last girl to shoot was a tiny point guard. She truly didn't have the strength to make the shot, so they tried to substitute for her. I told them not a chance. She had to make the shot—that was the deal. She backed up from the half-court line, ran up, and lugged the ball over her shoulder just to get enough power to make it to the goal. We all watched the ball arc and then swish right through the hoop."

They all felt like they were in the twilight zone. The girls were laughing and celebrating while Jim was scratching his head. He checked his wallet; he didn't even have $1,000 to make good on his word at that moment.

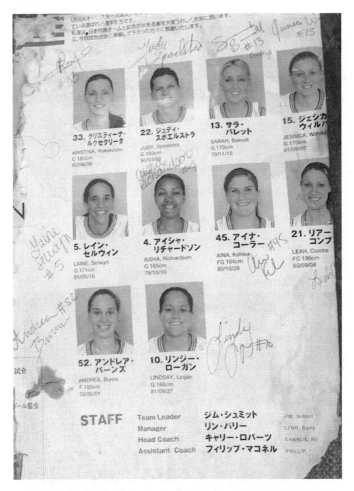

The half court wonders—this roster survived a fire

"It's a fact," Jim says. "They all made it! The odds are so slim. You couldn't get 10 professional NBA players to do that. The girls went 10-for-10 from half court. I wouldn't believe it if I hadn't seen it with my own eyes. I had to make arrangements that night to get the money because my word is my bond. They each got $100. I'll never forget that. It was incredible!"

Tom Fields recalls a less pleasant memory: a time when Jim was pick-pocketed at a food market. "Jim had a gold-banded watch that was inlaid with diamonds taken right off his wrist and his wallet taken out of his back pocket. Later on, when thinking back, we remembered there was a large group of kids in their 20s following us around. My wife and I got a lot better at spotting pickpockets in our later travels, thanks to that experience."

Jim says, "When I first started going to China, I was told you didn't have to worry about anyone touching you. And it was true. I would wear my nice jewelry and I never had a problem. Ten years later...things had changed, I guess. And one day, they made a haul off of me."

Rex and Marty saw changes too. They learned more Mandarin, made more friends, bought more antiques, and returning to the U.S., they opened their Asian import shop in Fairhope, Alabama. They also watched the city of shanty structures transform into a city of shiny, new apartments surrounded by cars in preparation for the 2008 Olympics. Rex describes this transforma-tion as "the destruction of a living museum." Nevertheless, Beijing became and still is Rex and Marty's second home.

Jim also made trips to China with people that he hadn't thought about in years. The U.S. basketball teams always traveled with a doctor, and on one occasion, Bruce had asked an orthopedic surgeon based out of Lake Tahoe, Dr. Watson, to accompany them on a trip. Dr. Watson was a bit hesitant to accept the invitation. He mentioned to Bruce that maybe he shouldn't go to China because Jim might be mad at him.

Nearly 20 years prior to this conversation, Jim had been dating a woman named Sherri, and they were living together. Jim and Sherri had started a casual relationship. "She had a great smile and a great figure," Jim says. At some point, Sherri needed to attend to a medical ailment and she went to see Dr. Watson who ended up falling for her. Sherri moved out of Jim's house and into Dr. Watson's house. She got a ring from the doctor, and eventually, a marriage certificate, too.

Years later, when Dr. Watson found himself in China with Jim—the man whose girlfriend he stole and married—he observed that Jim didn't seem to harbor any animosity towards him. Dr. Watson finally asked Jim, "You mean you're not mad at me about Sherri?"

Jim had replied, "No. Not at all. If a woman doesn't want to be with me, then I don't want to be with her. It's that simple."

A grin came over Dr. Watson's face. He looked at Jim and said, "You know Jim…you cost me a million dollars." It turns out that Sherri and Dr. Watson had divorced, and Sherri had made out with a nice lump of money.

Jim then realized that Dr. Watson had been concerned about this for many years. Yet, it never had made Jim mad. Jim hadn't spent any time being concerned about Sherri leaving him for Dr. Watson. Meanwhile, Dr. Watson seemed to have felt some guilt over the circumstance. Jim's capacity to accept, let go, and move forward without a grudge or any feelings of angst are often surreal to those he meets.

Traveling with Eric Elkaim

Jim's experiences traveling internationally with good friends and new friends had become a highlight of the first part of his 21st century, yet China wasn't the only place Jim traveled.

"I took a trip to Venezuela with this tall basketball player. I can't remember his name. He was a tall, black guy that stood out in Venezuela. There was concern he would be kidnapped for ransom. When we went out to dinner or a club, we had guards with big guns escort us around. That was a new experience," says Jim.

He enjoyed the new adventures, the unusual stories, and the foreign cultures and people he met along the way. When he returned back to the U.S., it was business as usual. Jim was enjoying his relationship with Margaret, juggling a lot of projects, and had never been more successful. At 65 years old, Jim had amassed a $50-million empire and it was all achieved in kindness and generosity. He had never once cheated or manipulated his way to a profit. Jim always stayed busy, dreaming up the next ideas and following through on the old ones, too.

Chapter 43:

THE MOGUL

Clifford admiring the hand carved doors at the Suttle Lake Lodge

"It took me over a decade, maybe longer, to get the permits to build on Forest Service land, but I did it. I built the lodge at Suttle Lake," says Jim. He was very pleased with the finished product and the opportunity to see his vision come to life. Since 2005, guests have enjoyed Suttle Lake resort and its cozy, yet grand, lodge for communing and lounging.

Guests enter the 10,000-square-foot Suttle Lake Lodge through hand-carved wooden doors with designs that depict the lore of the American West. Whether it's skirted in snow in the winter or surrounded by green grass in the summer, the rustic lodge is warm and welcoming. There are many fireplaces, carved railings, wooden plank floors, and large windows with a scenic view of the forest.

The lodge has a great room, a conference room, and 11 bedrooms. The design of the lodge was intended to complement its surroundings; the wood exterior, simple rooflines, and asymmetrical floor plan replicate the traditional Craftsmen-style of national park lodges. The Suttle Lake Lodge serves as the relaxing hub for a tranquil resort: a place where kids can play lawn games in the summer and build snowmen in the winter, and adults can take in some placid moments and peaceful breezes off of the glassy lake.

"The logs...those massive logs and the carvings are my favorite part of that lodge," Jim says.

While Jim was working on making his vision a reality in Suttle Lake, he continued balancing various real estate projects with Del Mathews and Tom Fields. At this point, Jim had also invested in nearly half of the real estate investments that Del owned in Yakima, Washington, including a massive 230,000-square-foot building that held the antiques mall, a train mall, and a casino. In addition to these Yakima properties, Jim was the largest investor in the USBA and a primary investor in a sports complex in Eugene, Oregon. He also owned a smattering of homes on the West Coast, including the custom log home he was building outside of Lake Tahoe, in Genoa, Nevada.

Inspired by Suttle Lake Lodge, Jim began building a grand log home for himself outside of Lake Tahoe. This private log home would be the culmination of all his design dreams contained in one immaculate structure. Like Suttle Lake Lodge, Jim's log home would eventually become one of his most beloved projects.

Present-day Genoa, Nevada, is a charming town. Located a half-hour's drive east of Lake Tahoe, it was originally founded as a trading post during the pioneer and gold rush days in the mid-1800s. In 1855, the settlement was named after Genoa, Italy, the birthplace of Christopher Columbus. "It's very historical. I bought land here because of the history and it's an easy drop over the hill from Lake Tahoe. It has ties to Snowshoe Thompson," Jim says.

Genoa is home to the grave of Jon Torsteinson-Rue, better known as Snowshoe Thompson. Snowshoe was born in Norway in 1827 and died in the U.S. in 1876 after becoming a local legend. He would brave every kind of weather to carry and deliver mail, medicines, newspapers, and other items between Genoa, Nevada, and Placerville, California. He would make the approximately 80-mile trip crossing the Sierra Nevada Mountains in three days, even during the winter. He would trudge along on long homemade wooden skis with little rest and simple provisions. His physical stamina and aptitude for surviving in the harsh conditions of the mountains are legendary in Nevada.

Finally, Jim explains why he began his masterpiece log cabin in Genoa. "I was building it for myself. It was a huge house for one person. I knew I wasn't going to have kids, so it had one very grand bedroom and another little bedroom. The size of the house was 1,500 square feet. The front doors were carved and there was a separate three-car log garage. I had old cars; I wanted a big garage. The logs came out of a 100-year-old fir forest in Oregon. Fir logs will last forever; they're heavier and bigger. Once the logs were all selected, they were sent to my place in Lakeview, Oregon, where the house was actually built. It sat there for a year to let the logs settle, then it was disassembled and relocated to Genoa. The logs were numbered and put back together like a Lego project. It was very expensive and first class.... Some of those logs were 48 inches in diameter."

When the costly project came near completion, Jim realized he could use a little extra cash to help finish the log home. He wanted to include beautiful carvings, complementary rustic furniture, western collectibles, and have proper landscaping in the yard.

Jim was aware of a fellow, or Mr. C, who had been doing well in the Lake Tahoe area. He had just sold the Lake Tahoe Marina, so Jim figured he was sitting on a lot of money. While they were not strangers, they had never been in a business partnership before. Nevertheless, Jim decided to approach Mr. C to ask for a $100,000 loan to finish up the Genoa log home. Jim offered to guarantee the loan with his personal furniture and pieces of his antiques collection selected for the house. Mr. C agreed to the loan—the beginning of their first partnership. Jim was able to complete the deluxe log cabin, and he scattered a number of old wagons on the property to fit with the luxurious pioneer theme he had designed for himself.

Jim had never been so pleased. His log cabin was a far cry from the log cabin where he was born and raised for the first few years of his life. It was exactly what Jim had imagined, and he was proud to welcome friends and guests to see it.

Jim was also an investor in a handful of other properties in and around South Lake Tahoe, including the old Tahoe College. Jim and Tom Fields had bought the College as a redevelopment project in the 1990s, years after teaching there when it originally opened. Decades before, Jim had also purchased the quaint Carson River Resort with a few partners.

Carson River Resort is a rustic campground near Markleeville, California, the county seat of Alpine County. The Resort has tent sites and recreation vehicle camper sites. For those who prefer a proper roof overhead, there's also the choice of a half dozen aging, but quaint, wooden cabins and one special riverfront cabin. Jim fortuitously discovered this property as he was out driving, looking for a ranch to buy at a lower elevation than Lake Tahoe.

"There was a lot of snow this particular winter…it must have been around 1970 or so. I drove south on Highway 89 and down through Markleeville and came across this little resort out in the middle of nowhere along the Carson River. There was a little gas station and a store."

Jim stopped and inquired about any nearby ranches for sale with the elderly, crumpled man sitting at the front of the wood-sided store. The local fellow was unaware of any ranch land for sale. He informed Jim that his wife was ill, and he was considering selling his little resort. Jim dismissed the idea until he started looking around. Once he learned that the resort had about a mile of riverfront property on each side and he spied a streamside wooden cabin, he started giving the idea a little consideration. He looked around at the massive pine trees dotting the quiet valley, the meandering river hibernating under the snow and ice, and the picturesque cabin tucked in a small crevice of the Sierra Nevada mountain range.

This riverfront cabin appeared as if dated back to the silver mining days of the 1860s that had originally put Markleeville and nearby Silver Mountain on the map. The homesteaders that had moved to the region to find silver soon scurried away when the endeavor proved unprofitable, in part because of the demonetization of silver in 1874. Nevertheless, a few hardy stragglers remained behind in Markleeville. They subsisted by making a living in the ranching and lumber industries that supplied the more successful operation, the Comstock Lode mines, located northeast of Carson City, Utah. The Comstock Lode mines produced more than $500 million in silver and gold in a few decades and are said to have effectively ended the California Gold Rush.

The population that stayed behind in Alpine County grew from about 200 souls in the early 1900s until it stabilized at a population size of about 1,200 people countywide. Under 5 percent of the land in Alpine County is available for private ownership, meaning there are few opportunities to purchase land in this pristine section of the mountains.

Jim says, "I saw that old, dilapidated cabin and it probably had bats in the belfry. It had the most beautiful setting. The wood was all chewed up. I loved the cabin and knew I could fix it up and make it a neat place."

The cabin was a simple structure; it only had three rooms and a small front porch facing the river. While it was large enough that it could hold a family, it was just cozy enough to encourage occupants to spend much of their time outdoors when the season allowed. Jim's visionary mind was kick-started by that cabin, and his idea rapidly grew into a new, unforeseen plan.

"I came back to the man and asked if that cabin was part of the resort," says Jim.

The fellow responded that it was. Jim had promptly asked the man, "How much for the resort?"

Confused, the man had replied, "I thought you didn't want a resort."

"I don't, but I want that old cabin."

Jim was serious and he had the means to get it. Jim struck a deal with the owner, put a few partners together to make the purchase, and they became members of a rather exclusive club—landowners in Alpine County, California.

"I had Bob Lindner Sr. and Bob Jr. help me fix up that cabin with knotty pine interior. We called in the East Fork Hilton as a joke. There are six Sears & Roebuck log-sided cabins on the resort too," Jim says.

The Carson River Resort became a small attraction for visitors and travelers who were looking to escape from civilization. They came to enjoy the quiet and solace of the river, the setting, the therapeutic mountain air, and the other like-minded folks seeking the same environment. Alpine County is a destination sought for outdoor recreation and thrives on tourism. With no traffic light, bank, or even a supermarket in the whole county, those visiting get a true taste of a relaxed rural lifestyle.

After any length of history, the folklore and myths that inevitably arise are fun to pass around and contemplate. "I was told that Patty Hearst stayed there when she was on the run. I can't verify it…there's no way to prove it," says Jim, laughing. "Who knows, maybe D.B. Cooper stayed there too. Some say Bigfoot is walking around Carson River."

Patty Hearst was the granddaughter and heiress of publishing tycoon William Randolph Hearst. She was kidnapped in February 1974 from her Berkley, California, apartment. Her abductors were members of the Symbionese Liberation Army, a group of Berkley radicals that was founded in 1971. This group demanded a number of ransoms from the Hearst Corporation in exchange for Patty's release. However, after about $15 million had been paid to the agitators, Patty refused to leave the group. She preferred instead to join their crusade and requested her ransom amount be donated to charities. Approximately 19 months after her kidnapping, Hearst was arrested by the FBI in San Francisco. She testified that she was a victim—brainwashed by the group. She was sentenced to 35 years in prison and released only 22 months later.

Even more outrageous is an event that took place several years prior to the Patty Hearst kidnapping saga. On November 24, 1971, a businessman named Dan Cooper, dressed smart, boarded Northwest Orient Flight 305 from Portland, Oregon, to Seattle, Washington. He walked down the aisle of the plane while clutching a briefcase and took his seat in the last row. After take-off, Mr. Cooper explained to the flight attendant that he had a bomb when he proceeded to open the briefcase and show her the bomb. Then he started making his demands.

Mr. Cooper's demands were arranged—land in Seattle and board another plane with an assigned flight crew. The new plane was to have a briefcase with $200,000 and four parachutes and the pilot was instructed to fly towards Mexico City at an altitude not higher than 10,000 feet with the cabin depressurized. Around 8 p.m., Dan Cooper stepped out of the airplane with a parachute strapped to his back and a case full of cash. The plane was somewhere between Seattle, Washington, and Reno, Nevada.

Despite extensive searching, neither Dan Cooper (more commonly referred to as D.B. Cooper in media reporting of the story) nor his money was ever found.

The remote and secluded location of the Carson River Resort made it attractive to all kinds of people that wanted to establish a secluded place of acceptance and comfort. "One gay group offered to buy the resort from me so they could make it their own special community. Another group made an offer and thought the deal had been made, but it hadn't, and they put a swastika flag on the flagpole. It seems they were a Nazi group," says Jim.

The number of visitors to Carson River Resort ebbs and flows. In the spring and summer, it's busy with fly fishermen and campers. During winter it is mostly vacant; the cold air and snow fill the spaces between the handful of hearty recreational vehicles and cabin campers. The Carson River Resort opportunity fell into Jim's lap because he stopped to talk to an old man sitting on an old porch, down a faraway two-lane road.

In addition to all the properties that Jim owned was his massive, ever-growing collection. "I had a lot of collectables. I figured I could sell an item a month and live comfortably for two hundred years," says Jim. There was both buying and selling. Jim was always doing both and coming out ahead. His collectibles were now doubling as his personal insurance plan.

Jim's instincts were sharp, and his decisions were sound. However, in 1979, Jim chased after an opportunity that left him short of breath and money and it all started with the U.S. being short of gas.

Chapter 44:

THE LUCKY

In 1979, the United States was facing an energy crisis as a result of a shortage in the global oil supply that was directly related to a decrease in Iranian oil production. The following year, the oil crisis was exacerbated by the war between Iran and Iraq. The war brought oil production to a near halt, and Americans found themselves waiting in long lines again for gas, similar to what had happened during the 1973 oil crisis.

"There was a big gas shortage. Huge! The whole country was running out of gas," Jim says.

As a result of the shortage of oil coming from Iran, oil production in the U.S. and other countries began to increase. Big American oil companies, including Texas Gulf, Chevron, and Shell, were busy problem-solving and searching for hidden caches of energy within American borders. Extraction in some locations required innovative methods that compressed and removed the oil from the rock or shale buried under the surface. These oil companies found plenty of sources of fuel in Alaska and in the small town of Rock Springs, Wyoming, among other locations.

In 1980, while people were waiting in long lines to fill up their gas tanks, Rock Springs was a town just shy of 20,000 residents. The rumor was that Rock Springs was about to get a whole lot bigger after oil companies came in to gather up the energy resting dormant near and under the town.

"I was told the oil companies would buy every house I could build," says Jim. He jumped on this project, knowing it would result in a grand payoff. He gathered five partners and went to work. As an experienced land developer, Jim knew he was up for the job. "I put everything on the line in fine print, all my houses, cars, real estate…everything. My guesstimate was that we all would get a 10 percent return on the investment, but we had a lot of work to do and fast."

Jim rallied investment monies from his partners, bought a few hundred acres of land off of Interstate 80, and budgeted money to build an off-ramp for the development and a school—virtually an entire town. He was working over-time, excited to see his plan turn into reality. It was the biggest development project he had ever worked on, and he was capable and confident that he had a thoughtful plan in place. Jim was on the verge of building the first of hundreds of structures when things went bad.

"Within two months of starting on the project, there were no gas lines. Those oil companies picked up their equipment and were gone. There I was sitting on all this real estate… I was going to lose everything," Jim says.

His six-month project fell flat. He hadn't seen it coming, of course. He promptly switched into recovery mode. As good fortune would have it, a builder named Pulte Homes caught wind of Jim's debacle and expressed interest in purchasing the land from him.

"Out of the clear blue, I got a call and an offer to buy the land. I have no idea why they wanted to buy it, but I was ready to sell. I flew to Denver, Colorado, in my jet. After meeting with Pulte Homes, I made the deal. I remember it cost $2,500 to refuel the jet and I put it on my charge card." It was the best high-priced gas money Jim ever spent.

Jim adds, "When I was recruiting investors, I had verbally explained they would likely make 10 percent on this investment. Of course, that's before everything happened. I was so thankful I was able to provide money back to all the investors; I didn't care that I lost my investment. Everyone was so thrilled to get their original investments back, and not lose on the deal. Well, everyone but one guy."

Instead of being thankful about getting his money back, this one guy kept whining and moaning that Jim had promised a 10 percent profit. While Jim tried to explain a number of times that they were all lucky that they got out of that mess and got their money back, this guy simply would not go away.

"I was so happy I wasn't taken under that I just paid him off. I never forgot it and a few years later when he wanted to partner with me again, I declined. This was one of the scariest investments of my life."

Although different properties came in and out of Jim's life, there were a couple properties that were particularly special to him, including the Lake Tahoe House in Tahoe Keys. It was his home base in Lake Tahoe for several decades before he decided to sell it. Fortunately, he was able to sell it to his good friend, Bob Lindner, who grew up remembering it being the cool house down the street. Bob and his wife completely rebuilt the house. The redesigned house has large windows for soaking up the Lake Tahoe view, a classic 1927 Hacker triple cockpit ski boat that doubles as a bar inside the living room, and memorabilia from their friends and the bygone Jewelry Factory days. The Lindners maintain an open-door policy for Jim, who will never be considered a stranger on that property as long as they live there.

Tom Fields maintained his conservative approach to investments over the years. He participated in some of the deals Jim made with Del, opted out of others, and made some separate investments. Tom recognized that Jim and Del were the big idea guys; his role was best served in watching the numbers and attending to the details. Tom says, "It went pretty good through most of the 1990s. All of a sudden, I didn't have the checkbook anymore, and I wasn't sure what was going on. It made me uncomfortable." However, Tom started feeling Del was more cavalier in his investments, which didn't match up with Tom's personal, more cautious investing style.

Jim, on the other hand, trusted people with investments and money based on a mere handshake. Del says, "He had about $8.5 million in the banks. If I would have been a crook, I could have stolen him blind."

Unfortunately, Jim was not immune to being taken advantage of. In his early Tahoe days, there was the bartender Dick who absconded with a lump of money from Yank's Station when Marty was bartending there. She says, "He is not a great judge of people because he doesn't judge people. Sometimes he gets taken for a ride. He always wants to see the good, and he thinks he can find the good other people can't see. He likes to open doors for people."

A handful of summers after the bartender took off with the money, Jim was driving along I-80 and stopped off in one of the ski resorts nearby. Jim and his travel companion were out looking around at some shops and came across a jewelry shop. In the shop sat the bartending thief. Jim and the thief made eye contact. Jim remembers, "He turned 40 shades of red. I just looked at him and said 'How ya doing?' a bit sarcastically, then walked away. Whoever I was traveling with asked what that was all about, and I told them the story."

There was another fellow in Lake Tahoe swindled Jim out of $10,000. After Jim bought the Tahoe College building, he remodeled the Student Union building, turning it into a bar and restaurant. Jim was traveling frequently to Hawaii, so he found a partner to help him manage the project.

"I didn't know him very well, but he was a Mormon Bishop. It wasn't even a question...I trusted him. I can't remember his name—he owned a dry cleaning business. We had a shared account so he could manage the project while I was traveling," Jim says.

Jim opened up a checking account with his partner's name on it and deposited $10,000 into the account to start the remodel. A week after opening the checking account, Jim returned to Lake Tahoe and found that the remodeling project had been halted and he could not find his partner.

"I checked the account and the money was all gone. I went to the police and asked for help finding him and they laughed at me. They said, well, the guy's name was on the account so he didn't necessarily steal the money," says Jim. Jim never saw that guy again.

Del recalls a different instance, "When we had the museum in Central Oregon, there was a guy there we called Jon the Barber. I can't recall the specifics, but Jon the Barber ended up finagling $120,000 through a real estate transaction with me. I had one bad business deal with him and never trusted him again. Jon the Barber later came to Jim and asked to borrow money to get out of some trouble. I warned Jim about him, but Jim didn't see the harm in helping out. Jon the Barber gave Jim some deeds of trust in exchange for cash."

As Del anticipated, the deeds were phony, and Jon the Barber got away with another scam. Jim lost a nice sum of cash because he was kindhearted and trying to help a fellow in need. Del felt strongly about going after Jon the Barber and approached Jim to see if he wanted to be involved. Del says, "I suggested Jim give me his paperwork to be part of my case, though he told me, I don't want you to get stressed out about it. Go on home and I will deal with it."

"Yeah, Jon the Barber probably screwed me a few times. I think he ended up going to jail," Jim says. "I'm sure there were a few more people that took advantage of me, I don't let it bother me. I just thought it was their problem, not mine."

There are always scammers looking to take advantage of generous people: the cold and calculated individuals, the brazen and unapologetic types, and the basic petty thieves. Despite the bad apples out in the world who took advantage of Jim's kindness and generosity, he continued to give.

Money to Jim was just money. He had lived without it before, and while he enjoyed the ability to take care of people and be a provider, it was not the root of his contentment. When people take advantage of Jim, he does not hold onto regret, he simply lets it go. Jim explains, "I never beat myself up, because I know I'm doing the best I can. I don't dwell on the past. I don't avoid things either. If something bothers me, I go on the offensive and do something about it. If you're a good honest person, you can be happy. It's a choice. People can be rewired—I had a lousy childhood and I turned my life completely around when I went out on my own. I rewired myself after childhood. I get through all the tough times, even when I have been taken advantage of, by thinking positive."

Chapter 45:

THE MENTOR

In 2002, Brad Kanis graduated from a Southern California high school while in the midst of some emotional times. His sister had passed away his senior year of high school, and his parents were in the throes of a divorce. He was an exceptionally tall, all-American kid. Although he may have been confused about his future, he was cognizant that his height—7 feet 1 inches —and his basketball skills were means to an end. Perhaps these attributes could help him get into college and earn a degree.

A young prospect, Brad Kanis

Brad started his freshman year at Irvine Valley College living with his mother. He squeezed college basketball practices and games in between classes and work. By his sophomore year, he was unable to balance all the demands.

"Basketball was a hobby and it started getting in the way of my work," Brad says. That was also about the time that "my brother gave me a business card with a picture of Yao Ming and Jim." Of course, he had no idea who the fair, middle-aged man standing next to Yao Ming, only a little over half his height. However, like most of America, he knew who Yao Ming was.

Jim met Brad's brother, Chris, when he dropped in to get his laptop fixed at a computer store in Huntington Beach. When Jim saw this tall kid, working on computers, who he guessed was around 6 feet 8 inches tall, he asked Chris if he played basketball. Chris said that he was a soccer player, but suggested that Jim should see his brother, Brad, who was taller and a basketball player. Jim then handed over his business card to Chris and asked Chris to have his brother contact him.

Brad got the card from his brother. "I took it to my coach. He thought it was for the military and threw it away. I believed my coach and kept on living my life."

It wasn't long after that when Brad's coach told him to choose work or basketball. Brad made what he thought was the most responsible decision and chose work and was then booted from the team.

As good luck would have it, Jim ended up back in the computer store in need of some additional computer technical help. He asked Chris why his brother never called. Chris dialed Brad on the spot and they made an appointment for Brad and Jim to meet. Brad recollects, "The first time I met Jim was in a McDonald's parking lot. He explained that he was very serious about basketball and likes to help people. I liked Jim the first time I met him."

The second time Brad met Jim was at a Wahoo's Fish Taco restaurant, not far from his mother's house. Angelo was with Jim and they set up a few exercises to measure Brad's athleticism. "They were measuring my vertical jump in a parking lot," Brad laughs.

Brad was halfway through his sophomore year when he heard Jim's sales pitch and took the sparkling bait. Jim explained that Brad could come up and help at the United States Basketball Academy during the busy summer months and continue his own basketball training. Jim volunteered to help Brad if he wanted to pursue basketball.

"Brad was helping his mother who had gone through some tough times financially. I thought I could help him out and get him into basketball," says Jim.

"I was kind of lost when I met Jim. I didn't even think basketball was an option. He told me I could be a pro and make a lot of money doing this. He seemed so sure; it gave me confidence," says Brad.

With so little to lose, Brad felt this was an opportunity he should take advantage of. He was appreciative of the chance to give basketball another attempt, and he was certainly willing to do the work.

"I lived in Eugene at an inexpensive house owned by one of the assistant coaches at the Academy. Jim paid my rent, my food, and my school. I would work out with Charlie Roberts every morning and then practice with my team after."

Jim remembers, "I brought Brad up and took care of him. He turned out to be really good. I thought he might possibly make the NBA. Kareem Abdul-Jabbar taught him how to do a sky hook."

Though, not everything was about basketball. "He was always inviting me over to his house on the Blue River. It was a beautiful house. I remember there was a nice Chris Craft boat out in the river. It was funny…here was this boat and there was hardly any room to drive it on that river," Brad recalls.

"The McKenzie River runs into a hydroelectric dam, and right in front of my house, there was a small pool of a lake," where Jim kept his boat at the dock.

Brad remembers catching trout from the river, and then cooking and eating them right on the back patio. He remembers Jim's little dog Buddy, and how he would carry that little dog around with him everywhere in a little bag, on planes, and in the gym. Brad also recalls the stories Jim told him about making his start in real estate, his story about Elvis cooking him eggs for breakfast, and how Jim often carried around pictures of his friends in a briefcase and on his RV.

"There were hundreds of pictures plastered all over Jim's RV. And I got a pair of Clifford Rays shoes that were left at his house. Jim gave them to me." Brad also remembers a good life lesson that Jim taught him which he still practices, "He taught me to plan my day. You've got to make your list every day. I plan my days better because of him."

Maybe most important, Brad learned from Jim that being a businessman didn't have to be a suit-and-tie affair. One could be successful in sneakers and shorts working in a job they actually enjoy. This lesson on top of his positive experience at the USBA stuck with Brad the most.

All of Brad's time spent practicing at the USBA and studying to finish school proved worth the effort. After buckling down to finish a college degree in business, he returned to the USBA to train with a Chinese pro team and attend a pro exposure camp. "All the agents tried to sign me. I signed on with the Houston Rockets for a summer league and then I went to Uruguay."

"I took him under my wing and got him through college. I thought he might make it in the NBA and arranged a tryout for him in Houston," Jim pauses. "Although that didn't work, he played in Europe for a while."

Basketball led Brad on a world tour playing for teams in Uruguay, Qatar, Syria, Taiwan, Japan, Kosovo, Morocco, and Spain. "To be completely honest, Jim Schmit is the reason for that. Jim put that idea of basketball in my head. He's made such an impact on my life," Brad says.

Three years after discovering Brad Kanis, Jim headed to the USBA with Eric Elkaim to check in and watch the players attending a recruiting camp. There was a tryout camp with about 100 of the best players available from college and guys cut from the NBA. Agents were on hand selecting players for teams in China. The typical big centers caught the eyes of the agents, yet there was one kid that caught Jim's eye.

Another kid, referred to as Jay, had a stack of honors and recognitions from Mount Vernon High School in Mount Vernon, Washington. He would help lead the Bulldogs through an undefeated season all the way to the 2001 High School State 3A basketball championship his senior year, averaging 15 points per game and four assists as a guard. He was not an imposing figure on the court at a lean 6 feet 1 inch tall, but his game intellect, court awareness, leadership, and tremendous athleticism, including a vertical jump of over 40 inches, was hard for any spectator to miss. He also took scholastics as seriously as athletics and graduated from high school as an Honor Roll student. By his senior year, colleges near and far had a keen eye on Jay and were hoping to recruit him to their respective universities.

Jay chose to stay on the West Coast beginning his college career at the basketball powerhouse of Gonzaga University as a freshman *red shirt* in Spokane, Washington. He played on the court for Gonzaga the following season as part of the team that advanced to the second round of the NCAA tournament before being knocked out of the bracket by Arizona. He then played on and off for a few different mascots from San Jose City College in San Jose, California, to Brigham Young University, and Azusa Pacific University in Southern California. He experienced a lot of court time and refined his game when not recovering from pesky injuries sidelining him here and there. Jay wrapped up his college game days in 2006, but he hoped to keep playing ball as long as he could.

His tenacity to play and attend college is impressive given he made opportunities for himself on his own merit and motivation with a few good guides along the way. He had an atypical childhood, originally born in Tijuana, Mexico, growing into a model mix of his black father and white mother. His nomadic childhood kept him meandering from school to school to school amongst the western states through his formative elementary and early teen years. Fortunately, he identified a talent for basketball and settled in to play under a good coach at Mount Vernon through high school and then on to college.

Post-college days found Jay at the USBA scrimmaging to fulfill his hope to stay in the game. Standing out in these USBA tryouts would allow him to continue to play in China. Standing out, however, would prove challenging given his height disadvantage.

By the time Jim arrived, Jay had made it through the first week of camp and ranked as a top pick. The second week would end in a pick or no pick determined through games and drills and practices. Between court time, Jay would continue to dine in Schmit Hall with his friendly competitors.

Jim pulled into the USBA in his monstrous Prevost motorhome he called his bus, and parked it near Schmit Hall. Hardly a bus, the Prevost was a luxury motorhome nicer than most brick and mortar houses. It was outfitted with all the latest technology and features one wouldn't dream to find in anything on wheels. Jay remembers Jim's bus and thinking, "Wow, someone important is here."

As usual, Jim stopped in to spectate. "They had two games going for a few days. I was up on who was good and who was better. Jay was one of the best players there."

Jay proved sharp and decisive on the court playing a tight point guard position. His sinewy, athletic frame kept him a step ahead of the other players although he was a runt compared to the big fellows. His game wit and intuition clearly stood out and he was hopeful he would be selected to play in China.

Jay recalls being in the midst of a game when an agent requested to meet him. Jim watched this clean-cut kid with a sunny smile intelligently chat up the agent; Jim took a liking to Jay immediately. He also knew something Jay did not; the agent would not pick him.

"They were only looking for seven-foot tall guys for China and he played the point guard position. He was probably the best player in the camp, but they were looking for *bigs*," Jim says.

Jay remembers meeting Jim, "There was this guy waiting behind me, pacing a little back and forth. And when I was done talking to the agent, Jim said, 'Excuse me, young man, my name is Jim and I enjoyed watching you play. If you don't get drafted to play in China, don't be discouraged because it's a big man's market. They want the giant guys. So don't be offended. I just wanted to tell you that because you are a phenomenal player and deserve to go, but I just know how these things work.'"

Here was this stranger volunteering up this valuable and rather disheartening information. It was a bit odd and also much appreciated. Jay, in turn, asked politely for an introduction. Jim introduced himself and invited him over to the bus. They shook hands and parted ways.

Jim was right; Jay was not selected for a team. After receiving this news, Jay stopped by Jim's bus to say hello and Jim invited him in. Jay entered a strange, lavish world, "There were televisions coming out of the ceiling and marble floors. I immediately realized he was really wealthy. And I remember he told me, 'One day you will be on to the next chapter of your life. If you decide to go into real estate give me a call.' He handed me his business card with a picture of him and Yao Ming on the front. It was folded because Yao Ming was twice as tall as Jim."

Jim says, "I remember he was disappointed about not being picked. He said he was broke. He had already envisioned playing in China and now his next step was uncertain."

Jim felt for the kid and mentioned the discussion to Eric Elkaim. Before Jay left the USBA, Eric Elkaim found him, Jay says, "and pulls out $1,000 in cash and hands it to me. I asked him what it was for and Eric told me, Jim is a good friend of mine. He made me into a millionaire and he asked me to look out for you. If you ever need anything, a car, a job…let me know. Here's my phone number."

Jay tucked these two valuable business cards away in a safe place and continued on for the next few years to play basketball overseas, including in Israel and Mexico. The man that handed Jay a pile of money as a kindhearted

255

gesture was privileged with having Jim as a mentor as well and was doing his part to pay it forward.

"When you have a friend that makes you a millionaire, then you like to help them," Eric says.

Jim admits, "I'm not sure I really mentored Eric. I guess he did spend a lot of time with me and see my success. He would ask me why I did the things I did and made the choices I made. I guess I taught him a lot that way. He was always picking my brain."

Another young man who enjoyed observing and picking Jim's brain was Hayden Watson, the son of one of Jim's own mentors, Bob Watson, from Jim's early salesman days. The Watson family relocated to central Oregon largely because of Jim informing Bob and others of the opportunities near Redmond in the early 1990s. Hayden credits Jim's influence as being a big factor on why he and his successful company have been based in central Oregon the last 30 years.

"I remember Jim driving up to our house in Santa Cruz in the late '60s. He was driving this crazy Excalibur-looking car—it was impressive. He wore this amazing gold watch and had a little dog with him," says Hayden of his first memory of Jim.

After first meeting Jim, Hayden remembers him being around a lot more, so much so he started to feel like an uncle. Hayden would observe Jim's enthusiasm and never-give-up attitude, his ability to bring people together, and his general excitement for life each day. Jim also taught Hayden the importance of first impressions and looking sharp. Following college, Hayden moved into the family business and adult life realizing, "My dad had a lot of interesting friends and thought a lot of Jim. I was getting my real estate license and knew my dad was a great salesman, but he told me Jim was the best salesman he ever met, that I could learn a lot from him. That was saying a *lot*—my dad knew thousands of people in real estate sales."

During Hayden's impressionable early career days, he recalls that unusual era in central Oregon as a comedic wild west when his father and unique friends were making things happen. "They were remodeling gas stations. Trading watches, cars, deeds, motorcycles, guns, silver. Jim had this crazy museum and Olaf in this cowtown nowheresville. They were the rainmakers. They faced all the naysayers. It was an interesting time for sure."

This made Hayden realize you could do anything and he continued to soak up the habits and methods of both Jim and his own father. "I remember one morning Jim was over early and I had been in the shower. Jim said something about how he could get ready with a three-minute cold shower in the mornings; in part because he had to growing up and also because he didn't want to waste time. I was super impressionable and those little things were motivating to me." When asked if Hayden thinks of Jim as a mentor, he replies, "He absolutely is one of my mentors. He is such a unique individual—he's been inherently present his whole life, very engaged and not distracted. He's so thankful and good about telling people he loves them."

If one considers a mentor as an experienced and trusted advisor, Jim has mentored countless friends, acquaintances, business partners, and even strangers through the years. Jim always appreciated the individuals he considers his mentors, like Jim Wilson, Bob Watson, and Loren Bamert and the others that greatly influenced him, such as his grandfather, Henry J. Kaiser, and the mystery man with the gold nugget watch. He was happy to motivate and encourage others by guiding them with lessons he had learned and sharing his experience and knowledge. He never tired of it. Mentoring, motivating, and providing opportunities was and still is one of Jim's favorite ways to give to others.

Bruce O'Neil sums it up, "If he believes in somebody or something he's always stepped up and helped in whatever way he could. He's really a selfless guy. He loves adventures, people, and causes. He's always going to give to people."

Chapter 46:

THE GIVER

The one thing that makes Jim the happiest is giving. On top of guiding good friends into profitable partnerships, he did much to help both friends and strangers in times of need. He also enjoyed giving to a good cause, like rebuilding the bridge at Smith Rock State Park or donating $10,000 to help preserve the historic Thunderbird yacht, a famous floating Lake Tahoe landmark.

The Thunderbird was commissioned by the reclusive George Whittell specifically for cruising to and from his estate on Lake Tahoe. In 1940, Whittell received the 55-foot wooden speedboat with mahogany hull and stainless-steel crown—stylized after the fuselage of a DC-2 airplane. He enjoyed it liberally for a year until he tucked it away, out of sight when World War II erupted because he was concerned the boat would be used or cannibalized for military purposes. To keep it safe he hid it in the boathouse.

It was rare to see the Thunderbird out on the lake after World War II. Whittell's increasingly reclusive nature and health issues left the Thunderbird collecting dust in his boathouse. In 1962, Bill Harrah purchased the iconic boat and refurbished it back to its glistening reputation. He used it to host celebrities like Sammy Davis, Jr. and Liza Minnelli, among others. Each winter Harrah saw to it that the Thunderbird underwent extensive maintenance. The yacht eventually fell into the ownership of the Thunderbird Lodge Preservation Society after a number of owners following Harrah. The society raises much needed money through donations and hosting events aboard the elegant 16-passenger boat.

"We had the honor to go out for a cruise on the Thunderbird in Lake Tahoe," Jim remembers. "I called up a bunch of friends and they stayed at my big house and we had a great time. It was a big deal."

Jim and Margaret treating a crew of friends to a cruise on the
Thunderbird Yacht in Lake Tahoe

Sometimes giving meant a lot more work than simply donating money. Tom Fields says, "Jim and I hosted a golf tournament to benefit the American Cancer Society. We sponsored it with our own money and unfortunately spent too much money on prizes and didn't charge enough for participation the first year."

As usual, Rick brought the star power for the tournament and encouraged friends and celebrities to attend. That first year Jim and Tom simply donated money to the foundation. They learned their lesson and the next year they minimized the cost of the prizes and charged more for the attendees, which resulted in them happily writing a large check to support the American Cancer Society the subsequent years the tournament was held.

To help maximize the donation to the American Cancer Society, Jim did some recycling. "I had all of these snowmobiling trophies from years of racing. We decided to reuse them. We took the snowmobile toppers off and screwed on golf toppers and then replaced the little plaques with funny awards like best dressed, or hole in one, or best golf cart driving, and so on." The participants liked the random awards and they all knew that the money was going to a good cause, which was the ultimate purpose of the tournament.

Tom remembers, "Even in the beginning, when we didn't have much, Jim was always doing something generous for people. I would find donations for charities in his checkbook regularly." Later, and as the money piled in, Tom notes, "Jim had probably 50 different accounts for charities."

One day a woman and her wheelchair-bound son came into the real estate office. Jim spoke with the mother and found out her son suffered with cerebral palsy affecting his coordination and mobility. The guy really wanted a three-wheeled bicycle to travel on instead of a wheelchair. "That same day, Jim drove to Reno to buy this guy a three-wheeled bicycle and delivered it to his house," Tom says.

Glenn Lucky found such empowerment in his new three wheels that in 1988 he cycled across 12 states in three months to raise over $10,000. He rode 3,648 miles from the Nevada State capitol to Washington, D.C. to raise awareness for cerebral palsy research. "I remember seeing him on the news riding his three-wheel bicycle across the country. It was amazing!" Jim smiles.

"I once got a letter from a mother telling me her very athletic son had diabetes and he needed a pump. She was asking for my help to get her son a diabetes pump. I bought one for her son. Those pumps were expensive, about $5,000 each, I think," Jim says.

Jim knew of and connected with a Portland Trailblazer professional player that had diabetes. Together they started a program to buy diabetes pumps, or insulin pumps, for kids in need. "I bought pumps for years, probably about one a month," Jim estimates.

Jim had a soft spot for people with disabilities or health issues. He had experienced his own scary health issue and was empathetic to people in need of moral and oftentimes financial support.

Jim's little neighbor from the early days in the Tahoe Keys, Laura Larson, had a grand crush on Jim. She says, "He was my dream man when I was a little girl. I remember my friend and I dressed up for Halloween and we walked over and knocked on his door. I was dressed as a Genie and he told me I looked beautiful and gave me a kiss on the cheek. And…he gave us the BIG candy bars, not the little ones."

A few years later, Laura was sick with a ruptured appendix at the age of nine. Two surgeries were required at the local hospital in Tahoe, yet neither fully worked due to infections. Laura's parents sought out a surgeon in San Francisco Children's Hospital yet needed quick and safe transportation to get her there. She was suffering greatly.

"All I remember was waking up in an ambulance with tubes in me. Then I saw Jim, he squatted down next to me and asked, 'How are you doing?' I looked at him and looked away. I didn't know what to say because I was so sick."

Unbeknownst to Laura, Jim had offered to fly her to San Francisco in his plane with his pilot. Once there she underwent the third surgery and recovered months later.

"I never knew until many, many years later that it was Jim that flew me to San Francisco. I finally put the pieces together."

It was a life-saving flight. Laura's recovery was slow but progressing. Her mother stayed on a cot near her hospital bed to tend to her, while her father visited as much as physically possible between maintaining a job and household in Lake Tahoe. Laura's recovery involved a lot of tubes and monitoring, and her father would call and ask her how she was doing, checking in all the time. One day, she finally had the tubes removed and was able to walk and move. Her father called to ask about her progress and she changed the subject because she wanted to surprise him when he came to visit.

"The next time he came to the hospital I saw him, I stood up and we walked towards each other. He knelt down and embraced me. That is my favorite memory of my father. My favorite memory of my father is in a way, due to Jim," Laura appreciates.

Years later, Laura had the chance to reconnect with Jim in 2012 when she was in Lake Tahoe for a class reunion and Jim was visiting friends. They talked for a while and Laura mentioned her father. Jim made it a point to call Laura's father and say hello and reconnect. The two men had a great deal of respect for each other.

"Jim once warned my father to avoid doing business with a certain guy on the North Shore, but he did it anyway and he lost a lot on that deal. Jim was a very savvy businessman," Laura says.

Laura had discovered another depth to Jim as she grew into an adult and filled in the blanks through conversations with her parents. When she reconnected with Jim, she asked him directly about the flight to San Francisco. According to Laura, Jim replied that he had flown so many people to so many places for so many reasons…he didn't remember that flight in particular.

In 2014, Laura's father passed away the day before her birthday. He was cremated and his ashes were up in Lake Tahoe, though Laura was living in Southern California. She did not want to have his ashes mailed. She had called Jim to give him the news about her father passing and after providing details, including the logistical issues in retrieving his ashes. Without hesitation, Jim volunteered to go pick him up.

"He drove 800 miles to Tahoe to get my dad's ashes and then brought them to me. He is very generous—totally non-judgmental. He would help anybody that needed it, no matter what. He's an incredibly compassionate, giving individual. Jim has a special place in my heart."

Jim never had a close bond with his own father yet truly respected the men that were loving fathers to their children. One of the closest father figures Jim had was Bob Lindner, Sr.

Bob Jr. recollects the time his father had a heart attack. "He was only 51. In fact, he had the first signs of the heart attack when Liberace did the show at the opening of the Liberace Room in The Jewelry Factory—The first Liberace Museum."

Jim immediately called Doctor Albo to treat him. Doc made the house call and helped Bob Sr. recover from the ordeal. Bob Sr. kept selling jewelry until his massive stroke 18 years later.

"We tried everything to help him get better," Bob Jr. says, touched by the memory. The Lindners tried medication, diet, acupuncture, and other treatments. The Houston Rockets used this magnetic machine to help the athletes recover from injuries, so Jim bought it and flew it to Lake Tahoe for Bob Sr. to try. He used it a few times, but it was hard to tell if it helped or not. The expense of the treatments, the machine, the medical bills, and so forth added up quickly. It was an inelastic expense as the Lindners planned to take every measure they could to help Bob, Sr.

"Jim gave us all the money to help my dad. He cared about him like a father. He's done that for other people too," Bob says.

"It makes me happy to see other people happy. To see them succeed or get better. I've never been good at receiving. It makes me uncomfortable because I want to be the giver," Jim explains.

Of course, where there are givers, there are always takers.

PART III – RAGS

A truly happy person is one who can enjoy the scenery while on a detour. – Unknown

Chapter 47:

THE SILENT PARTNER

In the heart of Washington state, about 60 miles southeast of Mt. Rainier, lies the city of Yakima. Yakima sits in a valley that's wrapped in 300 days of sunshine and a pleasant, mild climate. When Yakima was first incorporated in 1883, it was called Yakima City. There were homes, stores, churches, hotels, a bank, and a basic town infrastructure that supported around 500 inhabitants. The Northern Pacific Railway Company came roaring through just as the city was being established. However, the railroad opted to build its train station four miles north of the city because land was cheaper and more plentiful. Proximity to the railroad encouraged some Yakima City residents to move to the new town of North Yakima.

Teams of horses relocated more than 100 buildings by pulling them over rolling logs for four miles. Some companies were even rumored to have continued carrying on their business activities as usual while their buildings were being moved to the new location.

In the beginning, there was some animosity between Yakima City residents and the residents of the new North Yakima town. However, the fertile valley was ripe for farming, and within a few decades, the two towns grew into one thriving in agriculture.

The presence of a railroad and an irrigation network attracted farmers to the area. They found success growing a cornucopia of grains, vegetables, fruits, and apples. In the early 1900s, there were numerous refrigerated warehouses located near the railroad depot; this area was called Yakima's *Produce Row*. These large buildings held the local crops from surrounding farms, and workers packaged the produce to prepare for shipment. After that, they transferred the produce into railcars for nationwide distribution. The railroad depot also had passenger service and was considered the city of Yakima's front door. It bustled with life and energy and welcomed short visits from Presidents Teddy Roosevelt and William Howard Taft.

Fast-forward 100 years from the opening of the Yakima Depot: the year is 1986, and Jim's friend Del Mathews had become one of Yakima's kaleidoscope of characters after purchasing a large warehouse in the city. This massive building—four stories, a block wide, and two blocks long—was located adjacent to the railroad depot, and it sat on some property leased from the Burlington Northern Santa Fe Railroad. The faded words *Blue Ribbon Yakima County Horticulture Union* were stamped at the top of the red brick warehouse, marking a bygone era. Instead of produce, the building now held countless antiques, the new sign on the building read, *Yesterday's Village*.

"I originally bought Yesterday's Village about 10 years before I met Jim. Then he gave me some of his property, so we swapped. I gave him part-ownership in some of my property in Yakima. We comingled assets, but it was in my name," Del remembers.

Jim could visualize the potential in the space and location, and he happily joined in on the project. He provided finances and collateral for Del's real estate holdings in Yakima.

Jim says, "The antiques mall must have had hundreds of vendors. It was in this historic, old warehouse where all the apples had been brought in, stored, and packaged for shipment on the railroad in the past. It was huge. It had three-foot-thick insulated walls and thick floors for cold storage."

In addition to the antiques mall, Jim and Del rented office space to bring in steady revenue. Plus, the building was so colossal that there was room in the basement to store both Jim and Del's extensive collections. They walled off some of the basement to store their collectibles, locked up some of the collectables, and installed an alarm system.

Del says, "We had pallet racking, and we put all of our stuff in there… kind of on display. It took hours to walk through it. Friends would want to come see it, and I would give private tours. It included all of my antique toys."

"I put all the items from the old Fantastic Museums in there. It moved around, but it ended up in the Yakima building for storage." Jim estimates his portion of the collection exceeded over $2,000,000 in worth.

Together, Jim and Del continued to acquire more buildings and parking lots in downtown Yakima. They leased railroad property and managed a few adjacent railroad land parcels. For years, Del would inquire about purchasing the land that Yesterday's Village sat on from Burlington Northern Santa Fe Railroad, although the railroad never expressed interest in selling.

One railroad lease was a piece of property that had out-of-service train tracks with a couple dozen old trains parked in line. It was called the Track 29 Train Mall. Track 29 first opened in the fall of 1987, under the vision of John Edwards. Mr. Edwards collected different railcars from all over the nation and relocated them to Yakima. His eclectic mix of vintage passenger cars, freight boxcars, World War II-era Army hospital cars, and a bright red caboose housed various businesses, including little shops, restaurants, and a daycare. There were nearly 50 employees who worked at the Track 29 Train Mall. They pleasantly hosted customers as they ducked in and out of the railroad cars from a level wooden board walk. People enjoyed strolling amongst the timeworn, immobilized trains and searching for treasures, food, or the children they had dropped off at the daycare established in a few repurposed vehicles.

"One of the best Mexican restaurants in town was at Track 29," Jim says.

On the next block, there was another out-of-service track. It had several staged, silver parlor railroad cars that sat behind a hulking train engine. The engine looked like a smirking cyclops, bemused and satisfied with its retired life. The train set was entirely painted with matching blue-and-green striping, and it housed Del's personal office space. Jim says of Del's unique office, "It was plush. Del used one parlor car as his office with fine antiques and the nicest things from our collection. He had a beautiful Tiffany Lamp on his desk, along with the Hindenburg gauge I found years before. The other car had a conference table and a desk for a secretary and Mr. Peepers—well, that's what I called him. Mr. Peepers was Del's bookkeeper, and he wore big, thick glasses."

Doug Nelson was Mr. Peeper's real name. Doug says, "Working on those railcars was kind of like being on a ship. Space was premium; we had stuff stored in cubby holes all over the place. You'd be surprised where we'd make cubby holes. One time, a guy came inquiring to buy those train cars for his rail museum. He told us there were worth about $200,000 each."

Doug started working for Del in 2000. He was the property manager, accountant, and Del's all-around go-to man. Doug collected the rent from all the tenants and ensured the facilities were clean and functioning. From the day he started, he kept a close eye on the books and understood the inner workings of all of Yesterday's Village's finances.

As time passed, Del and Doug discovered that office tenants were more lucrative than the antiques mall. As they found more office tenants, including government tenants, the footprint they dedicated to antiques shrank. They completed renovations to provide more office space, and an increase in tenants finally led Del to purchase more property for parking spaces.

For over a decade, the management of the Yesterday's Village building and its adjacent properties ran smoothly; tenants made payments and business carried on as usual. Investments and business in Yakima were going well, and Jim kept in touch with Del from afar. Jim visited Yakima on occasion to say hello, but the Yakima properties were managed and run by Del.

Chapter 48:

THE PREY

As the 1990s came to an end, the nation entered a new century after success-fully avoiding The Year 2000 Problem, or Y2K. However, the nation would face many other misfortunes in the first decade of the new century. There were huge economic costs that resulted from the technology bubble that burst in 2000, then the country was unhinged by the September 11, 2001, terrorist attacks. Incidents of scandalous accounting fraud were uncovered at multiple top American corporations at the same time the U.S. was waging war on Iraq. Mother Nature ushered in Hurricane Katrina in August 2005, which drowned entire swaths of America's Gulf States and its residents; the loss of life and property damage was devastating.

Up in the Northwest, Jim remained focused on his real estate endeavors: swapping, trading, and selling properties as usual. In 2005, when the Great Lodge at Suttle Lake first opened, Jim had made a deal to sell the resort to a woman who had been involved with the property and was as emotionally invested in the resort as Jim had been. A key part of the deal was an agreement that would allow Jim access to his lake-view cabin forever.

"It was a very successful and popular resort. I sold it to a gal that ran it into the ground. She never paid me, and she filed for bankruptcy. I never got my money," Jim says. What could have been a profitable and advantageous sale turned into a big loss for Jim. While it was frustrating, Jim shook it off and moved forward.

Meanwhile, Jim decided to sell his McKenzie River house in Oregon for no particular reason other than that he had enjoyed the place enough and was ready to let it go. The buyers, a coupled referred to as Mr. and Mrs. D, had a reputation as being real estate-savvy. Mr. D markets himself as a successful real estate salesman, hosting motivational seminars on sales strategies and guidance in initiating and elevating one's career. His website boasts a phenomenal real estate career and says that he logs approximately 200 sales a year.

Jim was pleased that Mr. and Mrs. D were going purchase his house saying, "He was an upstanding person, and he traveled around the world teaching people how to be successful in real estate. I thought he was as good as gold. I was wrong."

To make the deal, Jim called and informed the bank up-front that he was making a contract to sell the property to Mr. and Mrs. D. The couple agreed that they would go to the bank and take over the note and property payments. It is unclear what Mr. and Mrs. D did or did not do to keep their end of the deal.

Jim presumes, "Well, I guess maybe they went into the bank and didn't qualify to take over the note, or maybe he didn't even go. So the property was left in my name. They moved in and they were supposed to make mortgage payments to the bank each month, but didn't. They ruined my credit. Period. It was a mistake on my part to trust them."

Not long after Mr. and Mrs. D effectively killed Jim's credit, a cost previously unknown to Jim emerged related to the Sportsplex in Eugene, Oregon. Jim and Del had put a lot of work and money into fully remodeling the indoor tennis complex into a multi-sport facility, including basket-ball courts, indoor soccer, exercise equipment, a food court, and a state-of-the-art gymnastics center. They had made it into a first-class complex after investing $12 million into the facility over a number of years. As the Sportsplex was being finished, the City of Eugene informed Jim about some required landscaping.

Jim remembers, "The landscaping cost another $500,000, which we didn't have at that moment. Eric Elkaim sponsored that part; he wrote a $500,000 check. Looking back, it feels like that was when things started to change for me."

In the late 2000s, a great opportunity had appeared at Jim's doorstep in the form of Jay, the talented basketball player Jim had met years before at the USBA. After several years of playing basketball and a knee surgery, Jay decided to retire his sneakers. He was looking forward to a business career and took the initiative to write a business plan for a technology concept. In contemplating how to get started, Jay recalled the conversations he had had with Jim and Eric years before.

Jay was living in Southern California at the time. He recollects, "I went looking for Jim's business card and I wasn't sure where it was. I looked in one possible place. When I opened up the cabinet, it fell out in front of me. It was meant to be." Jay called Jim, who was staying in Malibu, and Jay soon found himself presenting his business plan to Jim.

"I got to his condo and there was a thick book on the table. He saw me looking at it and said it was his taxes. It was thicker than a silver dollar and bound like a bible and when I opened it his net worth was shown as $50,000,000. I'll never forget what he told me next… 'When you make a lot of money, your tax book will be this thick,'" says Jay.

Jay presented his business plan, a plan half as thick as Jim's taxes. Jim asked what Jay needed. Jay explained it would take $82,000 to get started.

Jay remembers, "Jim took the plan, opened it, and flipped through it in seconds, as if it were a magazine. It was the hardest thing I'd ever done, and he barely looked at it."

Jim wasn't interested in the business plan; he was interested in the success Jay projected for the business. He wanted to know how much money this business would make. Jim wanted to know if Jay could turn his domestic business plan into an international business plan that would work in China and other countries.

Jim directed Jay to, "Take that million-dollar business plan and incorporate China and make it a billion-dollar business plan. Then we're in business."

Jay went home, beefed up his business plan, and got Jim's initial investment of $25,000 to start developing and creating the business. Jim was happy to be the investor and leave the execution to Jay. "He motivated and inspired me so much in that moment that all of the doubts and critics went out the window. I knew he was the right investor and I knew moving forward it would work out no matter what."

The timing was a bit unfortunate as Jim did not have the cash he wanted to work on the start-up with Jay. However, this did not deter them. They decided to move forward on a smaller scale to get their business in motion.

Jim had always seen a lot of opportunity in the USBA, especially when he initially invested in it. He had orchestrated the development of the small campus of cabins and basketball facilities and felt positive about the great value in the property predicting it would easily sell for a profit. Unfortunately, a strong offer never came together and by the mid-2000s, the USBA was not doing well. "I felt bad because I got my friends involved with the USBA. They were losing money, but I was proud of my reputation that nobody would ever lose money with me; I was bound to maintain it," says Jim.

The USBA stock had lost half of its value since Jim's initial investment, when he had encouraged his friends to buy into the property. While many of the investors were Jim's friends, there was another investor who was an acquaintance of Jim's from Southern California. He seemed like a nice-enough guy and he seemed serious about investing.

Jim wanted to be sure and take care of the investors. He says, "I started giving my stock to my friends. I wanted my co-investors to be whole."

Since the stock had lost about half of its value, Jim gave nearly all of his stock to his friends. He wanted to double the amount they had invested so at least they would break even with their investment. Jim's strategy would ensure his investing friends would get their money back when the USBA sold.

While no one was particularly happy about how the USBA deal was going, Jim's friends remained patient. However, the acquaintance investor from Southern California grew especially unpleased and decided he wanted out of the USBA venture.

"He decided he wanted his money back, plus profit. He started harassing me and Del. He got weird," Jim recalls. It started to get especially serious when Jim received phone call threats from this man. It was concerning enough that Jim began to worry about personal safety.

"It put a lot of pressure on me. Eventually, I convinced Del to buy him out of his USBA stock for a lot of money…probably $1 million or so. It was also a big reason I broke up with Margaret. I was a bit worried about her safety."

Despite the breakup, Jim and Margaret remain friends, and he continues to stay in touch with her. Plus, he occasionally swings by Huntington Beach to visit her, Gina, and Angelo.

Chapter 49:

THE PROBLEM SOLVER

Good news arrived for Del and Jim in May 2008: the railroad finally agreed to sell their land to Yesterday's Village. Del and Jim negotiated a price of $1.3 million, with a $100,000 earnest money deposit. The railroad accepted and set a deadline for the full payment. This purchase would make the Yesterday's Village property more valuable and eliminate the monthly lease payments. They anticipated they would save $12,000 in overhead costs every month. Most importantly, owning the railroad land would make the property more appealing to buyers when Del and Jim were ready to sell. After all, real estate is always for sale at the right price.

In December 2008, a property appraisal identified that Yesterday's Village holdings, including ownership of the railroad property, was worth $21.1 million; it was twice as valuable as it had been in 2000. Of course, purchasing the railroad property did not happen overnight.

As it happened, Del had spent $1 million on the USBA just before getting word of the railroad's intent to sell their property to Yesterday's Village. The timing left Del with no cash to make the railroad property purchase. Unfortunately, Jim was in a similar, cash- strapped situation.

Additionally, there was a requirement written into the ten-year government leases for two of Yesterday's Villages' largest office tenants that the property owner had to cover deferred maintenance items—like new painting, carpeting, and wiring for the latest technology—before the lease could be renewed. The leases were up for renewal around 2008. While there was a trusted full-time maintenance man on site, these types of projects were beyond his capacity. Contractors would have to be hired to manage these large-scale maintenance projects, and the estimated price was $240,000. This was a hefty expense for Yesterday's Village; yet it was important because these government tenants paid approximately 90 percent of the revenue on the property.

Del needed to strategize a way to finance both the railroad property purchase and the cost of the deferred maintenance. He approached the bank, requesting a loan to cover the cost of both expenses. Del received a verbal agreement from the bank that they would finance the $240,000 deferred maintenance. To Del, this made total sense; financing these costs would continue to be a good investment for both the owners and the bank. Plus, since the mid-1980s, all the monthly mortgage payments for Yesterday's Village were provided on time. Del, along with Jim as a partner, owed $9.5 million on the property, which was worth an estimated $21.1 million. Since they had been good and reliable bank customers, they did not foresee any issues getting financing through the bank.

When the bank never fulfilled their side of the agreement for the $240,000 loan, Del approached the bank again, inquiring about refinancing the property. The bank, however, did not maintain their verbal agreement. Meanwhile, Del's government tenants were growing restless while they were waiting for their required maintenance—after which they would renew their long-term leases. On a separate note, the bank made no promises or progress to finance the railroad property purchase either.

The days were ticking away, so Jim and Del requested two extensions for the railroad purchase deadline. Luckily, both were granted. Meanwhile, the government tenants supplied a letter expressing their concern about the delay in the deferred maintenance. The tenants communicated that the continued delays may lead them to cancel their leases. It was time for Del to do some problem-solving and come up with funds outside of the bank to cover the deferred maintenance.

Jim says, "None of my closest friends could write a check for $1.2 million at that time, including me. But I knew Mr. C was sitting on a lot of money because he had just sold the marina." It was the same Mr. C as who had helped Jim finish his dream log house. Jim approached Mr. C about being a partner and fronting the $1.2 million for the railroad property purchase. After Mr. C expressed interest in the opportunity, Jim brought him up to Yakima for a show-and-tell on his investment. In the end, Mr. C agreed to the partnership and purchased the railroad land on February 9, 2010, just before the railroad's final purchase deadline.

The purchase was made in Mr. C's name with a gentleman's handshake that Yesterday's Village would provide monthly payments to him until they obtained money to purchase the property out right. Mr. C's involvement was intended to be a quick fix—a way to buy Yesterday's Village more time to find an investing partner for the railroad property purchase. All in all, it was a good deal for Mr. C because he was getting monthly payments. Additionally, he would make a little money when he eventually sold the property back to Del and Jim.

They had one problem solved, but the deferred maintenance issue remained a dilemma. Del had pleaded his case to the bank and made additional requests for the $240,000 loan, yet he couldn't wait any longer. When he felt the tenants were about to walk, he made a risky decision that was a gamble with the bank. Del knew that the loss of the government tenants would be a significant blow to their property income, therefore starting in June 2010, Del decided to skip three monthly mortgage payments of approximately $89,000 each. He would use that money to finance the deferred maintenance items instead, which was now two years overdue.

Del had explained his plan to the bank. However, this decision pushed over the first domino in a long line of ugly dominos.

Doug sums up the situation, "From the time I started, Del and Jim were constantly talking about acquiring the railroad land. About a decade later, the railroad finally made a one-time offer to sell, but the bank would not give us the loan even though they had made a verbal agreement—although a verbal agreement doesn't mean a whole lot to a bank. Del made the good argument that the banks financing of the railroad property purchase and deferred maintenance would give the bank better collateral on the property. In the end, the bank never made good on their verbal agreement and Del decided to forego three monthly property payments to pay for the deferred maintenance. Jim brought in Mr. C to purchase the railroad property with the agreement that once Yesterday's Village got financing, they would purchase the land from Mr. C."

Chapter 50:

THE CHALLENGED

At the same time as Jim and Del sealed up a partner for the railroad purchase, there were two parties that were interested in purchasing the Yesterday's Village property. Although neither purchaser finalized their offers in writing, one potential buyer communicated that they had found nothing to interfere with their closing after they had completed their investigation. This party had proposed to provide a hard-closing date for purchase once the credit markets calmed down.

The potential buyers were hesitant for a good reason; one of the industries that was positively flourishing throughout the decade would soon fall dangerously flat due to various banking and financial services factors.

Generally, throughout the 2000s, the housing market was booming: home values were high, and just about anyone with a pulse could purchase a house because of low or zero down payment qualification requirements and low initial interest rates. These low initial interest rates would last for a few years, but usually after that would bump up to normal, higher rates. Many new homeowners were purchasing homes well beyond their budget, due to somewhat distorted marketing tactics. It was unclear to many of these new homeowners that their payments would increase within a few years of their purchase.

Several years after the low initial interest rates increased, the numerous homeowners who were once able to pay their mortgages were now unable to make their payments. A trend of new loan defaults started in 2007. Many loans became delinquent, and major national and international financial institutions found out that much of their real estate holdings were worthless. Like a house of cards, these assets crumbled en masse, eventually leading to the Great Recession, the largest economic recession in the U.S. since the Great Depression in 1929. One of the major differences between a recession and a depression is time—a depression is simply a prolonged period of recession leading to a major decline in employment. Very few people proved to be immune from this recession as citizens nationwide with vast and varied fortunes were all impacted.

Del explains, "When the market dipped in 2008 and 2009, I thought we would dodge that bullet. We were collecting $500,000 a month in projects, and we had long-term leases with our big tenants." Better yet, their long-term leases were with government tenants, typically less susceptible to economic downturns.

"I had the impression things were being handled in Yakima, so I didn't worry about it much," says Jim, who was managing a few of his own challenges.

It was a stressful time, but Del and Jim were thankful they had brought in Mr. C to purchase the railroad land under the warehouse building. Certainly, Mr. C's support would give them some leverage to work with the bank. After all, foreclosure is a losing situation for both the lender and the owner. Usually, neither party truly wants to reach that point.

Jim was facing a new reality; money was tight and he was the one asking to borrow money rather than being the lender. He was struggling to balance all of his projects and problem-solve the challenges. Normally he had enough to go around, though with money due for Suttle Lake, the credit debacle caused by the Mr. and Mrs. D regarding the McKenzie River house, the additional and unexpected costs to finish the SportsPlex, manage the USBA, and the money Jim invested in Jay's business plan, he was losing ground.

"It was the perfect storm; everything was happening at the same time," Jim says. Jim had been in one serious financial pickle before, and he was able to wiggle out of it. He was always very capable of covering financial losses because he had saleable property as a way of generating cash quickly. Plus, he had his museum and collectables that could act as an insurance plan for covering the costs of any unforeseen expenses, payments, or tacky and threatening investors. He felt certain he could sell off portions of his museum for cash.

Chapter 51:

THE UNDERDOG

Back in Yakima in late 2010, after Yesterday's Village had resumed its normal monthly property payments, Del and Doug were informed that the bank planned to foreclose on the property. By the end of March 2011, Yesterday's Village had opted for voluntary bankruptcy proceedings after being advised to do so from a local attorney, whom we will refer to as Mr. A.

Voluntary bankruptcy, as opposed to involuntary, has some benefits. These kinds of proceedings are typically more orderly and entail an amicable settlement of the debtor's obligations. In voluntary bankruptcy, the debtor can request a Receiver, which the court has to approve or disapprove.

The Receiver—a person appointed by a court to manage the affairs of a bankrupt business or to care for property in litigation—has a lot of power in bankruptcy dealings. After the court judgment approves the Receiver, that individual can seize and liquidate assets and also take control of funds and deposits. In addition, the Receiver is to act in the interest of both parties: collect without interference on behalf of the creditor and protect the debtor from other overzealous creditors. Precisely because it is a powerful role, it is critically important for the individual selected as the Receiver to remain objective to the parties involved. A good Receiver understands the law and remains fair; they do not use the situation to take advantage of the debtor.

Del chose to use Mr. A as the Receiver because he was a local bankruptcy lawyer. As a lawyer, he would likely be approved by the court without question. He also seemed to be supportive of Del's plan to save the property.

Following Mr. A's guidance, Del's plan was that the voluntary bankruptcy proceedings would hold off the foreclosure for enough time so that Jim and Del could obtain new funding to pay off all Yesterday's Village's delinquent expenses owed to the bank. Bankruptcy proceedings normally take around six months or longer with a complicated case. It was a risky strategy, but Del felt Mr. A's advice was sound and believed it was the best way to manage their situation rather than being forced into bankruptcy.

In the long term, Del hoped to sell Yesterday's Village, assuming they were able to get the financing and modernize the property. In 2008, the property was appraised at around $21.1 million. With some improvements, Del estimated the property would be worth around $25 million; he was optimistic that it had doubled in value in a little over a decade.

Shortly after selecting Mr. A as the Receiver, it became clear that he was not going to help Yesterday's Village very much. Doug says, "The Receiver had some close friends that did not like Del at all. So right off the bat, the Receiver was negative and anti-Del."

Mr. A made a court appointment on Friday and the following Monday he issued a letter to Del informing him he was not allowed on the property. From that point forward, Doug started printing checks for Mr. A to sign instead of Del.

"When Mr. A took over as the Receiver, all the paperwork was filled out and in the court before there was an opportunity for Del to sit down and review it. All the account signatures were changed and Mr. A was in total control of the property," Doug explains.

Doug witnessed a lot of what he perceived as questionable and unfortunate decisions made by Mr. A. From Doug's point of view, many of Mr. A's actions appeared to be cavalier and illogical, as if his newfound power over Del and Yesterday's Village gave him an opportunity to act with malice.

It began to appear that Mr. A no longer supported Del's original plan to buy time to find financiers to and pay the money due to the bank. It was also thought that Mr. A turned off the alarm system in the basement of the warehouse building and unlocked the doors to Jim and Del's personal collections and many collectables disappeared. However, in backing up a bit, when the former maintenance manager retired, Yesterday's Village hired a young man to replace him. Jim and Del suspected that this young guy may have had sticky fingers; he was one of very few people with access to Jim and Del's locked collections.

Doug says, "That employee—when he was fired—stole the shop truck. When it was recovered, there were no tools."

Also, because Jim and Del owned the building, they had never thought to draft up a formal lease for use of the basement space. By the time Jim and Del learned about items missing from their collections, Mr. A had total control of the property. Jim attempted to file a police investigation on the stolen items, but the police did not accept Jim's report because the property was under Mr. A's control. In order for a police investigation to become necessary, Mr. A would need to file the report on the stolen property because he was in charge of the property and these items fell under his ownership. Mr. A did not file a police report and no investigation was conducted.

Another example of Mr. A's obstructive actions included the decision to bring in a real estate management company to replace that maintenance fellow instead of another maintenance guy. The management company was supposed to collect rent, pay bills, and take care of the property's maintenance. Under this new system, Mr. A had to approve all maintenance orders. This led to a delay in the response to routine maintenance requests. With a diligent maintenance employee available on-site as was previously available, maintenance requests were promptly addressed.

"It was a nice bonus for our tenants to have a maintenance guy on hand. As a result of Mr. A's new maintenance arrangements, one State department got tired of the poor maintenance and moved out—that was a big lease lost.

Mr. A was paying probably $10,000 monthly to this real estate management company who wasn't doing much at all. A good maintenance guy would have done a much better job for half that," Doug justifies.

Doug suspects that contract with the overpriced management company went on for about 15 months likely costing up to approximately $150,000.

In an interesting and surprising twist, on August 5, 2011, the bank purchased the railroad land from Mr. C for $3.6 million. This felt like a particularly grand insult for Del. It is unclear why the bank made this decision in 2011 after they had denied the same opportunity to Del a year and a half before. In the end, the bank opted to purchase the property from Mr. C for twice as much as what was initially requested by Del in the form of a loan for Yesterday's Village.

Doug contemplates, "I'm not sure. Up through the bankruptcy in March 2011, Mr. C was on board with holding the land for Yesterday's Village. But based on people I've talked to and rumors, I'm left with the impression that Mr. A talked the bank into making the deal with Mr. C. Forget friends and promises...Mr. C took the money and ran."

Mr. C may have decided to sell because it seemed like a simple business decision. He had the chance to double his money while his business partners struggled with their finances. Mr. C may have simply been taking care of his own interests. However, at a time when Del and Jim needed his good word the most, Mr. C sold out.

That is something Jim would never dream of doing to another person. "My word is my bond," Jim says. Unfortunately, this is not a personal policy all people follow.

"I knew when Mr. C sold the railroad property it would be hard to recover. I was scrambling, thinking what do I do? We attempted a last effort to find an investor, but nobody could buy at that time. We realized it was over," Doug says.

Doug's last day working on the train for Yesterday's Village, under the care of Mr. A, was September 30, 2011. The last domino had fallen.

Chapter 52:

THE ADAPTABLE

Without monthly income from Yesterday's Village flowing in, Jim was unable to make payments on many of his other projects. Very quickly, the banks started repossessing his properties. His financial *ship* was sinking fast and none of his ideas were able to plug the holes in the boat.

One day, Jim was in a beauty parlor getting a haircut in South Lake Tahoe, "There was this beautiful woman in another chair and I had my Yorkie named Buddy sitting on my lap."

The beautiful brunette walked over to meet Jim and professed her love of Yorkies.

"She asked me what I did and I said, 'I'm really good at losing money.' Then she told me, 'We should get together, I'm really good at making money,'" says Jim.

Jim couldn't believe a beautiful woman like Debbie Hammond was single when they met. He describes her as a stunning brunette and the kind of person that commands the attention of a room without intending to. "She has an *it* factor that is hard to explain. She still does," Jim says.

Debbie had a home in Lake Tahoe and plans to be there for a while. She and Jim became quick friends and began traveling, visiting parks, and enjoying the scenes of nature—as well as each other's company.

Jim recalls being out on a bike ride with Debbie when she got a call. "There was a lady in front of Debbie's Tahoe house asking how much it was. Debbie explained it wasn't for sale. Here I was in need of money and I couldn't give my real estate away. Debbie didn't need or want to sell her property and was getting an offer," Jim laughs.

Although she had no interest in selling her Lake Tahoe home, she decided the offer was impossible to pass up. Within 30 days, she had received a cash check and was packing up to leave Lake Tahoe.

Jim suggested that she buy another house in Lake Tahoe, but Debbie opted to head back to South Texas and be near her aging mother. Jim offered to take her and her dog, Buster, to Corpus Christi, Texas, on his bus (one of the items the bank had yet to snag). Unfortunately, only a few hours into their trip, Buster suffered a heart attack or a stroke. Debbie made a fast decision and walked into the local medical center for treatment.

Jim recalls, "We go into this little hospital with this little dog. It's not a vet clinic. It's a human hospital. Debbie looks like a million bucks—she had her jewels and diamonds on; she always looked classy, not extravagant. She tells the staff her dog is dying and somehow gets a heart surgeon to revive this little dog." Jim pauses and says, "Nobody else could pull that off. That is the power of beauty."

Little Buster didn't have many heartbeats left after his revival; he ended up passing away shortly thereafter. Debbie was heartbroken. She wanted to bury Buster locally, so she hired a boy to bury her dog in Tonopah, Nevada, where Buster's remains remain.

As much as he liked Debbie, after a few days in South Texas Jim realized it simply was not his place. It was flat, hot, and humid. He headed back up to Lake Tahoe to see what, if anything, he could salvage from his disappearing assets. As he usually does with the women he dates and cares for, Jim maintained a close friendship with Debbie.

Chapter 53:

THE FREE SPIRIT

*Jim testing his belief that "real" wealth
is family and friends*

Although some people, including Del, suggested that he try to fight Mr. A and the bank with a team of lawyers, Jim declined to do this. Instead, he got on his bus and drove south to Long Beach, California.

Jim shrugs, "I just started signing things over. I didn't put up a fight; the banks had me. I just didn't want to spend the next five years of my life fighting in a court. I knew it wouldn't be worth it even though we had a good case."

Jim believes that opting to release all of his possessions—in addition to not pursuing a lawsuit—may have saved him years of exposure to negative people and greedy, false accusations.

Jim found a nice camping spot that wasn't far from the RMS Queen Mary, a famous cruise ship-turned-hotel permanently docked in Long Beach. He started riding his bike everywhere for exercise. On his bike rides, he came up with many plans: how to save what he could, new business ideas, his recovery and return to wealth, and the idea to cycle all the National Parks. He also began adjusting his lifestyle so he could live within his new means. He supplemented his monthly Social Security checks by selling some of his jewelry and other valuable items still in his possession. He became a frugal spender and regular at the local dollar store.

For Jim, this new world was an adventure: a new challenge, a new experience, and a new beginning. In this situation, some people might crumble in agony, feeling shameful or embarrassed and have a hard time adapting to a new way of life after decades of extravagance. Unfortunately, Jim watched Del fall into a state of despair, obsessing about the loss. Even more tragic, Del developed some significant health issues.

Jim took the defeat in stride; he accepted it and owned it. He hopped on his bicycle under the palm trees in Southern California and pedaled himself into better physical shape than he'd ever been before.

On his bike rides and during the time he spent in his bus, Jim began to see the beauty of this simple life. He was no longer burdened with piles of possessions, mortgages, bills, and the heavy responsibility of ensuring that all of his friends and employees were taken care of. He was absolutely free. There were no meetings, problems, or possible business opportunities tugging him from one location to another. It was the first time in a long time that Jim had the luxury of being present in a location for more than a few nights. For Jim, it was kind of like a vacation.

He did retain some of his previous habits; his daily to-do list, his eye for opportunities, and the continued progress of a few unfinished business transactions. Jim had not given up; he had simply adapted. He was looking at life with a new perspective, and he was curious and eager to test his capacity to move forward and start his next empire. Although now, once he attained his next fortune, he planned to manage his money differently.

On a pleasant evening in the middle of summer 2012, Jim was just finishing up his long bicycle ride when he ran into a sun-kissed blond named Angel. She was closing down her sunglasses kiosk for the day.

"I thought, oh no I was just closing," says Angel, remembering Jim riding up. She was ready to go home, "Then he started asking me the most unique questions. Once he started talking, I told him to hang on—give me 15 minutes and let me close." Angel is a petite Californian with a bright smile. Her upbeat mood and cheerful demeanor match Jim's personality well.

Jim remembers meeting Angel and thinking, "She was a cute little blond with a lot of spirit."

After closing her kiosk up, Angel met Jim in the shadow of the iconic Queen Mary. The Queen Mary has been in Long Beach since retirement in 1967 after 1,001 trans-Atlantic crossings. She is a ship grander than the Titanic at over 1,000 feet in length and younger by 24 years setting out for her maiden voyage on May 27, 1936. During cruising days, the ship was capable of carrying 3,212 passengers and crew within her lavish art deco interior. Many celebrities enjoyed luxurious travel aboard the Queen Mary including Bob Hope, Fred Astaire, Bing Crosby, Audrey Hepburn, and Elizabeth Taylor, to name a few.

Jim and Angel discussed business ownership, life experiences, and their own short-term plans for the future. Angel expressed how she was looking forward to owning a little place in a tranquil location one day. She talked about how well her sunglasses kiosk had done and that she was thinking about her next step. Meanwhile, Jim divulged the unusual predicament he was in and the loss of his fortune. He also mentioned how he was planning to auction off Elizabeth Taylor's dressing trailer. He'd owned the trailer for years and had stored it near Lake Tahoe. It was an easy decision for Jim to sell the trailer. "That's when I was losing my shirt. I needed the money."

After meeting Angel, Jim returned to Lake Tahoe so that he could haul the trailer down for the auction with a borrowed truck. Bob Lindner joined Jim at the auction; he added some Sammy Davis Jr. and Liberace memorabilia to sell. Jim also invited Angel to the auction in Los Angeles. She surprised herself by accepting the invitation; after all, it sounded fun to her.

In seeing the trailer for the first time, Angel says, "I was stunned and amazed. It was this big, beautiful travel trailer—36 feet long—with these elaborate pink Corinthian columns. You can't make this stuff up."

The trailer—referred to as the Love Nest when Elizabeth Taylor owned it—resonated with Angel. She saw the entrepreneurial potential in the trailer, which got her thinking. In addition to being impressed with the trailer, Angel was also impressed with Jim's towing and parking skills. Jim informed her he had not lost his prize-winning tractor pulling and backing-up skills that he had learned in his Future Farmers of America teenage years.

"It turned out the auction was a disaster. Things were not selling for what they were worth. It was poorly run," Jim remembers. When the trailer went up for auction, Jim devised a plan with Angel. Because it was being sold for so cheap, Jim suggested that maybe Angel could buy it and make it a profitable asset.

There was some back and forth, but Angel eventually won the bid for the trailer.

Angel became the new owner of Elizabeth Taylor's Love Nest. Within days of acquiring the trailer, a movie production company working on an Elizabeth Taylor movie contacted Angel because they wanted to buy the trailer. Instead of selling it, she worked out a deal to rent it to the production company working on the movie. Soon, Angel found herself on another random adventure with Jim.

Angel reflects meeting Jim, "It seems all of this happened in a week. It was like a tornado hitting my life when we met. We got to know each other pretty well in that one week. You can't help but love him."

With the Elizabeth Taylor trailer checked off his list, Jim had other business to attend to. He hopped in his car and drive north with Angel accompanying him. Jim was planning a whirlwind expedition to continue saving as many of his remaining properties as possible from repossession. He hoped that his friends and acquaintances would buy his properties, or his share of them, before the banks snagged them all up. While this strategy worked for some of his properties, others were lost to the rules of the bank, the tragedy of the economy, and unforeseen circumstances.

Angel was introduced to Jim's vanishing wealth. Together they visited a number of his treasured spots, including the Carson River Resort, Lakeview, the USBA, and Suttle Lake Resort. He also took Angel to Drew's Lake while they were passing through Lakeview, Oregon. He showed her a piece of property with some lovely pine trees standing like sentinels over the lot. Jim referenced the fact that she had told him she liked trees. Then he handed Angel a piece of paper. She looked at it and was shocked to see it was the deed to that lot on Drew's Lake. Those were her trees now. He had given her a piece of land within weeks of meeting her.

On the trip, Jim and Angel made time to enjoy bicycle rides and hikes between trying to save Jim's properties and visiting Jim's friends. At one point, Angel received a call from the production company that was renting the Elizabeth Taylor trailer. "They told me the trailer had been vandalized. It was trashed. I couldn't believe it."

The well-preserved Love Nest would not return to Angel in the same pristine condition in which she had lent it to the studio. The trailer was in a state of disarray: broken dishes, furniture, and decorations, ruined linens, cigarette burns on the vanity, and worse. These were relics that could not be replaced. Angel was dumbfounded. It was wrecked inside.

"Everyone pointed fingers at everyone else. So, I went to the media. I got an agent and she set me up to tell the story," Angel says.

Before she knew it, Angel was riding in a limousine on her way to a number of media interviews. After *Showbiz Tonight*, she was interviewed by *Nightline* and *CNN News*. In the long run, Angel achieved her goal; the studio producers called her and gave her money for the damages.

"It was my 15 minutes of fame. It was quite an amazing experience," she remembers.

Once the trailer was returned to Angel, she and Jim cleaned it up so that it looked nearly as good as before. Along the way, Angel and Jim's relationship swiftly developed into a romance.

Jim says, "I remember walking across the street to a pizza place in Long Beach and looking at her. I told her; you were worth all the millions I just lost." He meant it from the bottom of his heart. He realized that if he hadn't been in such dire financial straits, he never would have never been out bicycling in Long Beach and run into Angel near the Queen Mary.

"Something good always comes from something bad," Jim says.

Chapter 54:

THE HUMAN

While he is usually exceptionally positive, Jim is not immune to disappointment and frustration. He has had his moments of experiencing awe and disbelief at what transpired in just a few short years—he went from $50 million to living off of social security.

During the downfall of Yesterday's Village, Jim was afforded the opportunity to go and get his collectibles from the Yakima Building, or what was left of them. After he was granted permission to collect his things, he scurried up to Washington only to find a fraction of the collectables he had originally stored there.

"It bugs me a little that all that stuff was gone. We had a doll collection worth a lot of money—it was gone. Every once in a while, you'll see a doll sell for $10,000 on the *Antique Roadshow* and I just know I had that doll. We had hundreds of them. I'll watch a car auction and see a car sell for a million dollars and think, gosh I used to have that car," Jim says, sharing a rare moment of disappointment followed by a whiplash snap back to reality.

"I just had to let it go…that's history," he says.

Jim salvaged what he could. He saved a few remaining lonely dolls, a taxidermized Kodiak bear, several pedal cars, a few stacks of old toys, some movie memorabilia, sporting goods, and a few Jones Fantastic Museum remnants—including Olaf. He moved the last bit of his collection to a storage unit in Gardnerville, Nevada, for safekeeping.

Like the massive Yesterday's Village buildings and its tenants and collections, the popular Track 29 Train Mall was also now subject to Mr. A's destructive touch. Doug explains, "Some of the Track 29 tenants were occasionally behind on their rent. But Del and I would work with them and allow a payment plan."

After Mr. A's arrival, Doug was directed to request all tenants pay all their back rent within a short period of time. Otherwise, they would be moved out. Doug hated giving this news to the tenants. They were good people running good businesses.

Doug gave all the Track 29 Train Mall tenants letters informing them that their leases were ending. The popular Track 29 Train Mall became local history. There was a last-minute effort to raise money to save the red caboose, unfortunately, the majority of the train cars were sent to scrap. A photograph posted online by the City of Yakima on September 18, 2013—titled *Trashing Trains*—shows the lonely red caboose next to a construction crane brought in to dismantle the other railcars.

It was unfortunate that these railcars were not saved by any interested parties as a way of preserving some local history. In addition, the sale of these railcars could have contributed to the debt that Yesterday's Village owed the bank. Del says, "Mr. A ran off the tenants, and the collections and the trains disappeared. He completely destroyed the relationships we had established. The big tenants decided to move out and, all of a sudden, the building was empty and worth much less. They ended up selling the empty building for a deficit and now it was on us to make up the difference in what the bank lost. And one of the worst parts was that Jim had guaranteed this note by cross-collateralizing his other properties."

It could be said that Mr. A was creating a worse situation for both parties, and this seemed to be in direct opposition to the responsibilities of his role as the Receiver for the bankruptcy court proceedings. As a result of Mr. A and the bank's decisions—which appeared to be riotous and contradictory—the value of the Yesterday's Village property was being diminished.

If Yesterday's Village had been left with the Del and Jim, they would have worked tirelessly to continue to pay off debts and build value with personal interest. However, that would not be the case. This large piece of Jim and Del's real estate portfolio was now officially history.

Chapter 55:

THE SIMPLE MAN

In order to make ends meet, Jim started selling his jewelry. "I had quite a bit of gold jewelry—rings, necklaces, bracelets—and I just started selling it. The store would weigh it and buy it."

Jim was with Tom Fields when he mentioned how he planned to sell his gold nugget watch that had been custom-made by Bob Lindner. While this watch was significant to Jim because it symbolized his success, he was ready to sell it off to make ends meet. Tom offered to buy it for $2,000. Jim was happy to get the cash and sell it to a friend. That money could go a long way at the dollar store for the next few months. He also needed a little cash to court his lady.

Jim took Angel to New Orleans for Mardi Gras in 2014. First, they met up with Rex and Marty to enjoy a little Southern hospitality in Alabama. After that, they headed west to Louisiana. The two couples piled into a big truck and drove from Alabama to New Orleans to stay at a friend's guesthouse for the Mardi Gras festivities. They were privileged to receive invitations to a Mardi Gras ball and dressed up in their fineries for a nice formal night out.

Angel says, referring to Rex and Marty, "They treated us like gold.... I bought the most beautiful dress I have ever had in my life. I was glittering, and Jim was all dressed up. It was fun!"

Jim looked dashing in a sharp tuxedo; Angel wore a floor-length gown. They were a handsome couple. Jim smiles, "I'll never forget that moment. I was madly in love. It's amazing how a single person can impact everything."

The following day, they celebrated Mardi Gras with the rest of the city by watching the parade. The four friends had packed up the truck. They left Marty's little dog in the vehicle while they were out cruising the neighborhood on bicycle and watching the festivities.

"It was a great event. We got piles of beads. But when we came back— the truck was gone. And Marty's dog was in the truck! I lost $1,000 in cash, and Jim lost some jewelry, a Rolex watch, and some nice suits," Angel says.

Angel and Jim at Mardi Gras

The truck had been stolen from its parking space, which was only a half block from a police station.

"We had to call the police. The dog was found, but the rest was gone. I was more worried about Angel and my friends losing their stuff than my stuff. I was used to losing stuff by then," Jim says.

When Jim and Angel first met, he was living in his high-end, fancy Prevost motorhome, or his bus. Over the years, Jim had plastered the outside of his bus with pictures of his family and his friends, and it became a mobile tribute to his memories. There was a phrase on the back of the bus: *Real wealth is one's family and friends!*

"The bus with the pictures got repossessed. He couldn't make the payments on it anymore. It was sad," says Angel, recalling a time not long after they met.

With his shelter gone, Jim rented out his friend Pam's Lake Tahoe house. This house was next door to the house he used to own, the one he had sold years before to his good friend Bob Lindner. Jim stayed there for a time, and Angel came up to visit. Mostly it was Jim that was back and forth, driving from Lake Tahoe to southern California to see Angel. She lived in Laguna Beach and the location began to grow on Jim. However, Jim's constant companion had made his last trip.

"Angel was with me when Buddy died. I had to put him to sleep," Jim says. Buddy had lived a long, good life. After a bit of a mourning period, Jim knew he needed another sidekick. He found his furry friend east of Reno near a little airport.

"The people there that took care of the airplanes had little Yorkie pups. They were tiny. There was only one girl. I had to come back in a few weeks. I bought her and named her Gidget. I don't know how I came up with the name," Jim says.

Gidget weighs three pounds as a fully grown dog. She is a Teacup Yorkie, and her slight stature and gender perfectly fit her name, which is derived from the combination of the words *girl* and *midget* or a little girl with big ideas. It originates from Frederick Kohner's 1957 novel about a petite surfer girl and her Malibu surfer friends. The name became even more fitting when Jim and Gidget started spending a good part of their time near the ocean in the surfer haven of San Clemente. In between bike rides, they cruised around in his Doval Shadow in the warm sunshine near the pier. They also spent a lot of time hanging out with Angel.

"You know, there are dog breeds for hunting and guarding and retrieving and searching and so on…there's a dog breed for every sort of function. The purpose of a Yorkie is to look at you and simply love you," Jim explains.

When Jim got Gidget, he bought a little, brown pet-carrier shoulder bag that also doubled as his briefcase. The middle pocket was for Gidget and on the outside pockets were for his yellow pads, pens, mobile phone, and all his other basic necessities like a tangle of keys. He took that bag everywhere and in it quietly hunkered Gidget.

It was a blessing for Jim to have his new dog friend because Jim and Angel's romantic relationship was coming to an end. "He was 19 years older than me. We gave it a try and we love each other. Jimmy is my dream man, but not really romantically. Now we have a close friendship and we are business partners, too," Angel explains

Angel bought into Jim's old Carson River Resort. For a few years, she helped manage the place. She also helped Jim buy a kick-around car since his Doval Shadow is not ideal for driving around in bad weather. Jim also signed over the remainder of the museum to Angel to protect it.

Although their romance ended up concluding in the fall of 2014, Jim decided to stick around in San Clemente—just a few miles south of where Angel lived. Angel introduced him to a friend, and her friend lent Jim a small room with a garage parking space for the Doval.

In his tiny room, he had a futon, television, a hotplate, a small refrigerator, and two random pedal cars from his museum. The walls were decorated with pictures from his high-rolling days with high-rolling people. The pictures represented a bygone lifestyle—bouncing between seven homes, selling millions of dollars in real estate, and lending friends, and sometimes strangers, thousands of dollars without much consideration.

Jim designed a new daily routine and he set up a new office. As usual, he woke up early curious about the day ahead and contemplated new ideas. Every day, he wrote down what he wanted to accomplish on his yellow pad, what calls he wanted to make, and what business opportunities he planned to check on. On sunny days, which is most days in Southern California, he made a peanut butter and jelly sandwich, dressed in his cycling gear, loaded up his road bike on the back of his Doval Shadow, and drove to the San Clemente pier. He unloaded the bike, strapped a small leather pouch onto his chest, and gently slipped Gidget in her pocket. Together, they headed out for a long bike ride.

When they returned, they sat in the sun making phone calls, chatted with anyone and everyone wandering by who stopped to look at the Doval Shadow, and checked in on how the USBA sell and web company were progressing with Bruce and Jay respectively. Jim also gets creative and considers how he might sell and profit from this storage room full of old earrings he had acquired at some point of his life. He contemplates his next big idea. He tells stories about his unusual life to strangers with time to sit and visit. One day, that stranger was a writer.

Making phone calls from his San Clemente, California "office"

Gidget ran over to a woman who strolled down the hill and gazed at the ocean. The woman with reddish hair and freckles could not help but notice Gidget's tininess and stooped to pet her. Then she saw Jim seated by the Doval Shadow and he introduced himself.

"What kind of car is that?" she asked petting Gidget. Jim answered and provided some details on the Doval. Then Jim asked her what she was doing. She replied that she was out checking the surf, which was no good, so she sat down to chat.

"What do you do?" Jim asked.

"I'm a writer," she replied.

"Do you write biographies?" he inquired.

"No. I'm a technical writer. I work from home and write railroad safety reports. I do hope to make a living writing fiction someday."

"If you ever decide to write biographies, let me know…I've been told I should write one."

Several hours later, Laynie D. Weaver had learned much about the rise and fall of Jim Schmit. She had learned his greatest regret was not journaling more and that his main hope was to fall in love with the right woman. Yes, it was quite interesting, this man, this car, and this teeny, tiny dog as a caravan out to start over.

A year later after a friendship had blossomed between the two, Laynie walked up to Jim one random day and simply mentioned, "Let's talk about a book."

Jim responded, "My biography?"

"Yes. Are you ready to start it?" she asked.

"Yes," Jim confirmed.

Laynie explained that she had never written a biography, but she was willing to give it a shot. Jim explained he had no money to pay her and a lot of time to be patient. Together, late in 2015, they started collaborating on his life's story.

Having started on his biography, Jim felt this project served as a good substitute to satisfy his regret of not journaling. Ultimately, this meant there was only one thing left to do.

Chapter 56:

THE HOMELESS

Jim and Clifford Ray at Carson River Resort

Although Jim's schedule no longer required him to zip from place to place to do business, he still had nomadic tendencies. After a few months in Southern

California, he was ready to go north to Lake Tahoe. He also sometimes opted for trips to Arizona, Texas, or Alabama to visit his close friends there.

In Tahoe, he kept himself busy helping Angel run the Carson River Resort. He made reservations and became the handy man—repairing leaky roofs and plumbing, landscaping, and cleaning.

Jim reconnected with an old buddy of his while he was at the Resort. Olaf, the petrified Viking, came out of storage and he stayed at the Resort for a short period of time. With his big circus banner lashed to the side of the resort store, he became a roadside attraction. Behind it—in the cold shade—was Olaf, laying just as still as before.

Jim remembers, "There had been a large forest fire not far away from the resort. I put him out as a fundraiser. I was hoping people would stop by to look at him and leave a donation to help replant trees. And he did! Olaf raised several hundred dollars."

Jim maintained his headquarters in a large bus that his friend Eric Elkaim had loaned to him. Inside the bus were his last bits of personal possessions, outside of the collection he had stored in Gardnerville, Nevada.

The items he appreciated the most were his pictures because they were the closest thing to a journal. They captured memories and stories that he would likely forget without an image to prompt them. The pictures surrounded him like a cocoon. Also, part of his décor was a tiny Christmas tree that sat on the kitchen table.

"Christmas trees make me happy," Jim explains. He often leaves one up throughout the year. "I got the idea from Clifford Ray. He always has a Christmas tree up."

Jim decided to open up the Fantastic Museum in Gardnerville, Nevada. He found an affordable space to rent that was a 30-minute drive from the Carson River Resort. After hauling them collection out of storage, Jim dusted off the remaining items and moved everything into the new, temporary museum for display. In a small town like Gardnerville, the museum quickly became an attraction; it was even featured as a story in *The Record-Courier* local newspaper paper.

A week before Jim planned to open the museum, in September 2016, he was doing his last bit of set-up. He got an unexpected call from Angel at the Resort; she was anxious and told Jim that there was a fire at the Resort. For a place surrounded with pine trees and forest tinder, a fire in the August summer heat was bad news.

Jim locked the museum up and hopped in the Duval with Gidget to drive back to the Resort. When he arrived, the firefighters were on the scene putting out the blaze. A fire had started in the maintenance shed. It had then burned down the small structure and one neighboring cabin. In addition, it had ignited Jim's bus, which happened to be parked right next to the maintenance shed. All of Jim's personal belongings on board—including his bicycle and treasured pictures—were ashes.

"I thought I was poor before. After that fire, I was like a brand-new baby. I didn't even own a toothbrush. Just a few years ago, I had seven houses. Then, in one day, I didn't even have a bus to sleep on anymore. I was actually homeless," says Jim.

*Reading through the Fantastic Museum inventory
before opening in Gardnerville, Nevada*

Like back in his college days, Jim found some necessities at the dollar store and the local Salvation Army. Then, Jim moved into his latest temporary home—an available and furnished room that was conveniently located above his new museum in Gardnerville. His close friends pitched in and gave him a little spending money to get back on his feet. Before long, he had some basics: hairbrush, toothbrush, a few pair of shorts and shirts, socks, underwear, some sheets and blankets for his apartment, a cheap stationary bicycle, a little bit of cookware, bread, peanut butter, and jelly.

Jim marched on and turned his attention to the museum. After waking up in the morning, Jim ate his eggs and vegetables and then walked down-stairs to open the museum. He donated half of the $5 museum entry fee to a local charity even though he could have used all of the money himself. Jim provided visitors with pamphlets and sometimes, he even led tours. He would tell guests personal stories about many of the items. He ended his tour in the small tomb-like basement where Olaf rested. Kids and adults enjoyed the random, pop-up museum, and it kept Jim busy.

It was open only for a little bit. Jim knew this was his final museum; he was ready to let go of it all. Plus, he could use the cash.

The museum closed after Jim found a buyer for the entire collection in the spring of 2017. He sold everything, including his dusty old friend Olaf. Now, Jim had a nice wad of cash that he could live off for a little while. As part of the sale, Jim acquired a used bus. The bus would serve as his new headquarters at Carson River Resort. He set it up and moved in and within less than one year of the fire that burned up his belongings, Jim had a new little spot to lay his head and welcome guests.

Unfortunately, he would find that not all future guests would be genuine and authentic individuals.

Chapter 57:

THE CRIME FIGHTER

On Friday, November 30, 2018, Jim sat in a courtroom in Dallas, Texas. He was watching as the trial judge sentenced 37-year-old Desiree Boltos to 263 years in prison. She was found guilty on six counts of organized crime and money laundering. The witness that sealed her fate was Mr. Jim Schmit.

Nicknamed the Sweetheart Swindler by the press, Boltos was a con artist and a thief. She was a married woman who took to seducing older men for money. Then she gambled much of it away in Las Vegas. While there were only a handful of victims that were represented in this particular case, there were possibly up to two dozen more that had not, or would not, come forward.

In the courtroom, Boltos appeared frumpy and unkempt. Her hair was stringy, and her face was pudgy and plain. Her appearance in court was a far-cry from the pictures that she posted and shared with her targets to begin her scam. Boltos used various online dating websites and coincidental encounters to attract her victims. Her victims were primarily wealthy, older men—both married and single. She changed her looks and her names, and she came up with stories to prey on her victim's weaknesses. She gave them the intimacy many of them lacked and desired. Her routine was to gain their trust and confidence first. Then she would tell her victims that she needed money for an illness, a business investment, or another emergency. At this point, if the men were married, she sometimes blackmailed them. However, many of these men freely gave her money. After taking it, she would disappear. Clearly adept at picking targets, Boltos filtered through many fellows. She made a luxurious living from this illegal racket.

In Boltos' defense, she claimed these alleged victims voluntarily gave her the money, and there is no crime in dating and love. The unfortunate truth was this did seem to be the case for all but one victim; Jim broke the mold. It was Jim's testimony that made a critical difference in the case.

When Jim was put on the stand to testify, he explained the events surrounding his encounter with the disreputable Desiree Boltos. Jim's shared the summary of his testimony several days after the trial:

> It was a day or two before my birthday in July 2017 when I got a call on my cell phone from this woman, Desiree, who said she had met me years before when she was traveling through the Carson River Resort near Markleeville, California. She asked if I remembered her and I didn't remember her because I meet a lot of people there—which is true.
>
> She continued to talk, saying she thought I was a special guy, someone that really stood out to her. She said that she wanted to come back through and say hello.
>
> Then she sent me a picture. She had on glasses and lipstick and had a nice smile. She was nice-looking, but I did not recall meeting her. She was kind on the phone, and at her consideration of coming back up, I thought—plenty of people come and stay at the resort, that's what it's for. If she wanted to come up and stay, that was fine by me.
>
> She flew into Carson City from Las Vegas, and I picked her up from the airport. She carried a purse and an overnight bag for the trip. We talked on the way and she was well-spoken. She seemed intelligent and interesting. It all started with normal small talk and then, as the hours crept by, she started talking

about her interior decorating business. Her stories were impressive: the places she had decorated and the people she mingled with. She explained that she had an opportunity to work with Steve Wynn for a decorating project in Las Vegas, but needed an investor to provide her the initial $100,000.

I said, well, there was a day when I could help you, but I don't have any money anymore. I told her I had lost my money during the recession years. And that was that. There was not much more to talk about on that subject.

She stayed with me in my RV one night. I have friends stay with me all the time. I offered her the bedroom in the back of the RV, but she opted for the couch in the front claiming to be claustrophobic. That night we both slept in our own spaces.

The next morning, she told me she had recently found out the people renting her house in Dallas missed a few payments and the bank was going to take the property if she didn't come up with some money to cover the missed payments. She said that $15,000 would save her house. She asked me if I would write her a check for $15,000 to save her house.

I once again explained that I did not have that kind of money, and, no, I could not write her a check for $15,000. I felt bad for her. There was a time and place in which I could have easily helped her; there was a time and place in which $15,000 was a drop in the bucket for me.

Strangely, as it so happens, I had just sold off some of the last of my collection and I did have $15,000 on me, but it was to cover my living expenses. I did feel bad for her, that she traveled all this way thinking I could be an investor, and I couldn't help her with her house. So I offered to pay for her flight. I asked her how much it was, and she said $2,000. My first thought was, that's an expensive flight from Vegas, but maybe it was so expensive because it was a last-minute flight. I don't know...I didn't worry too much about the expense.

So, I went back to my bedroom in the RV where I had my money stashed, along with a couple of signed, blank checks I had on hand for resort bills and payments. I was in charge of the resort because the manager was away at the time. I took out $2,000 in cash and stashed my money back away. I walked towards the front of the RV where Desiree was sitting. I gave her $2,000 cash in $100 bills.

Then I got to thinking, maybe I need to hide my money a little better. I just got this feeling. At some point, I went back casually and hid the rest of the cash and blank checks in my socks and underwear drawer.

A little while later, I suggested we go to town for lunch. She put on a pretty dress—it was low-cut in the front—and we drove a few miles into Markleeville. We had some drinks. Then we walked across the street, and I introduced her to some of the locals.

When we returned to the resort, I told her I had about an hour of work I needed to do in the resort store. So, I left her in the RV and walked to the store about 100 feet away. I did my work and returned an hour later.

When I came back, I found her out in the car, with suitcases packed and the engine on. She had Gidget inside too. She was ready to go and I didn't think much of it.

I grabbed my bag and we headed back up to the airport for her flight. When we got there, she started rummaging through her bag to find her ID. She put her bags on the hood of the car and asked me to go through her overnight back to check for it.

I thought that was weird, but I did, shoving her clothes around a little. Then she asked me to go through her purse, and I did. As I was looking through her purse, she said she found it, in some pocket of her overnight bag.

Then she said goodbye and walked towards the terminal doors.

I was almost back to the resort when I got a call from the store. They said the beer vendor needed a payment. When I got back, I went straight into my RV to get a blank check to pay the vendor. It was then I noticed all the cash was gone. I knew she took it. There was no one else that could have taken it.

I called the Alpine County Sheriffs' Department and they came out and took a report. I pretty much knew I'd never see that money again. Boy, I was really hoping to catch her.

I came up with a strategy to be nice and also get her to confess to her thievery. I gave her a call and asked her if she took my money. She denied it. She said that I had looked through all of her stuff and if she had it, it would have been in her bags. Then she diverted; she said she had seen a suspicious-looking guy walking around in a blue shirt at the resort before they left for the airport. Maybe it was him.

I asked if she would take a lie detector test and she said sure. I got ahold of a lie-detector guy. He said he traveled to Vegas regularly, and he would be happy to meet her there. I told Desiree who said she would certainly meet up with him because she did not take the money.

I gave her number to the lie-detector guy. He called her a few times, but she never answered. I maintained communications with her, calling her every so often. I continued to push the lie detector option. Of course, she kept coming up with excuses.

For some reason she kept taking my calls to proclaim her inno-
cence. So I kept calling her.

*Jim's sleuthing and honesty help
put a con artist behind bars*

Naturally, Jim shared all the information he had with the Alpine County
Sheriff's Department that set off a domino effect to help crack the case. A
little over one year later, Jim found himself sitting in a courtroom testifying
about how the cunning, lying Desiree Boltos had stolen $13,000 from him. It
was the one clear case in which she had taken money from someone; it had
not been gifted out of kindness or for sexual favors. After all, there was no
sex involved in Jim's case, and he never once told her he would give her more
than $2,000 to reimburse her for the flight she may or may not have taken.

At the end of the trial, Jim summed it up in an interview with the local
press: "She found out that I didn't have big money anymore, so she was very
disappointed…she's very cunning, I mean so convincing. I consider myself
half-smart and she was so good."

Chapter 58:

THE DISAPPOINTED

In early 2019, Jim learned more disappointing news about a friend and business partner that he had trusted wholeheartedly. Over the decade they had been in business together, Jim had invested over $300,000 in the company he shared with Jay. For years, Jay kept promising Jim that their business was ready to launch in the next few months, yet nothing ever happened. Jim kept his faith in Jay because he knew he was a smart kid.

In the eyes of a few of Jim's friends, Jay did not add up. He was full of empty promises and never delivered. Jay continued to accept money, and he had plans to spend it in odd ways that were mismatched from the company model. He was also never available for Jim. Jim likened him to Facebook founder Mark Zuckerberg, but when he was quizzed by a rather astute technologist, his answers fell flat. A few friends around Jim continued to raise and communicate their concerns about Jay. However, Jim truly wanted to believe in this business and partnership.

Finally, after not receiving any responses back from Jay for an extended period of time, Jim drove to his house in Los Angeles. He knocked and knocked and knocked. Finally, a neighbor came out to see what was going on. Jim inquired about Jay's whereabouts and the neighbor was convinced Jay was in his apartment just not answering the door. Jim continued the discussion to get more information. He discovered that the neighbors had witnessed a rough crowd coming and going from his place for a while. The neighbor also said that Jay had one time knocked on their door and asked for a syringe.

Jim had to face the fact that Jay was having problems and pulling away. He continued to call until he finally got a hold of him through texts. Jim's correspondence focused on asking Jay if he was okay. Jay claimed to have had a car accident that resulted in injuries that required surgery. Jim asked him if he was addicted to pain medication, but Jay denied anything was wrong and stopped replying to Jim's inquiries.

Jim continued to call. Finally, after more prodding, Jay admitted that he was having drug problems. Jay was admitted into a drug rehabilitation program and Jim was glad to hear that he was trying to help himself. At the same time, Jim wanted to understand the state of the business. Jay said that he had had to sell everything—even his computer—but the business was stored safely in the *cloud*. Jim turned to salvage mode; he was hoping to save anything he could of the business. In a last attempt to save what he could of their business, Jim bought Jay a new computer, and after delivering it to the halfway house, he instructed Jay to provide him with a copy of all the work he had done for their business.

Jay disappeared for a final time and has yet to return any of Jim's calls. Jim was able to stay informed of Jay's whereabouts through one of his friends. Last he heard, Jay is alive and is living with his mother. However, Jim doesn't know anything about the business. Jim was disappointed that he had trusted Jay. It seems he invested in a young man who squandered all of his money on drugs.

PART IV – RICHES

"Real wealth is one's family and friends."
—Jim Schmit

Chapter 59:

THE OPTIMIST

During the 2017 Christmas holiday season, Jim received a very special package in the mail—a present to himself. After unwrapping it, he was pleased to see the item looked exactly as he remembered it. It was a little out-of-date, but he happily fastened it on his wrist and smiled.

Despite the theft of a good chunk of his money a few months before (by the con woman Jim helped put away), Jim had just enough tucked away to buy his gold nugget watch back from Tom Fields. He felt better with it on his wrist; it matched the only other piece of jewelry he had kept—his gold nugget ring. All other jewelry had been purged for cash in order to support his daily expenses over the past several years.

For a fleeting moment, he wondered if all his money would flow back to him now that he had his watch back. Then he shrugged off the thought. He knew that building up his fortune would require the same effort as before by recognizing opportunity and making deals. Plus, a little luck had never hurt him either.

Things were starting to look up. Jim was enjoying his winter in San Clemente. He was conducting his usual routine—wake up early, watch the news, do his exercises, make a peanut butter and jelly sandwich, drive down to the San Clemente pier, take a bike ride, make his phone calls, talk to strangers, and enjoy the sunshine. On one of these seemingly typical mornings, something quite atypical occurred. Jim was up extraordinarily early—before the news—and he was clicking around on his phone when he saw a website with a listing that announced *Doval Shadow for Sale*. He read on. It was exactly like his Doval, but it was brand new. It had only 36 miles on the odometer and a red interior instead of a black interior. The price for the vehicle was listed at a fraction of the cost that Jim had paid for his car in the early 1980s. He blinked, cleaned his phone screen, and looked again.

"It was impossible! I couldn't believe the price and the low mileage. The phone number listed was based in New Jersey, so I waited until 6:00 a.m. to call, which was 9:00 a.m. on the East Coast."

Jim talked to the owner for a while. He discovered that the new owner had bought it for his wife because he thought it was a beautiful car. He had bought it at an auction in Texas, sold by the U.S. Marshal Service. After having it shipped to New Jersey, he discovered that his wife did not want it. She was uncomfortable driving such a long car.

"I told him I would send him a deposit that day to hold the car. I wanted to make sure it was new, so I called up my New Jersey friend, Michael Herring. As it so happened, he lived only about ten minutes away from the car's location. Michael stopped by for a look, and he told me it was brand new and looked good."

Jim immediately discussed making the purchase with the owner. He called in a favor with Angel about acquiring the vehicle. Within days, the purchase was made, and the vehicle was shipped to San Clemente, California.

Jim was a proud owner of 11 percent of all the Doval Shadows ever made in the world saying: "There were only 18 of these cars ever made and who knows how many still exist today. This one was brand new, it was located in the States, and it was being sold for a fraction of its worth. Mine is number 18 and this one happens to be number 17. I tried to figure out who the previous owner was, but I never could. I figured if the U.S. Marshall takes your car, you've probably done something bad. I've got more enjoyment out of the Doval than any Ferrari. Everyone loves that car. It's fun to drive. But this new one is in storage."

Jim will take special care of the car and has given it to Erik Elkaim. Jim says, "I want to make things right; I want to give him back the money he loaned me years ago."

In addition to a new car, Jim was gifted a small log cabin thanks to Rick Barry. Rick had done some advertising for a company that made log cabins, and they gave him an excellent deal on purchasing one. Rick had arranged for a small log cabin to be transported and delivered to a spot of Jim's choosing. Not surprisingly, Jim was looking at having it delivered to Carson River Resort. Unfortunately, Jim's new partner in the resort, a man named Philip—who had bought Angel out of her share—was being very uncooperative with Jim and the rest of the owners. This was posing a challenge for where Jim wanted to place the cabin.

Jim had brought Philip in with the hope that he would help build up the resort and also make much needed repairs and enhancements. Instead, Philip began making poor decisions and pushing away the original investors, including Jim. Jim was so disappointed—one of his oldest investments and his favorite resort was now being mismanaged by a man he thought was going to be a good partner.

Jim started to consider other locations for his new log cabin. However, he did not have to think about it long; while the cabin was in transit on a semi-truck, it burned to the ground. His home was once again in ashes.

He had his old watch and his new car, but some of the same old problems. Jim was distracted by the log cabin mishap one morning while he was sitting in his office near the San Clemente Pier—or the picnic tables he visits daily before and after taking is bike ride when based in San Clemente. A pretty brunette had stopped to look at the ocean and take some photos. Her hair was fixed, her outfit nice, her figure slim. That's the day Jim and Gayle Martz met.

"I like to go down to the Pier in the morning, when I'm in San Clemente, to look at the ocean. On January 7, 2019, I meet this man, and it was like a total connection. He looked at me and said, 'I'm going to spend the rest of my life with you.' We took a picture that day and when I left, I couldn't stop thinking about him," Gayle says.

Gayle—who splits her time between Paris, France, and San Clemente, California—had been seeing an advisor, a very spiritual woman, to help her make some major decisions after selling her company in 2016.

"My advisor told me many times that a wonderful man was coming into my life. I was told we would be connected in our hearts and souls, and that we would be free together." Gayle dismissed these comments. She was not looking for a man; she was concerned with business.

Gayle returned to the Pier the next day and saw Jim again. They exchanged numbers and began texting. She wanted to keep meeting up with him in person, but she had a trip arranged to Paris. They stayed in touch via text messages and phone calls and through talking, they became very close very quickly.

Gayle with KoKo and Jim with Gidget near the Pier in
San Clemente, California where they met

"He wrote so beautifully and honestly. It was so weird. It feels like we've known each other a lifetime. We can talk about anything: business, relationships, travel, pets, problems, the books we are writing… Anything! He's fun and he gets my humor—even my dark humor. I can joke with him very freely. I guess I had a heads up, but I mean really?!"

Jim reflects, "When I met Gayle, I knew she was special. She is so smart, fun, and classy. We had a lot in common from the start. She loves dogs. In fact, she made a very successful business around dogs and pets. She travels. She is so positive. It's amazing. I can't believe we met each other."

When Gayle and Jim are together, you can see how they reflect each other. They are both loyal, smart, honest, kind, and generous people to a fault, and trusting. Their playful conversation keeps them connected—even when they are apart. They enjoy their time together, but they also respect that the other has their own ambitions and a separate path to take. They regularly invite each other to join along on a work trip or an adventure, but they do not take offense when one declines. They accept each other fully and indisputably.

In the short time they've been together, they have traveled internationally, met and doted on each other's dogs, introduced each other to close friends, and talked every day.

As Gayle puts it, "We don't have to be together physically, because we are totally connected anyway. We can be ourselves. We can make odd situations funny."

Jim says, "We talk all the time. She is my best human friend. Gidget is my best dog friend, of course."

"I'm devoted to my pets, and he loves his dog as much as I love mine. There is no one in the world that would understand that more than me. I completely understand," Gayle says. "Jim is a perfect addition to my life."

Jim's hope had come true. He found his lady.

Chapter 60:

THE CONTENTED

After meeting Gayle, Jim took a trip to visit her in Paris for a few weeks. Upon his return, he received a call from Rick Barry wondering if Jim knew of any land for growing hemp for industrial purposes. Before long, Jim was driving around Oregon, learning all about industrial hemp and how it could be used for cat litter. He reconnected with a lot of people back up in Oregon. While the hemp farming plan fell flat after about nine months of effort, it proved worthwhile. The hemp farming work and contacts opened up a different door to something Jim was really good at: real estate. It was time to dust off his old salesman skills; Jim wanted to get back to work developing and selling land.

In gratitude for all Jim had done to get momentum under the industrial hemp project, Rick Barry bought Jim a new bus to serve as his home. "It's so nice," Jim says, describing his new home. "Rick is a fantastic friend. He realized I wasn't getting paid for all the time I put into the industrial hemp project, and he wanted to make sure I was compensated somehow. So, he bought me my new bus. It is perfect!" Jim says. Then he turns to his latest, and possibly, his most exciting news in a long time.

"I'm working on a 2000-lot subdivision in Sisters, Oregon, with the Cyrus family who owns the land. Of all things, Aspen—Vicki's daughter that I helped raise in Lakeview, Oregon, years ago—married into the Cyrus family. I am heading up this real estate deal with a golf course and a club house. It's a beautiful complex," Jim explains.

The Cyrus family is an Old California/Oregon family and decedents from Lovina Graves and John Cyrus who met and married in the Gold Rush days. At 12 years old in 1846, Lovina Graves survived their family's western migration from Illinois to California as part of the Donner Party, just barely.

Jim also reconnected with Bonnie and Amber Thornburg while in Sisters, Oregon. He explains, "Amber is a cowboy and has traveled the world hunting and Bonnie is a beautiful and smart lady. Bonnie and my ex-wife, Vicki, ran the Duck Inn restaurant together in Lakeview, Oregon, when we lived there. I went up to their beautiful house the other day, and Amber had just been bucked off a horse. I think Amber's even older than me! They are a large land-owning family that has done well. They recently sold quite a bit of land to Phil Knight, the Nike founder. They are also extremely kind people."

The Thornburgs are looking to develop a large, five-star property with a Ritz Carlton on a large piece of their land. They want to include plenty of golfing and pleasant scenes. The Thornburgs, like the Cyrus family, have clout in the area, and both were planning attractive developments.

Jim explains, "Sisters, Oregon, is going to be like the Hollywood of the Northwest. There is so much potential here. I'm excited to see it through. All I have to do is make something happen, and I'll get a reasonable percentage of the deal."

With the Cyrus family's permission, Jim parked his new bus near the golf clubhouse that sits adjacent to the development project. The project has waterways, scenic views, and an amazing golf course that attracts golfers from all around. The location is a 30-minute drive from a number of big towns in the area and golfers happily drive that distance to play the course.

Once the permitting and approvals are completed for the development, Jim plans to camp out at the golf clubhouse. He already has lots of marketing ideas to sell lots.

"I'm going to put signs on each golf cart we rent and hand out flyers to all the golfers. I'm going to sell lots like I did in Lake Tahoe. Maybe I can get Bonnie to help start up the Club restaurant," Jim says, his mind rolling.

Jim's hemp and resort development plans hit pause with the outbreak of COVID-19 in early 2020. Since then he has been hunkered up at the USBA running the facility after Bruce O'Neil's passing.

Chapter 61:

THE RICH

In reflecting on it all—the rags-to-riches-to-rags adventure of his life—Jim remains hopeful that he will soon return to *riches*.

Jim says, "The biggest lesson I have learned is who my friends are. I always believed if you had one true friend, you were lucky. And if you had two true friends, you were really, really lucky. I have a dozen true friends. I'm the luckiest guy I know!"

Jim knows, without question, who his real friends are. They are the people who never abandoned him. They check on him daily, and they supported him through his wealthy and poor days. They are the people who still respect and admire him, call him for advice and support, enjoy his unbelievable stories, and are a part of many of them. They are the people who remain in his life as companions and confidants and make his life better. All the other business associates, acquaintances, and moochers have faded away.

The years that Jim spent strapped for cash have made him recognize the beauty of simple and healthy living. He no longer has dozens of employees depending on him or stacks of bills to pay. He says, "In some ways, losing everything has been a blessing in disguise. I never knew how much pressure I was under before."

While Jim was adept at handling the pressure with a positive attitude, he has been relieved of a great deal of responsibility. Regardless, Jim says that there are very few times in his life that he can remember being stressed. "I just don't let things bother me. It's not worth my time. I look forward and solve problems I can solve. If I can't solve it, I let it go," he says.

All of the happiness that bubbles out of Jim could make a person begin to wonder: How can one person be so happy?

When asked to explain himself, Jim fumbles for words, "I just know that it doesn't do me any good to dwell on the past. And I know that I probably wouldn't be sitting right here in the sunshine at the beach if I hadn't lost all my money. I'm healthy and life is good. It's that simple."

Maybe Jim is simply a genius…an optimistic genius. Many geniuses are adaptable, curious, versatile, outgoing, funny, driven, perceptive, patient, honest, self-assured, open-minded, and optimistic. Maybe Jim has subconsciously trained himself to effectively manage stress, while also remaining optimistic. Jim's optimism could be a refined skill, similar to Rick Barry's underhanded free throw or the rest of us tying our shoes. It's possible that through practice—and years and years of repetition—his attitude runs in automatic mode. Perhaps his mind has closed all possible doors to pessimism and stress.

Whatever the explanation is, it's clear that Jim's consistent state of happiness and effective management of stress is abnormal. Almost everyone else is seeking the secrets to a brain and attitude like his. A search on Amazon.com in February 2021 for books containing the simple subject of *happy* yielded over 70,000 results. Furthermore, consider all the businesses, services, and products that are designed to make our lives easier, less stressful, and, ultimately, happier. Happiness is a big business! If Jim could bottle up his stress management and happiness secrets and sell them as a product, he would be the richest man in the world.

Jim has Gidget, Gayle, his friends, bike, car, food to eat, and a bed to sleep in at night. He is still excited to get up every morning and see what the day brings. Maybe today will be the day the United States Basketball Academy is sold; then, he will be monetarily rich again. Maybe today will be the day he sells a lot in Sisters, Oregon, and regains momentum in his first real passion of real estate.... Or maybe not.

In the meantime, Jim continues his general routines. He cycles in the winter in Southern California and he spends time near Lake Tahoe and around Oregon during the summer. He keeps in close contact with his friends and continues to jot down ideas on his yellow pads. He also regularly hops in his Doval and heads out for a short or long road trip with Gidget. He talks to Gayle nearly every day.

Of course, Jim plans to be financially wealthier than before. However, this time Jim wants to do something different with his money. He plans to take his new bus, fill it with lots of gas, and drive all over the United States to cycle in all the national parks. His next collection will be one of miles on his bike and miles on his bus.

As for the rest of his money, he plans to give it away to his friends with only one exception; he wants to make good on a few debts he owes, including paying off the bank. The bank continues to call as part of an attempt to collect the estimated $2 million debt they believe is owed from the Yakima property debacle. Jim says of his debt to the bank, "I don't believe I owe it to them. But I just want them to stop calling me about it. I believe I am going to get rich again and die broke. I'm not going to leave with anything. I'm going to give it all away to my friends before I die."

Of course, Jim will need to budget some of his money towards his plan for cryopreservation, which is not cheap. Jim says, "When I first came up with the idea of being frozen, way back, it was no problem. I had loads of money." Though, now he is in a holding pattern. When he imagines what it would be like to wake up to a world full of strangers, he says, "I think it would be exciting to see what I missed out on."

Regardless of the day, Jim remains tenaciously happy. It may be more accurate to say that he is satisfied with his stress-free life, even as it has evolved from rags, to riches, to rags, and he hopes back to riches. He knows that every difficult time has led him to a new adventure and opportunity.

Unless cryopreservation goes awry, Jim's insatiable curiosity, his positive genius, and unbreakable friendships will be preserved with his frozen body. Still, he has countless more breaths to inhale, bike rides to take, and dollars to make before signing up for his frozen intermission.

AFTERWORD

The year 2020 was tough in many regards—Jim lost his good friends Del Matthews and Bruce O'Neil, the world shut down as a pandemic spread, the USBA struggled financially and barely survived wildfires that ravaged parts of Oregon, and Jim fought to keep his projects afloat.

Although, as this book was going to print, Jim texted me saying, "The property [United States Basketball Academy] has recorded thanks to Hayden. I'm now going to be a millionaire again until I give it all away. LUJIM [Love you, Jim]."

Still close friends—Rick Barry, Jim, and Gidget in front of the
Rick Barry Cabin at the United States Basketball Academy in April 2021

ACKNOWLEDGEMENTS

Naturally, without Jim Schmit there would be no book. Our serendipitous encounter led to this enormous and challenging undertaking. Having worked on this for over five years, I feel I now have a PhD in happiness, mindfulness, and well-being. Thanks for all you have taught me. We did it! Now, as the designated salesman for this project...Jim, please go sell lots of these books!

A Most Improbable Millionaire would not have been possible without all of the people interviewed to fill in the gaps between Jim's piecemeal memory. Your generosity with your time and words made this story complete. Enormous gratitude goes to, in no particular order: John Schmit, Gayle Martz, Bill Smith, Chips McAllister, Tom Fields, Hayden Watson, Pam Connolley, Aspen Nolan, Angel Algers, Kathy Lang, Rick Barry, Bob Lindner Jr., Douglas Nelson, Carl Fair, Brad Kanis, Vicki Morrison, Ken Madsen, Marty Leatherbury, Rex Leatherbury, Mildred Barrett, Clifford Ray, Jade Harris, Eric Elkaim, Deena Schwarte, Dick Schwarte, Bob Novasel, Laura Larson, Del Matthews, and Bruce O'Neil.

To my editors who tackled this messy manuscript like warriors: Megan Hard and Katelyn Peters. It has also been a pleasure to work with BookBaby and their fantastic staff that taught me the publishing process: Darcy Post and Damon Glatz and all the BookBaby support staff. In addition, Ariel Curry also served as an advisor on the publishing process.

My very talented sister, C. Courtney Weaver, designed the cover concept using photographs taken by Marcus Casian. Thank you both for a wonderful cover.

The Puyallup Public Library was a helpful source for verifying some of Jim's early years and stories. Their compilation of high school annuals is where I pulled Jim's senior photo. Thank you to Mikayla Kimery and Joshua Hemphill for digging into the *Ranger Roundup* newspaper archives at Olympic College to find Jim's published article 'Students Voice Opinions on Cheating.' These are the details that make a good story so much better.

This project would also have been much more laborious without the Internet. A very serious thank you to the Internet! A great deal of this research was conducted on my couch with careful consideration of vetted and unvetted resources. Much effort was taken to verify all of the stories told using legitimate sources to back up dates and events. There were only a few stories that could not be fully verified and in these rare cases, the stories were included on the premise of Jim's conviction. If a reader takes any issue or has additional factual evidence to verify a story, date, time, or event, feel free to email me at laynie@layniedweaver.com.

My reading friends provided feedback to me on various versions of this book—I appreciate the time you dedicated, even if just a little, to this project: Lori Glickman, Stephan Gridley, Geoff Carter, Steve Vondrak, Sarah Arnold, Bob Lindner, and Blaine Lourd. To my friends who kept asking me when the book was going to be done, which served as positive reinforcement and thoughtful accountability for me: Mary Vondrak, Candace Pattillo, Eric Larsen, Armando Acosta, Michele Anderson, Kevin Gaddis, Dain Pankratz, and Ream Lazaro. There are a few friends that were great at distracting me from writing; enticing me to some fun filled outing, travel adventure, or simply providing good company, and to them I owe some of my sanity: Rudy Velasco, Trip Owen, Molly Ware, Michelle Warren, Brian Sandberg, Bud Price, and Barry Friedman.

A special thanks to Clifford Ray for his patience—he knows what I'm talking about.

Meg Gibson Keese, my longest running friend who I met at the Beehive Preschool in our hometown of Sinton, Texas when we were four years old, said a dozen or so years later after our friendship began that she believed everyone had a book in them. I never forgot that. Thanks for that little bit of motivation that reflects how truly powerful words can be.

I am grateful for my full-time employer that permits and supports my biographical writing as a hobby. While I serve as a technical writer for work, I enjoy the different styles of writing I am allowed to tackle each and every day. I truly enjoy the industry I work in and the people I work with inside and outside of our company.

Thank you to David Byers, the ocean, and the mountains for keeping my physically fit and getting this introvert out of the house especially during the strange year of 2020. Thanks to all my dog friends that I love to snuggle: Bentley, Hayley, and, of course, Gidget. Thank you to the members of the Dirty Dirty Girls Book Club because you all make me laugh and are my girl squad. Thank you to all the failed romantic relationships that prevented me from taking even longer to write this book. Even you guys served your purpose—entertaining me and my friends with occasionally sad, but mostly hilarious dating stories.

Finally, to anyone I may have forgotten; thank you too!

Laynie, Jim, and Gidget at the top of Mount Tallac in 2017
with Lake Tahoe in the background

BIBLIOGRAPHY

The Immortal

'Can A Human Be Frozen And Brought Back to Life?' *Zidbits.* February 21, 2011. Retrieved from http://zidbits.com/2011/02/can-a-human-be-frozen-and-brought-back-to-life/.

Conradt, Stacy. 'The Quick 8: Eight People Who Have Been Cryonically Preserved (and one who wasn't).' *Mental Floss.* February 11, 2009. Retrieved from http://mentalfloss.com/article/20849/quick-8-eight-people-who-have-been-cryonically-preserved-and-one-who-wasnt.

Eveleth, Rose. 'Cryopreservation: 'I freeze people to cheat death.' British Broadcasting Corporation. August 21, 2014. Retrieved from https://www.bbc.com/future/article/20140821-i-will-be-frozen-when-i-die.

Chapter 1: The Son

Foster, S. Mark. *Henry J. Kaiser: Builder in the Modern American West.* (Austin, Texas: University of Texas Press, 1989), 196.

Puyallup Washington History. City of Puyallup. Retrieved from https://www.cityofpuyallup.org/524/History.

The Century Book: 1863 Escanaba 1963. City of Escanaba, Michigan. Retrieved from https://www.escanaba.org/sites/default/files/fileattachments/city_clerk/page/2311/the_century_book.pdf.

Weiser-Alexander, Kathy. 'Ezra Meeker – Oregon Trail Pioneer.' *Legends of America.* December 2019. Retrieved from https://www.legendsofamerica.com/ezra-meeker/.

Chapter 3: The Serviceman

Green, Mike. *USCGC Dexter (WAVP-385) (WHEC-385).* NavSource Online: Amphibious Photo Archive. March 5, 2021. Retrieved from https://www.navsource.org/archives/10/01/0118.htm

Chapter 4: The Editor

Address at University of Washington's 100th Anniversary Program. John F. Kennedy Presidential Library and Museum. November 16, 1961. Retrieved from https://www.jfklibrary.org/learn/about-jfk/historic-speeches/address-at-university-of-washington

Findling, John. 'World's Fair.' *Encyclopedia Britannica.* Retrieved from http://www.britannica.com/topic/worlds-fair.

'Jones Fantastic Museum Tour.' *YouTube.* March 20, 2010. Retrieved from https://www.youtube.com/watch?v=ZPvs8xkSWuY.

'Jones' Fantastic Museum Explained.' *Everything Explained Today.* Retrieved from http://everything.explained.today/Jones'_Fantastic_Museum/.

Schmit, Jim. 'Students Voice Opinions on Cheating.' *Ranger Roundup,* Olympic College—Newspaper.

Chapter 5: The Hawaii Bellhop

'American President Lines: The Last Ocean Liners.' *LastOceanLiners. com*. Retrieved from http://www.lastoceanliners.com/cgi/lolline. pl?APL.

Buchanan, Colin. 'The Mummy Song.' *YouTube*. October 22, 2013. Retrieved from https://www.youtube.com/watch?v=Cn7jTPj4zsg.

Giles. Jeff. 'Beatles Honored with Historical Marker at JFK Airport.' *Ultimate Classic Rock*. February 5, 2014. Retrieved from http://ultimateclassicrock.com/beatles-jfk-airport/.

Kelly, Jim. 'Last of 50s 'Tiki-style' Hotels to Disappear from Waikiki.' *Pacific Business News*. February 27, 2005. Retrieved from http://www.bizjournals.com/pacific/stories/2005/02/28/focus2.html.

'Maritime Monday for February 18th, 2014: Ship of State; Vessels Named for Presidents of the United States.' *gCaptain*. February 17, 2014. Retrieved from http://gcaptain.com/vessels-named-for-presidents-of-the-united-states/.

Rachel. *Willys Surrey Gala Jeep 1959-1964*. Kaiser Willys Jeep Blog. May 5, 2011. Retrieved from http://blog.kaiserwillys.com/willys-surrey-gala-jeep-1959-1964.

'The Beatles' American Invasion Begins.' *The Beatles Bible*. February 7, 1964. Retrieved from http://www.beatlesbible.com/1964/02/07/beatles-american-invasion-begins/.

'Why People Visited the Islands of Hawaii in the '60s.' *The San Francisco Examiner*. September 17, 1967. Retrieved from https://clickamericana.com/topics/travel-tourism/testing-aloha-spirit-hawaiis-tourist-boom-brings-growing-pains-1960.

Yoshihara, Mari and Yujin Yaguchi. 'Evolutions of 'Paradise': Japanese Tourist Discourse About Hawai'i.' *American Studies* 45: 3 (Fall 2004).

Chapter 6: The California Bellhop

'Beatlemania Invades Palo Alto: A Celebrity Story.' *Palo Alto History*. Retrieved from http://www.paloaltohistory.org/palo-altos-beatle-mania.php

Igler, Marc. 'Our Town: The Cabana's Return.' *Palo Alto Online*. December 30, 1998. Retrieved from http://www.paloaltoonline.com/weekly/morgue/page4/1998_Dec_30.TOWN30.html.

Chapter 7: The Salesman

Chandler, Rick. 'Tahoe Paradise One Man's Dream.' *Tahoe Daily Tribune*. December 19, 2001. Retrieved from https://www.tahoe-dailytribune.com/news/tahoe-paradise-one-mans-dream/.

Lane, Don. 'Lake Tahoe Facts and Figures. Lake Tahoe History.' Tahoe Regional Planning Association. Retrieved from http://www.webcitation.org/64PkFxgR0

McLaughlin, Mark. 'A Look Back at Mark Twain Adventures—and Tomfoolery—at Lake Tahoe.' *Sierra Sun*. December 8, 2014. Retrieved from https://www.sierrasun.com/news/local/a-look-back-at-mark-twains-adventures-and-tomfoolery-at-lake-tahoe/.

Vogel, Ed. 'Lake Tahoe: Twain Called it the "Fairest Picture the Whole World Affords".' *Las Vegas Review-Journal*. January 4, 2014. Retrieved from https://www.reviewjournal.com/news/lake-tahoe-twain-called-it-the-fairest-picture-the-whole-world-affords/.

Chapter 9: The Partner

Associated Press. 'New California College Plans Fall Opening.' *Lake Charles American Press Archives*. April 29, 1967. Retrieved from https://newspaperarchive.com/lake-charles-american-press-apr-29-1967-p-3/.

Chapter 11: The Dog Lover

Newsonen, Susanna. 'Why Dogs Make You Happy: Science Shows Why Your Four-Legged Friend Makes You Feel Good.' *Psychology Today*. September 30, 2018. Retrieved from https://www.psychologytoday.com/us/blog/the-path-passionate-happiness/201809/why-dogs-make-you-happy.

Chapter 12: The Tour Guide

Basketball Reference. *Rick Barry*. Sports Reference LLC. Retrieved from https://www.basketball-reference.com/players/b/barryri01.html

Whitaker, Mark. *Cosby: His Life and Times*. (New York: Simon & Schuster, 2014), 170–171.

Chapter 13: The Proprietor

Burns, Bob. *A Track in the Forest: The Creation of a Legendary 1968 Olympic Team*. (Chicago: Chicago Review Press, 2019).

Hauserman, Tim. 'Echo Summit 1968: Where America's Best Track Athletes Gathered During a Time of National Unrest.' *Tahoe Magazine*. August 22, 2018. Retrieved from https://www.tahoemagazine.com/echo-summit-1968-where-americas-best-track-athletes-gathered-during-a-time-of-national-unrest/.

Payne, Bob. 'Olympic Camp's Press Ban Unpopular.' *The Spokesman-Review*. August 16, 1968. Retrieved from https://news.google.com/newspapers?id=rztWAAAAIBAJ&sjid=dekDAAAAIBAJ&pg=7207%2C298421.

Underwood, John. 'Triumph and Tragedy at Tahoe.' *Sports Illustrated Vault*. September 23, 1968. Retrieved from https://www.si.com/vault/1968/09/23/617519/triumph-and-tragedy-at-tahoe.

Chapter 14: The Weatherman

Andrews, Evan. '10 Things You Should Know About the Donner Party.' *History*. January 30, 2020. Retrieved from http://www.history.com/news/10-things-you-should-know-about-the-donner-party.

McLaughlin, Mark. 'Hoping for Another Winter of '69.' *Sierra Sun*. January 6, 2005. Retrieved from https://www.sierrasun.com/news/hoping-for-another-winter-of-69/.

McLaughlin, Mark. 'Reign of the Sierra Storm King: Weather History of Donner Pass.' Sierra College: *Journal of the Sierra College Natural History Museum* 2 (1), Winter 2009. Retrieved from http://www.sierracollege.edu/ejournals/jscnhm/v2n1/stormking.html.

'Tahoe is Weather Perfection.' Mic Mac Media. (2005) Retrieved from http://thestormking.com/Sierra_Stories/Tahoe_Weather/tahoe_weather.html

Chapter 15: The Snowmobiler

$10,000 Castrol Cup Snowmobile Race program. (1971)

About USSA Prostar Series. United States Snowmobiling Association Prostar Series. (2019) Retrieved from https://ussaprostar.com/about/.

Chapter 17: The Boss

Associated Press. 'Moves In, Invests $2 Million: Millionaire Adopts Small Oregon Town.' *Los Angeles Times*. October 25, 1987. Retrieved from https://www.latimes.com/archives/la-xpm-1987-10-25-mn-16244-story.html.

Chandler, Rick. 'History of Tahoe Keys.' *Tahoe Daily Tribune*. December 19, 2001. Retrieved from http://www.tahoedailytribune.com/news/history-of-tahoe-keys/.

Chapter 19: The Customer

Lankford, Scott. 'Tahoe Beneath the Surface: The Hidden Stories of America's Largest Mountain Lake.' *Heyday.* (2010)

Suave Jewelry. Facebook. March 29, 2014. Retrieved from https://www.facebook.com/permalink.php?story_fbid=696949043676744&id=162026140502373, March 29, 2014 post, Suave Jewelry.

Chapter 20: The Outsider

'Bonanno Crime Family Leadership Timeline.' National Crime Syndicate. (2020). Retrieved from https://www.nationalcrimesyndicate.com/bonanno-crime-family-leadership-timeline/.

'Frankie Fanelli Biography.' International Movie Database. Retrieved from https://www.imdb.com/name/nm2042338/bio?ref_=nm_ov_bio_sm.

Penrose, Kelsey. 'Nevada Lore Series: 50 Year Old Tahoe Mystery Includes and Assassination, a Secret Safe, and Oprah Winfrey.' *CarsonNow.org.* November 8, 2018. Retrieved from https://carsonnow.org/story/11/08/2018/nevada-lore-series-car-bomb-assassination-secret-safe-and-oprah-winfrey.

'The Incredible History of the Cal-Neva Lodge on Lake Tahoe.' *SnowBrains.* April 5, 2015. Retrieved from http://snowbrains.com/the-history-of-the-cal-neva-lodge-on-lake-tahoe/.

Chapter 21: The Statistician

'1975 NBA Finals G4 Washington Bullets vs. Golden State Warriors.' YouTube. November 7, 2017. 01:56:00 to 01:57:49. Retrieved from https://www.youtube.com/watch?v=TUYMvxw-IMw.

Associated Press. 'Moves In, Invests $2 Million: Millionaire Adopts Small Oregon Town.' *Los Angeles Times.* October 25, 1987. Retrieved from https://www.latimes.com/archives/la-xpm-1987-10-25-mn-16244-story.html.

Basketball Reference. *Rick Barry.* Sports Reference LLC. Retrieved from https://www.basketball-reference.com/players/b/barryri01. html

Cannon, John. 'The 1975 NBA Finals – The Warriors Turn the NBA Upside-Down.' *Crossover Chronicles.* June 4, 2015. Retrieved from http://thecomeback.com/crossoverchronicles/2015-articles/the-1975-nba-finals-the-warriors-turn-the-nba-upside-down.html.

Cannon, John. 'The 1975 Western Conference Finals – Where the Magic Began.' *Crossover Chronicles.* June 2, 2015. Retrieved from http://thecomeback.com/crossoverchronicles/2015-articles/the-1975-western-conference-finals-where-the-magic-began.html.

Cannon, John. 'Who Were Those Guys? A Look Back at the 1974-1975 Warriors.' *Crossover Chronicles.* May 30, 2015. Retrieved from http://thecomeback.com/crossoverchronicles/2015-articles/who-were-those-guys-a-look-back-at-the-1974-1975-warriors.html.

Newhouse, Dave. 'Robert Albo, Esteemed Oakland Doctor, Passes Away at 78.' *East Bay Times.* February 21, 2011. Retrieved from https://www.eastbaytimes.com/2011/02/21/robert-albo-esteemed-oakland-doctor-passes-away-at-78/.

Chapter 22: The Entertainer

Ambrose, Stephen E. *Nixon, Ruin and Recovery 1973-1990.* (New York: Simon & Shuster 1991).

'George Whittell Jr.' *Online Nevada Encyclopedia.* Retrieved from https://www.onlinenevada.org/articles/george-whittell-jr.

Marquez, Heron. *Richard M. Nixon.* (Minneapolis: Learner Publications Company 2003), 93.

Penning, Robin. 'Lake Tahoe's Original Mansion Masterpieces.' Keeping Lake Tahoe...The Best Lake. April 15, 2013. Retrieved from https://robinpenning.wordpress.com/2013/04/15/lake-tahoes-original-mansion-masterpieces/.

'Thunderbird Lake Tahoe: Thunderbird Lodge History.' Thunderbird Lodge Preservation Society. Retrieved from https://thunderbird-tahoe.org/index.php/thunderbird-lodge-history-page.

'Vikingsholm Tahoe's Hidden Castle.' Retrieved from http://viking-sholm.com/#One

Chapter 23: The Entrepreneur

Associated Press. 'Gary Dahl, Creator of the Pet Rock, Dies at 78.' *National Public Radio.* April 1, 2015. Retrieved from https://www.npr.org/2015/04/01/396726696/gary-dahl-creator-of-the-pet-rock-dies-at-78.

Dahl, Gary. 'The Care and Training of Your Pet Rock.' Rock Bottom Productions. (1975). Retrieved from https://www.scribd.com/doc/252772385/The-Care-and-Training-of-Your-Pet-Rock-Manual-by-Gary-Dahl.

Chapter 25: The Patient

'25 Stimulating Facts About Moonlite BunnyRanch, Nevada's Most Famous Brothel.' Retrieved from http://vitalvegas.com/25-stimulating-facts-moonlite-bunnyranch-navadas-famous-brothel/.

Chen, Siyi and Allison Schrager. 'The Women of the Moonlite Bunny Ranch Brothel Answer Your Questions About Working as Legal Prostitutes.' *Quartz.* September 23, 2016. Retrieved from https://qz.com/779415/moonlite-bunny-ranch-revealed-what-its-like-to-work-as-a-legal-prostitute-in-nevada/.

Gannon, Megan. 'What Kind of Men Go to Prostitutes?' *Live Science*. March 25, 2013. Retrieved from http://www.livescience.com/28169-men-who-use-prostitutes.html.

RolandNote: Country Music Database Searches. *June Carter Cash Timeline*. RolandNote. March 7, 2021. Retrieved from https://www.rolandnote.com/people.php?scode=timeline&keyword=June+Carter+Cash&page=11.

Chapter 26: The Restaurateur

'Bob's Burger Express.' *Statesman Journal*. June 27, 2014. Retrieved from https://www.statesmanjournal.com/picture-gallery/news/local/heritage/2014/06/27/bobs-burger-express/11453471/.

Lynn, Capi. 'Flavor of Nostalgia Lingers.' *Statesman Journal*. August 22, 2014. Retrieved from https://www.statesmanjournal.com/story/living/2014/08/22/bobs-burgers-nostalgia/14445885/.

Reed, Katherine. 'Tahoe Keys Marina's Troubles Keep Growing.' *Lake Tahoe News Archives*. July 2014. Retrieved from http://www.laketahoe-news.net/2014/07/tahoe-keys-marinas-troubles-keep-growing/.

Chapter 27: The Friend

dm30418. 'All the Light We Cannot See by Anthony Doerr.' *Bulb*. September 6, 2017. Retrieved from https://www.bulbapp.com/u/all-the-light-we-cannot-see-by-anthony-doerr.

'Holocaust Encyclopedia: Dachau.' United States Holocaust Memorial Museum. December 5, 2006. Retrieved from https://www.ushmm.org/wlc/en/article.php?ModuleId=10005214.

Chapter 28: The Guest

'Bicentennial Ring.' Collection: Gerald R. Ford Presidential Museum. Wikimedia Commons. Retrieved from https://commons.wikimedia. org/wiki/File:Bicentennial_Ring.jpg.

Dunne, Dominick. 'Khashoggi's Fall.' *Vanity Fair.* September 15, 2008. Retrieved from https://www.vanityfair.com/magazine/1989/09/ dunne198909.

'Gerald R. Ford 38th President of the United States: 1974–1977. Remarks of Welcome to King Hussein I of Jordan.' The American Presidency Project. March 30, 1976. Retrieved from http://www. presidency.ucsb.edu/ws/index.php?pid=5768.

Lusher, Adam. 'Adnan Khashoggi: The "Whoremonger" Whose Arms Deals Funded a Playboy Life of Decadence and "Pleasure Wives". *The Independent.* October 19, 2019. Retrieved from https:// www.independent.co.uk/news/long_reads/adnan-khashoggi-dead-saudi-arms-dealer-playboy-pleasure-wives-billionaire-lifestyle-wealth-profit-a7778031.html.

Chapter 29: The Eyewitness

Higginbotham, Adam. '1,000 Pounds of Dynamite: On August 26, 1980, A Nevada Casino Discovered a Gigantic Bomb—and a Ransom Note—Sitting on its Second Floor. Here's What Happened Next.' *Slate.* August 3, 2014. Retrieved from http://www.slate.com/articles/ news_and_politics/crime/2014/08/harvey_s_wagon_wheel_bomb-ing_the_bizarre_but_true_story_of_a_crime_gone.html.

Kingman, Bill and Kathryn Reed. '85 Died 50 Years Ago in Worst Tahoe Plane Crash.' *Lake Tahoe News Archives.* March 1, 2014. Retrieved from http://www.laketahoenews. net/2014/03/85-died-50-years-ago-worst-tahoe-plane-crash/.

'Lawsuits Grounded Commercial Service in Tahoe for 20 Years.' *Lake Tahoe News Archives.* (July 5, 2012) Retrieved from http://www.laketahoenews.net/2012/07/lawsuits-grounded-commercial-service-in-tahoe-for-20-years/.

Worrall, Simon. 'Mistakes Led to Needless Deaths from the Worst Volcanic Blast.' *National Geographic.* March 20, 2016. Retrieved from https://www.nationalgeographic.com/news/2016/03/160320-mount-st-helens-eruption-logging-volcano-olson-ngbooktalk/.

Chapter 30: The Catch

Colacello, Bob. 'Anything Went.' *Vanity Fair.* September 4, 2013. Retrieved from http://www.vanityfair.com/news/1996/03/studio-54-nightclub-new-york-city.

Chapter 31: The Family Man

LaLande, Jeff. 'Lakeview.' *Oregon Encyclopedia.* Retrieved from https://www.oregonencyclopedia.org/articles/lakeview/#.YEWSRS1h3kI.

Chapter 32: The Collector

'Simplot Co. Buys ZX Ranch, One of the Largest U.S. Cattle Operation.' *Associated Press.* January 2, 1994. Retrieved from https://www.apnews.com/28aa47e4b5d0e39ba3bf67bad5f79751.

Bloom, Philipp. *To Have and to Hold – An Intimate History of Collectors and Collecting.* (New York: The Overlook Press, 2002).

'History of Plumbing in America.' *Plumbing and Mechanical Magazine.* July 1987. Retrieved from https://www.plumbingsupply.com/pmamerica.html.

'The First Zeppelins: LZ-1 through LZ-4.' *Airships.net.* Retrieved from http://www.airships.net/zeppelins/.

'The Hindenburg Disaster.' *Airships.net*. Retrieved from http://www. airships.net/hindenburg/disaster/.

Welch, Bob. 'The ZX Ranch: The Story Behind the Iconic Brand.' *American Cowboy*. May 16, 2017. Retrieved from https://www.amer- icancowboy.com/people/zx-ranch-oregon.

Chapter 33: The Curator

Associated Press. 'Moves In, Invests $2 Million: Millionaire Adopts Small Oregon Town.' *Los Angeles Times*. October 25, 1987. Retrieved from https://www.latimes.com/archives/la-xpm-1987-10-25-mn- 16244-story.html.

Malinowski, Terri. 'Medicine Show Glamour.' *The Northshore Citizen*. December 12, 1963. Retrieved from http://khs.stparchive. com/Archive/KHS/KHS12121963p03.php.

Robinson, John. 'Sights & Sounds from the Jones Fantastic Museum! Sideshow World: Preserving the Past…Promoting the Future. Retrieved from http://www.sideshowworld.com/45-DMCC/2014/ Jones/Fantastic-Museum.html.

Chapter 34: The Oregon Developer

'About TRPA.' Tahoe Regional Planning Agency. 2021. Retrieved from http://www.trpa.org/about-trpa/.

'Enterprise Zone.' City of Redmond Oregon. Retrieved from https://www.redmondoregon.gov/government/departments/ community-development/planning-division/enterprise-zone.

Chapter 35: The Visionary

'Japanese Instrument of Surrender.' National Archives Foundation. 1945. Retrieved from https://www.archivesfoundation.org/documents/japanese-instrument-surrender-1945/.

Robinson, John. 'Sights & Sounds from the Jones Fantastic Museum!' Sideshow World: Preserving the Past…Promoting the Future. Retrieved from http://www.sideshowworld.com/45-DMCC/2014/Jones/Fantastic-Museum.html.

'South Lake Tahoe, California Vacation Rental Property – Bob's at the Beach.' Show Vacation Rentals. (2021) Retrieved from http://www.showvacationrental.com/10231.

Chapter 39: The Fundraiser

'The Smith Rock Fire: Then and 20 Years Later.' *SmithRock.com*. August 19, 2016. Retrieved from https://smithrock.com/news-all/smith-rock-fire.

Chapter 40: The Gentleman

'Saving Grace: A Bitter Custody Fight Erupts Over Daughter Born After Divorce.' *Forty Eight Hours*. May 31, 2000. Retrieved from https://www.cbsnews.com/news/saving-grace/.

Chapter 42: The Traveler

'In China, Fairhope couple Marty and Rex Leatherbury Find Business and a Second Home.' *AL.com*. November 7, 2011. Retrieved from http://blog.al.com/live/2011/11/in_china_fairhope_couple_marty.html.

Chapter 43: The Mogul

Bilyeau, Nancy. 'The Only Unsolved Skyjacking Case in U.S. History Might Have a Break: "D.B. Copper" is Robert Rackstraw, a Vietnam Vet and Ex-CIA Operative, Investigative Team Claims.' *The Vintage News*. February 8, 2018. Retrieved from https://www.thevintage-news.com/2018/02/08/d-b-cooper/.

'Patty Hearst Biography.' *Biography*. June 17, 2020. Retrieved from https://www.biography.com/people/patty-hearst-9332960.

'Snowshoe Thompson, "Viking of the Sierra".' *SnowshoeThompson. org*. Retrieved from https://snowshoethompson.org/the-story/.

Suellentrop, Chris. 'What is the Symbionese Liberation Army?' *Slate*. January 24, 2002. Retrieved from http://www.slate.com/articles/news_and_politics/explainer/2002/01/what_is_the_symbionese_liberation_army.html.

Weiser, Kathy. 'Comstock Load – Creating Nevada History.' *Legends of America*. March 2020. Retrieved from https://www.legendsofamerica.com/nv-comstocklode/.

Chapter 46: The Giver

'Lucky's Famous Cycle to Debut at the Carson City's Nevada State Museum.' *Nevada Appeal*. June 17, 2016. Retrieved from https://www.nevadaappeal.com/news/2016/jun/17/luckys-famous-cycle-to-debut-at-carson-citys-nevad/.

MacLaren, Grant. 'Thunderbird.' *GrantMaclaren.com*. Retrieved from http://www.grantmaclaren.com/thunderbird/.

Chapter 47: The Silent Partner

'About Yakima.' City of Yakima. Retrieved from https://www.yakimawa.gov/visit/about/.

Kershner, Jim. 'Yakima—Thumbnail History.' *HistoryLink.org.* October 16, 2009. Retrieved from http://www.historylink.org/ File/9187.

Oldham, Kit. 'Northern Pacific Reaches Yakima City, Where it Declines to Build a Station, on December 17, 1884.' *HistoryLink.org.* February 18, 2003. Retrieved from https://historylink.org/File/5237.

'Save the Track 29.' Facebook. February 24, 2013. Retrieved from https://www.facebook.com/216227111852161/photos/ rpp.216227111852161/216277198513819/?type=3&theater.

Chapter 53: The Free Spirit

Duke, Alan. 'Liz Taylor "Love Nest" Trailer Trashed During Filming of Lindsay Lohan Movie.' *Cable News Network.* August 30, 2012. Retrieved from https://www.cnn.com/2012/08/30/showbiz/tay-lor-trailer-trashed/index.html.

Chapter 54: The Human

'Photo of the Week 9-18-13 Trashing Trains.' City of Yakima. September 18, 2013. Retrieved from https://www2.bing.com/ images/search?view=detailV2&ccid=36T6MnqN&id=9AF-CD9D68A0F48DC3C3D51FA24175D9075DDA21F&thid =OIP.36T6MnqNy61wldBlkjZBQwHaEd&q=track+29+ya-kima+scrap&simid=608039566473170237&selectedindex-=9&ajaxhist=0&mediaurl=http%3A%2F%2Fwww.yakimawa. gov%2Fmedia%2Fphoto-of-the-week%2Fwp-content%2F-blogs.dir%2F3%2Ffiles%2Fsites%2F3%2FPOW-9-18-13adj. jpg&exph=3023&expw=5013&vt=Default.

Chapter 57: The Crime Fighter

Brown, Vanessa and Scott Gordon. "'Sweetheart Swindler" Sentenced to 263 Years Behind Bars.' *National Broadcasting Company Dallas Fort Worth.* November 30, 2018. Retrieved from https://www.nbcdfw.com/news/local/Sweetheart-Swindler-Sentenced-to-263-Years-Behind-Bars-501655091.html.

Chapter 62: The Rich

Lebowitz, Shana. '8 Personality Traits of a Highly Intelligent People (Backed by Science).' *Inc.com.* July 21, 2016. Retrieved from https://www.inc.com/business-insider/8-personality-traits-highly-intelligent-genius-people-share-according-to-science.html.

Westergren, Jim. '24 Qualities That Geniuses Have in Common.' *JimWestergren.com.* Retrieved from https://www.jimwestergren.com/24-qualities-that-geniuses-have-in-common/.

PHOTO CREDITS

The two Christmas trees Christmas (Jim Schmit personal collection)   7

Senior year at Puyallup High School (Puyallup Public Library)   14

Ranger Roundup article (Olympic College Newspaper)   25

Palo Alto Times headlines following the Beatles departure
(Palo Alto Times)   42

Tippy, Jim's constant companion (Jim Schmit personal collection)   62

Jim, a friend, Pam, and Rick Barry in 1970 at Harrah's Hotel
and Casino (Jim Schmit personal collection)   65

The Market Campus Shopping Center (Jim Schmit personal collection)   70

Enjoying the snow (Jim Schmit personal collection)   74

Winter fun (Jim Schmit personal collection)   80

Pre-race meditation (Jim Schmit personal collection)   82

Marty and Jim dressed up (Jim Schmit personal collection)   94

Sailing with Scooter Barry (Jim Schmit personal collection)   97

Tom Jones and Jim wearing the latest fashion
(Jim Schmit personal collection)   104

Jim and Liberace at The Jewelry Factory
(Bob Linder, Jr. personal collection)   107

1975 NBA Finals Most Valuable Player, Rick Barry during his
locker room interview with Jim at upper right (YouTube) 117

Jim with the escaped buffalo (Jim Schmit personal collection) 128

Fiddletown hayride with the Barry kids
(Jim Schmit personal collection) 130

Mount Saint Helens before and after eruption
(Jim Schmit personal collection) 156

The Doval Shadow (Jim Schmit personal collection) 166

Tom Fields with Jim and Pepsi at The Fantastic Museum
(Jim Schmit personal collection) 171

Aspen, Jeni, Vicki, and Jim with Pepsi celebrating Jeni's Graduation
(Vicki Morrison personal collection) 186

The *Blue Boy* makes it to Shelter Cove
(Jim Schmit personal collection) 196

Jim and friend Arvydas (Jim Schmit personal collection) 209

Jim with Yao Ming and friends (Jim Schmit personal collection) 227

The half court wonders—this roster survived a fire
(Jim Schmit personal collection) 231

Traveling with Eric Elkaim (Jim Schmit personal collection) 233

Clifford admiring the hand carved doors at the Suttle Lake Lodge
(Jim Schmit personal collection) 235

A young prospect, Brad Kanis (Jim Schmit personal collection) 249

Jim and Margaret treating a crew of friends to a cruise on the
Thunderbird Yacht in Lake Tahoe (Jim Schmit personal collection) 259

Jim testing his belief that "real" wealth is family and friends
(Jim Schmit personal collection) 289

Angel and Jim at Mardi Gras (Jim Schmit personal collection)   299

Making phone calls from his San Clemente, California "office"
(Laynie Weaver personal collection)   302

Jim and Clifford Ray at Carson River Resort
(Jim Schmit personal collection)   305

Reading through the Fantastic Museum inventory before opening
in Gardnerville, Nevada (Laynie Weaver personal collection)   307

Jim's sleuthing and honesty help put a con artist behind bars
(Laynie Weaver personal collection)   314

Gayle with KoKo and Jim with Gidget near the Pier in San Clemente,
California where they met (Gayle Martz personal collection)   322

Still close friends—Rick Barry, Jim, and Gidget in front of
the Rick Barry Cabin at the United States Basketball Academy
in April 2021 (Jim Schmit personal collection)   331

Laynie, Jim, and Gidget at the top of Mount Tallac in 2017 with
Lake Tahoe in the background (Laynie Weaver personal collection)   335

ABOUT THE AUTHOR

Laynie D. Weaver is a technical writer and biographer. *A Most Improbable Millionaire* is her first book. A Texan by birth, she now resides in San Clemente, California and Mammoth Lakes, California when not traveling for work or leisure. Her best friend is Gidget.

www.layniedweaver.com